UNDERSTANDING
FAMILIES

UNDERSTANDING FAMILIES

Approaches to
Diversity, Disability, and Risk

by

Marci J. Hanson, Ph.D.
Department of Special Education
San Francisco State University

and

Eleanor W. Lynch, Ph.D.
Department of Special Education
San Diego State University

·P·A·U·L·H·
BROOKES
PUBLISHING Cº.®

Baltimore • London • Sydney

Paul H. Brookes Publishing Co.
Post Office Box 10624
Baltimore, Maryland 21285-0624

www.brookespublishing.com

Third printing, April 2007.

Typeset by International Graphic Services,
Newtown, Pennsylvania.
Manufactured in the United States of America by
Versa Press, East Peoria, Illinois.

All of the vignettes in this book are composites or fictional accounts
based on the authors' actual experiences. Individuals' names have
been changed and identifying details have been altered to protect
confidentiality.

The following people contributed photographs that are used to
illustrate points in this book: Nandan and Ashish Dixit, Marci J.
Hanson, Shelley Herron and family, Tsai Hsing (Summer) Hsia and
Harrison Liou, Rebecca Lazo, Eleanor W. Lynch, Greg Rapisarda,
Terry Joseph Sam, Catherine Thomas and Jeffery Vamos, and
Jeanne Wilcox.

Submitted excerpt from page 87 from DUST TRACKS ON A ROAD
by ZORA NEALE HURSTON
Copyright 1942 by Zora Neale Hurston; renewed © 1970
by John C. Hurston
Reprinted by permission of HarperCollins Publishers Inc.

Library of Congress Cataloging-in-Publication Data
Hanson, Marci J.
Understanding families : approaches to diversity, disability, and risk /
Marci J. Hanson and Eleanor W. Lynch.
    p.   cm.
  Includes bibliographical references and index.
  ISBN-13: 978-1-55766-699-4
  ISBN-10: 1-55766-699-7
    1. Family social work.   2. Family services.   3. Problem families—
Services for.   4. Family—United States.   I. Lynch, Eleanor W.
  II. Title.
HV697.H35 2004
362.82—dc22   2003045126

British Library Cataloguing in Publication data are available from the
British Library.

CONTENTS

ABOUT
THE AUTHORS

Marci J. Hanson, Ph.D., Department of Special Education, San Francisco State University, 1600 Holloway Avenue, San Francisco, California 94132

Marci J. Hanson is Professor of Special Education and Co-Coordinator of the Early Childhood Special Education graduate program at San Francisco State University (SFSU). Dr. Hanson received her doctorate in special education with a minor in developmental psychology in 1978 from the University of Oregon. She directs the SFSU Joint Doctoral Program in Special Education with University of California at Berkeley and is a member of the Child and Adolescent Development faculty of the Marian Wright Edelman Institute for the Study of Children, Youth and Families at SFSU. Prior to joining the faculty at SFSU, she worked as a research scientist in charge of the Early Intervention Unit of the Institute for the Study of Exceptional Children, Educational Testing Service, Princeton, New Jersey.

Dr. Hanson has been actively involved in teaching, research, and community service related to families and young children who are at risk of or who have disabilities. She served as one of the principal investigators of the Early Childhood Research Institute on Inclusion. She also has directed a number of federally funded personnel preparation and research grants in early childhood. Dr. Hanson has had extensive experience developing and implementing family and early intervention programs for infants, toddlers, and preschoolers who have disabilities and has directed two model demonstration early intervention programs. The programs with which she has been involved reflect the cultural diversity of the San Francisco Bay Area and elsewhere.

Dr. Hanson has lived in Austria and has presented and consulted widely in the United States and in India, Italy, Egypt, Spain, Australia, and New Zealand. She has contributed actively to the peer-reviewed professional literature, and she has authored, co-authored, or edited several books, including *Early Intervention Practices around the World* (Paul H. Brookes Publishing Co., 2003) with Drs. Samuel L. Odom, James A. Blackman, and Sudha Kaul; the *Me Too! Series* (Paul H. Brookes Publishing Co.,

2001), with Dr. Paula Beckman; *Atypical Infant Development, Second Edition* (PRO-ED, 1996); *Homecoming for Babies After the Intensive Care Nursery: A Guide for Parents and Professionals in Supporting Families and Their Infant's Early Development* (PRO-ED, 1993), with Kathleen VandenBerg; *Teaching the Infant with Down Syndrome: A Guide for Parents and Professionals, Second Edition* (PRO-ED, 1987); and *Teaching the Young Child with Motor Delays: A Guide for Parents and Professionals* (PRO-ED, 1986) with Dr. Susan Harris.

Eleanor W. Lynch, Ph.D., Department of Special Education, San Diego State University, 5500 Campanile, San Diego, California 92182

Eleanor W. Lynch is Professor of Early Childhood Special Education at San Diego State University (SDSU) and former Chair of the department. She received her doctorate in exceptional children in 1972 from the Ohio State University. Prior to joining the faculty at SDSU she served on the faculty at Miami University and the University of Michigan. She is one of the Regional Coordinators of the federally funded Early Intervention Distance Learning Program, a collaborative project involving five California State Universities and state partners.

Dr. Lynch has been involved in teaching, research, and community service that focus on improving the lives of young children who are at risk for or who have disabilities and their families. She directs the Early Childhood Special Education graduate program at SDSU and serves on the faculty of the SDSU–Claremont Graduate University joint doctoral program. In 2003 she was honored by SDSU as one of the Top 25 on Campus and received the 2003–2004 SDSU Alumni Award as the Outstanding Faculty Member in the College of Education.

Dr. Lynch has directed a model demonstration project and personnel preparation grants in early intervention and early childhood special education as well as a series of research grants on topics such as parental perspectives on special education, the status of educational services for children with chronic illnesses, individualized family service plan development, and the use of behavioral data and reflective practice to improve novice teachers' skills. She has served on numerous local and statewide committees and was one of the national collaborators on the Culturally and Linguistically Appropriate Services (CLAS) Early Childhood Research Institute.

Dr. Lynch has lived in and taught special education to college instructors in Indonesia, taught in American Samoa, given invited presentations in Australia and Taiwan, and lived in India while her husband served on a U.S. Agency for International Development project. She is the author of numerous articles and chapters and is a frequent presenter and workshop leader in the area of cultural competence.

Drs. Hanson and Lynch have also collaborated on *Developing Cross-Cultural Competence: A Guide for Working with Young Children and Their Families, Third Edition* (Paul H. Brookes Publishing Co., 2004), and *Early Intervention: Implementing Child and Family Services for Infants and Toddlers Who Are At-Risk or Disabled, Second Edition* (PRO-ED, 1995).

ACKNOWLEDGMENTS

We are most grateful for the opportunity to work once again with the staff of Paul H. Brookes Publishing Co. We would especially like to acknowledge the long-term help and support of Vice President Melissa Behm and Acquisitions Editor Heather Shrestha, who offered guidance, patience, and faith in us through several delays in the manuscript preparation. The editorial assistance of Senior Book Production Editor Leslie Eckard has been invaluable as well as enjoyable. We also would like to thank the design team and the other members of the Brookes family for their contributions.

Most of all we would like to acknowledge our own families—our parents, who taught us about love and values and who gave us safe "nests" from which we flew, and the families we have entered and created who give us the bonds of love and support.

We are most fortunate to work in occupations that bring us into close contact with many families who come from a variety of diverse backgrounds. We continually grow and learn from our experiences with these families, and we thank them for the contributions that they have made to our thinking and to this volume. Last, we would like to thank the families whose photographs are featured in this book; most of them are close family and friends, and it is a special pleasure to have their participation.

To the families into which we were born:

Max and Maxine Hanson, Laurene, and Brett
Leo and Virginia Whiteside

To the families we

have created
Laura and Jillian

belong to
Patrick Harrison and Erin

and
To the families with whom we have worked

INTRODUCTION

For many, the word *family* conjures images of love; smells of cooking wafting from the kitchen; and memories of comfortable relationships, special moments, joy, and grief. Others may be reminded of hard times, sadness, anger, and loss. *Family* simultaneously connotes one of the narrowest and one of the broadest concepts in the world. It may include only two people, a kinship network of biologically related or unrelated people, a tribe or clan, or even the human race. By whatever definition, however, *family* is central to the fabric of life and the social structure of cultures around the world. This book is about families in their many forms, their strengths and challenges, and the ways in which human service professionals can extend their effectiveness by working in partnership with families.

In the past, most fields of human service employed a *prescriptive* or *directive* model of service delivery whereby professionals assessed families' needs and made recommendations for prescribed treatments or services. Those methods have shifted to services that reflect *partnerships* between families and professionals and focus on families as *active participants* and *decision makers* in the intervention/treatment process. Consequently, a family-centered focus has become one of the benchmarks of quality in early intervention, education, health care, and social service programs and services.

The value placed on creating and maintaining family–professional partnerships has changed services and the ways in which they are delivered. An emphasis on working within the family context benefits people of all age levels from infants and toddlers to the oldest members of the community. It is an approach that acknowledges family strengths; respects and is aligned with family culture, language, and beliefs; and helps create interventions that are acceptable and realistic for families and individual family members.

Although a family-centered approach to intervention has become a hallmark of outstanding programs and services, it is seldom taught or understood from both a theoretical and practical perspective. Some textbooks, research studies, and university courses focus on family theory and its evolution over time. Others focus on strategies for increasing professionals' and organizations' capacity to function in more family-centered ways. This book joins theory with practice to assist professionals by providing a deeper understanding of families and the theoretical, sociocultural, and political influences that surround them. Although the authors' work experiences have centered on families of young children with disabilities, the book is designed to be read and applied by all who work with families.

PHILOSOPHY

This book is shaped by the authors' beliefs about families and the essential role that family members play in intervention. These beliefs have developed from providing services to families of children with disabilities; conducting research with and about families; teaching graduate classes on working with families in early intervention; listening to students as they attempt to reconcile recommended practice and reality; and seeking, coordinating, and experiencing services for aging or ill family members. This thinking has evolved over time. Although these beliefs will continue to be elaborated and evaluated while research, interactions, and changes in practice create new possibilities and new visions, several basic beliefs are foundational. These beliefs are emphasized throughout the book and can be summarized as follows.

1. Family–professional partnerships require that professionals acknowledge and respect each family's strengths, culture, language, and ability to make decisions that are "right" for that family. Family decisions may differ from those that professionals would prefer, but they are to be respected as the family's decisions.

2. All families have strengths. At times those strengths are overshadowed by difficulties that the family or an individual family member is confronting, but these strengths may be marshaled at another time in the family's life cycle.

3. When working with family members, it is essential to listen, follow their lead, and make their agenda a priority. Although professionals bring extensive knowledge, expertise, and experience to bear in their work with families, in general, each family knows what is best for them.

4. When working with a child with disabilities or another family member with special needs, professional support and recommendations must be consistent with the well-being of the entire family.

5. Families' lives are influenced by the sociocultural, economic, and political environment in which they live. Families are often forced to cope with external forces that may include nonsupportive and destructive factors. Professionals have the responsibility to help families understand and negotiate these influences in ways that give families more control and understanding of their life circumstances.

Before beginning Chapter 1, readers may want to examine their own and their organization's beliefs about families. Are beliefs consistent with those that underpin this text, or do they differ?

ORGANIZATION

This book is organized into eight chapters and a conclusion. Each chapter links theory and research to daily practice, but some focus more on knowledge and theory than practice. Others provide multiple suggestions and recommendations for improving practice. Chapter 1 introduces readers to the increasing diversity of contemporary families. Chapter 2 describes several major family theories, as well as frameworks for understanding and describing human development. These theories and frameworks underscore the service approaches advocated in this text. Chapter 3 focuses

on family systems frameworks and family functions—the roles and responsibilities that families in this society are expected to fulfill. Chapter 4
discusses families and disability and the ways in which disability may affect
the family system. Chapter 5 provides an in-depth discussion of risk and
resilience, with special emphasis on the effects of poverty on families. A
discussion of risk factors and their impact on families continues in Chapter
6, which focuses on the effects of addiction and violence on children
and families. Chapter 7 discusses the importance of building family–
professional partnerships, and Chapter 8 suggests strategies for forging
alliances and partnerships and for developing effective communication
between families and professionals. Each of these eight chapters includes
several activities to extend the discussion and apply the concepts discussed
in the chapter to one's own community or individual sphere of practice.
The book concludes with some final thoughts on working with families.

SUMMARY

Families are like the DNA of society. When programs and services are
designed for families as well as for individual family members and respect
the centrality of families in intervention, the quality of programs will
change and their outcomes will improve. It is the authors' hope that this
book will stimulate thought, alter policy, and change practice to foster
services that truly reflect family strengths and potential for adaptation
through effective partnerships with professionals in human services fields.

SECTION I

CONTEMPORARY FAMILY ISSUES

CHAPTER I

DIVERSITY IN CONTEMPORARY FAMILIES

Families bear the brunt of humanity's troubles. At their best, they make a profound contribution to the health of society and its individuals: preserving culture, values, ethics, and wealth; defending the weak; carrying out the great unpaid work of the world. At their worst, they resist change, restrict individual freedom, and indulge in prejudices that can lead to conflict. Their power to form and reshape human minds is forever being rediscovered. Good or ill, we cannot do without them—they are the building blocks of our world.
—JO BOYDEN (1993, p. 20)

Today, family diversity is the norm rather than the exception. No longer is it relevant—and perhaps it never was—to talk about the "American family" as something unitary. Families may be the building blocks of the world, but each block has unique characteristics. Families comprise different sizes, colors, and configurations. Throughout the world, the differences and the similarities in families are striking. In the United States as elsewhere, families share many characteristics and differ dramatically in others. If 10 strangers were asked to describe their families, they would probably give 10 very different descriptions. Even 10 close friends might be surprised at the differences among their families. This chapter examines family diversity and considers the implications for those who work with children and families.

DEFINING FAMILY

Each reader of this chapter has his or her own definition of family. The word *family* is usually associated with certain mental pictures or images. Often, the first picture that comes to mind is of one's own family—perhaps a mother, father, and daughter in a small, Midwestern town; a father and son living together in a city apartment; a house full of brothers, sisters, grandparents, aunts, cousins, and other kin; or a mother, stepfather, and children from previous marriages. Some may resemble the classically depicted nuclear family of a mother, father, and two children. For more than 10% of those envisioning their families, the picture will include at least one member with a disability. For many, the picture may look more like a kaleidoscope with an image that changes, blends, and redefines itself as parents, partners, and siblings change through divorce or death, remarriage, and often divorce again. Some images may even include pets as family members. With this bulging album of different family pictures that come to mind, it is no surprise that defining families is not an easy task.

A review of the range of historical and contemporary definitions of family suggests that little agreement exists among researchers and theoreticians. Burgess's 1926 work defined family as "a unity of interacting personalities each with its own history" (as cited in Gelles, 1995, p. 3). The *Handbook of Marriage and the Family* (Christensen, 1964) provided a much more restrictive view that defined family as married couples with children. Gelles defined family broadly as

> *A social group and a social institution that possesses an identifiable structure made up of positions (e.g., breadwinner, child rearer, decision maker, nurturer) and interactions among those who occupy the positions. The structure typically carries out specialized functions (e.g., child rearing), is characterized by biological and socially defined kinship, and often involves sharing a residence. (1995, p. 10)*

Each of these definitions creates a different lens through which to view families, and the picture that emerges shapes both policy and practice. For services to be optimal, society must recognize the remarkable range of family diversity and the many variations across and within families. Throughout this book the definition of family used is one developed as part of the authors' work in cross-cultural competence. In an earlier work, the authors state "a family is considered to be any unit that defines itself as a family including individuals who are related by blood or marriage as well as those who have made a commitment to share their lives" (Hanson & Lynch, 1992, p. 285). This definition is inclusive and allows for many different family configurations, from nuclear families to extended kinship networks to same-sex partners to a group of older adults who have chosen to live together. "The key elements are that the members of the unit see themselves as a family, are affiliated with one another, and are committed to caring for one another" (Hanson & Lynch, 1992, p. 285).

DIMENSIONS OF DIVERSITY

Family diversity is multidimensional. It is evident in family membership, sociocultural and socioeconomic status, language, culture and cultural identification, religion, race, ethnicity, values, and traditions. Families also differ in their organization—the way in which they get the job of everyday life done. In recent years, the diversity of families within the United States has increased, and this diversity is being acknowledged. The paragraphs that follow highlight some of the changes that have broadened the authors' understanding of families.

Family Structure and Membership

Although extended families with large kinship networks have been common among many Americans for centuries, they have received less attention than the small, nuclear, typically Anglo-European families glorified in the 1950s and 1960s. Indeed, the size and configurations of families have changed from both of these models. According to the report, *America's Children 1999* (ChildStats.gov, 1999), 68% of the children in the United States lived with two parents in 1998 compared to 77% of children living with two parents in 1980. Nearly a quarter (23%) of children lived with only their mothers, 4% lived with only their fathers, and 4% lived with neither their mother nor their father. The term *only* used in this sense is somewhat misleading, however, because it does not include others who may be in the home, such as grandparents, step-parents, and parents' same-sex partners. In fact, in 1990, 14% of the children who would officially be counted as living in a single-parent family were actually living with a heterosexual couple who had chosen not to marry or a couple who could not legally marry because they were of the same sex (Riche, 2000).

Increased Life Expectancy and Decreased Family Size

Two major changes in the United States over the past century have had a considerable impact on family constellation: increased life expectancy and decreased family size. In the early part of the 20th century, child rearing was a task that continued through most of an individual's adult life. People, especially women, tended to marry younger, start a family sooner, continue to have children over many years, and die younger than is typical today. As a result, direct parenting continued for many years. For most adults, this is no longer true. Americans, on average, spend 35% of their years between the ages of 20 and 70 in direct parenting roles (Riche, 2000). This figure varies considerably based on gender, race, and socioeconomic status, however. Because women are still more likely to retain custody of children in situations of divorce or separation, slightly more of their years than men's years are devoted to parenting. Men are more likely than women to remarry, and many of these remarriages include taking on the responsibilities of the new spouse's children. As a result, men are likely to spend twice as much time parenting nonbiological children as are women, and these parenting years are often concurrent with the parenting that they continue to provide for children from a previous marriage (King, 1999; Riche, 2000). African American men and women tend to spend more time in parenthood roles than do Anglo-Europeans. More affluent individuals tend to postpone marriage and childbearing and have fewer children than those who are less affluent, meaning they have fewer direct-parenting years.

Increased life expectancy also has contributed to changes in family composition. Because people are living longer and having fewer children, families span more generations but have smaller numbers in each generation. By 1990, in fact, the most common type of family, as defined by the U.S. Census Bureau, was a married couple living together with no children under the age of 18. According to Riche, "today's living family tree is taller than it used to be, but its branches are shorter" (2000, p. 22). These "taller trees" give rise to more opportunities for intergenerational contact and involvement in everything from recreation and education to various types of support. Many grandparents provide daily care for grandchildren, for example, and some provide financial support for adult children, grandchildren, and even great-grandchildren. These opportunities are made increasingly possible as Americans experience more active, healthy years.

Research findings suggest that each generation of Americans entering their eighties has fewer incapacitating conditions than the preceding generation (Manton, Corder, & Stallard, 1997). A study using health-related measures of the quality of life of older adults in their last year of life lends support to the previous findings. Adults older than 84 years who died in 1993 were found to have a significantly higher quality of life in their last year than those who died in 1986; and the quality of life for those 65–84 improved or remained unchanged in the same time period (Liao, McGee, Cao, & Cooper, 2000).

Divorce, Blended Families, and Single Parenting

Although statistics indicate that the divorce rate in the United States is the highest among industrialized nations, determining the actual divorce rate is not easy (Gelles, 1995). The marriage-to-divorce ratio in any given year would suggest that nearly 50% of all marriages end in divorce. Such a ratio is both inaccurate and invalid, however, because it compares the number of divorces among all married people to the number of marriages in a single year. The *crude* divorce rate presents the number of individuals divorced per 1,000 people in the population. Although this statistical approach improves on the marriage-to-divorce ratio, it, too, is inaccurate because unmarried people and children are included as part of the population. The *refined* divorce rate calculates the annual number of divorces per thousand using only married individuals older than 15 as members of the population (Gelles, 1995). Commonly used estimates of divorce rate range from 40% to 60% because of the various methods of calculation (Seibert & Willetts, 2000).

Regardless of the statistic that one selects, most divorces are followed by remarriage. Nearly 70% of men and 60% of women who divorce remarry other partners (Gelles, 1995), and remarriages often result in blended families. Blended families may include stepparents, stepchildren, and, often, stepbrothers and stepsisters. According to Ahrons and Rodgers (as cited in Seibert & Willetts, 2000), one quarter to one third of the children in the United States will spend some part of their lives in blended families. The complexities of blended families are not difficult to imagine: threats to emotional security imposed by new siblings and parents, changes in family rules and power structure, changes in available resources, multiple sets of relatives with whom to interact, moves back and forth from one home to another, and the residual issues related to the divorce. Although many families are demonstrating on a daily basis that these complexities can be managed effectively, blended families face an array of additional obstacles.

Single parenting often occurs for at least some period of time following a divorce, and it becomes a primary role in the lives of those who do not remarry, cohabit, or rely on members of an extended family or kinship network for co-parenting following a divorce. Census data from a March 1998 report indicated that single parents maintained 27.3% of family households with children younger than age 18 (Casper & Bryson, 1998). Women are more likely to be single parents than men; in the mid-1990s, more than 90% of children whose parents were divorced were living with their mothers (Gelles, 1995). The disproportion between single father and single mother heads-of-households can be accounted for by at least two reasons: 1) custody laws applied in divorce continue to favor women, and 2) fewer women than men remarry following divorce (Teachman, Tedrow, & Crowder, 2000).

Single parenting has been blamed for a wide range of societal ills, but studies do not support such a simplistic view. According to Furstenberg's research on families, "most indicators of declining well-being for children—low test scores, drug use, teen pregnancy, and growing crime rates—began to rise at the same time, or even shortly *before,* divorce and non-marital childbearing rates began to rise" (as cited in Coontz, 1995, p. K 10). For one thing, a majority of the disadvantages of single-parent families can be accounted for by poverty (Coontz, 1995). Financial resources are likely to decline for women following divorce; in fact, 46% of children in families headed by single mothers live in poverty (Children's Defense Fund, 2000). When researchers are able to control for poverty, loss of financial resources, conflict between parents prior to divorce, parenting styles, changes in school and area of residence, and social prejudice, these factors are found to be more highly correlated with children's behavioral and educational success or failure than is the factor of being raised in a single-parent family (Coontz, 1995). Coontz noted that "the *educational* status of a child's mother has more impact than her *marital* status on that child's welfare" (1995, p. 10) in determining child outcomes. Nonetheless, single parenting is not for the faint of heart. The sources of strain identified by Weiss in 1979 have changed little over the years: responsibility overload, task overload, and emotional overload.

The discussion of single parenting up to this point has focused on divorce and its aftermath; however, a large percentage of single mothers have never been married. Between 1959 and 1997, the number of unmarried women between the ages of 15 and 44 years who gave birth nearly doubled, with an average of 23.2 per thousand in the 1960s increasing to an average of 45.0 from 1990 through 1997. The increase is even more dramatic among young women between the ages of 15 and 19. Among industrialized nations, the United States has the highest rate of births to teen mothers (ChildStats.gov, 1999). In the 1960s, the average number of teens who gave birth was 17 per thousand compared to an average of 44 teens per thousand from 1990 through 1997 who gave birth (Children's Defense Fund, 2000). Trends in birth rates differ by race; births to teen mothers have decreased more among African Americans than among Anglo-Europeans since the mid-1990s (Gelles, 1995). It is not surprising that teens who give birth are typically unskilled and have limited education and inadequate resources to support themselves and their children (Gelles, 1995).

Grandparents as Parents

One of the outcomes of improved health, increased life expectancy, the high divorce rate among adults with children, and the increases in teen pregnancy has been an increase in the number of adults raising their children's children. In many families, grandparents have responsibility for raising their grandchildren, or even great-grandchildren, because of the biological parents' lack of competence or their incapacity through imprisonment, abuse, drug addiction, or psychiatric disorders (Bengston, 2001; Bryson & Casper, 1999). In other families grandparents become primary or co-parents when a teenager gives birth and continues to live with her parents or when a son or daughter does not have the financial resources to provide a home for his or her children. In 1997, nearly 6% of children younger than age 18 lived in homes headed by their grandparents (Riche, 2000). Grandparents provide a range of support to their children and their children's children, not the least of which is financial. Contrary to the

philosophy espoused by bumper stickers on recreational vehicles that say, "I'm spending my children's inheritance," many older Americans are providing monetary and other forms of support to the younger generation (Bengston, 2001). Even in situations in which grandparents are not immediately involved in supporting their children and raising their grandchildren, they play a role that Hagestad (as cited by Bengston, 2001), has titled the "Family National Guard." When their children, grandchildren, and great-grandchildren experience crises, many grandparents who would otherwise have stayed in the background marshal their resources to support the younger generation's well-being.

The importance and the complexity of the role grandparents play within families is especially salient when a child in the family is diagnosed with a disability. As parents struggle with their own grief, explaining the disability to the grandparents and other extended family members and helping them cope with their disbelief and disappointment can put additional strain on the family system. From the grandparents' perspective, it is painful to see their children suffer when there is nothing that they can do to make it right (Morton, 2000). One of the roles of early intervention for young children with disabilities and their families is to provide the facilitation and support that enable families to understand and respond to their child's unique needs more effectively. In a small, informal study of families of young, deaf children, the grandparents' supportiveness increased by one third in families who participated in early intervention (Morton, 2000). Support from grandparents can be practical or emotional. Despite the many ways grandparents can provide support, however, few studies address the kinds of support that most grandparents provide (Baranowski & Schilmoeller, 1999). (For a comprehensive discussion of families of children with disabilities, see Chapter 4.)

The Sandwich Generation

The converse of older adults serving as the Family National Guard occurs when parents are providing care and support to their children as well as their aging parents. This population of people engaged in such double duty has been described in the popular press as the "sandwich generation." For these families, juggling jobs, children, and the needs of frail, older family members is challenging. An estimated 9 million baby boomers and those close to the same age find themselves in the middle of the sandwich. Although both men and women are affected by their parents' aging, women are more often squeezed in this multigenerational sandwich. Seventy percent of the caregivers are women, and 60% of these women work full time (McCombs, 2001).

The day-to-day needs associated with care of older parents, such as monitoring medication, making doctor's appointments, conducting business, maintaining a social support system for place-bound older adults, ensuring physical and psychological safety, and advocating for the care that is needed is demanding and exhausting (McCombs, 2001). But, in some respects, the role reversal is even more difficult than the daily demands. Watching one's own parents become dependent is heart wrenching.

Same-Sex Parents

Family membership is also changing in terms of gender makeup. Increasingly, same-sex couples are establishing families that include children. Children typically become part of a gay or lesbian family through second-parent adoption or co-parent adoption (Crawford, 1999). Second-parent adoption most often occurs when a child from a previous marriage is adopted by the new same-sex partner just as one partner may adopt the other partner's child in a heterosexual marriage. In a number of states, it is legal for gay or lesbian couples to adopt, as co-parents, a child who is not biologically related to either. The importance of the right to co-adopt cannot be underestimated because it provides both parents and child with the same rights as those afforded to children and parents in a heterosexual partnership (Crawford, 1999). In addition to adoptions of children from heterosexual relationships and traditional adoptions, an increasing number of lesbian women are choosing to have children via donor insemination (Patterson, 2000). Of the research available comparing children of gay men or lesbian women with those of heterosexual couples, no significant differences emerged in psychosocial development, gender identity, separation-individuation, locus of control, intelligence, self-concept, personality, or moral judgment (Ahmann, 1999; Patterson, 2000). The greatest concern is not with gay and lesbian families, but with societal perceptions and persecution.

Implications for Service Providers

Families in the United States were never as monolithic as nostalgic politicians and screenwriters would have the public believe. Diversity in family size, membership, and intergenerational involvement has always existed. The diversity of family structures that is publicly acknowledged has increased dramatically since the middle of the 20th century, however. The challenges, failures, and successes that have emerged as family structures have evolved have given us new ways of defining, studying, and working with families. These new paradigms have, in turn, taught us that there is no "right way" to be a family.

SOCIOECONOMIC DIFFERENCES: THE DOLLAR DIVIDE

In 1999, the median household income for white, non-Latinos; African American; and Latino families was the highest ever recorded, and the median income for Asian American and Pacific Islander households equaled the highest since recording began (U.S. Bureau of the Census, 2000) (shown least to greatest in Figure 1.1). In *Money Income in the United States: 1999*, a report issued by the U.S. Bureau of the Census (2000), the median household income for white, non-Latinos was $44,366; for African Americans, $27,910; for Latinos, $30,735; and for Asian American and Pacific Islanders, $51,205. The average household income from 1997

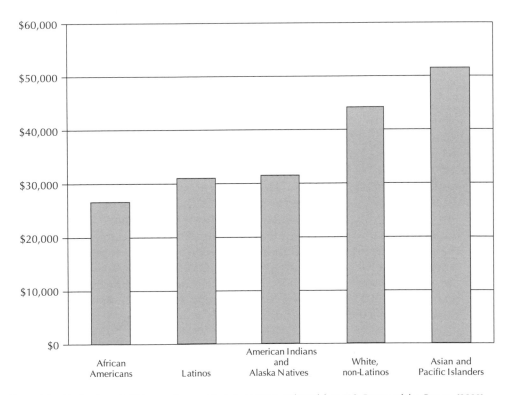

Figure 1.1. Median household income by race/ethnicity in 1999. (Adapted from U.S. Bureau of the Census, [2000]. *Money income in the United States.* Retrieved May 7, 2001, from http://www.census.gov/hhes/www/income.html.)

through 1999 for American Indians and Alaska Natives was $30,784. (These figures are based solely on money received and do not account for taxes paid or noncash benefits received such as fringe benefits that are part of an employment package or the variety of public assistance programs such as Medicare, Medicaid, supported housing, or food stamps.) Although 1999 capped 5 years of increases in household income (U.S. Bureau of the Census, 2000), the numbers cannot be taken at face value. Even in the midst of an extended period of strong economic indicators, not everyone profited equally. The median income calculations are made on household income—the aggregated income for all members of the household— therefore it is critical to know the average size of households to determine how each group is doing on a per capita basis. Viewed this way, the order changes. White, non-Latinos had the highest median income per family member ($23,798), with an average household size of 2.47 members. Asian American and Pacific Islander households followed with an average household size of 3.13 and a median income of $21,635 per person. African American and Latino households had lower median incomes per person. African Americans averaged 2.75 household members and a median income of $13,987 per person, while Latino households averaged 3.49 people and a median income of $11,598 per person (U.S. Bureau of the Census, 2000). Comparable data are not available for American Indians and Alaska Natives or for families who listed more than one race or ethnicity. These numbers must be interpreted with extreme caution, because each ethnic group is extremely heterogeneous. Within each, some members are very affluent, whereas others are extremely poor. The figures do demonstrate that there is considerable inequity across ethnic groups in median per capita income, however (shown least to greatest in Figure 1.2).

Inequities also exist between male and female workers. The number of women and men in the workforce is fairly comparable: Of the approximately 71 million women 15 years of age and older who worked outside of the home in 1999, 57.3% of them worked full time and had a median income of $26,324. Their earnings were statistically unchanged from the previous year. The real median income of the 73.3% of men who worked full time in 1999 was approximately $10,000 higher at $36,476, and had increased slightly from the previous year (U.S. Bureau of the Census, 2000). Although the numbers of women in the full-time workforce continues to grow, the female-to-male ratio of earnings dropped between 1996 and 1999, and women continued to be underpaid as compared with their male counterparts. The differences between male and female workers in a wide range of occupations was highlighted in a survey conducted by the U.S. Department of Labor and reported in *Money for Women* magazine (Daragahi, 2001). In all 10 occupations reported, the median weekly salaries for men were higher than those for women.

Income Diversity in the United States

The late 1990s brought a strong economy in which the overall wealth of the nation grew; unemployment was low and there was little inflation.

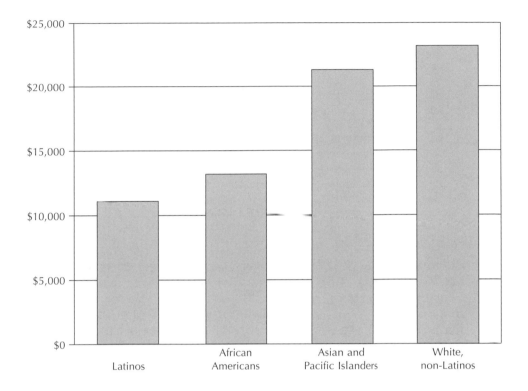

Figure 1.2. Median per capita income by race/ethnicity in 1999. (Adapted from U.S. Bureau of the Census, [2000]. *Money income in the United States.* Retrieved May 7, 2001, from http://www.census.gov/hhes/www/income.html.)

Newspaper headlines and stock market reports were rosy; but in many instances, the words of an old adage were accurate—the rich got richer and the poor got poorer. During that time, the gap between the wealthiest 5% of American families and the poorest 20% reached a 52-year high (Children's Defense Fund, 2000). In 1998, families in the top 5%, with annual incomes averaging $246,520, made nearly 20 times more than families in the bottom 20%, whose incomes averaged $12,526 (Children's Defense Fund, 2000). Middle-income families also lost ground. Although the annual, median income for the typical family with children in 1998 reached a new high of $45,422, much of this can be attributed to an increase in the number of women joining the workforce or increasing the number of hours that they spent in paid employment (Children's Defense Fund, 2000).

Official and Unofficial Characteristics of Poverty

The causes and consequences of poverty in the United States have been known for decades. Robert Hunter, a well-known sociologist (who wrote eloquently about poverty but was opposed to immigration), described the conditions of families at or near poverty in the 1900s in ways that would be startlingly accurate today:

[T]here are great districts of people who are up before dawn, who wash, dress, and eat breakfast, kiss wives and children, and hurry away to work or to seek work. The world rests upon their shoulders; it moves by their muscle; everything would stop if, for any reason, they should decide not to go into the fields and factories and mines. But the world is so organized that they gain enough to live upon only when they work; should they cease, they are in destitution and hunger. The more fortunate of the laborers are but a few weeks from actual distress when the machines are stopped. Upon the unskilled masses want is constantly pressing. As soon as employment ceases, suffering stares them in the face. They are the actual producers of wealth, who have no home nor any bit of soil which they may call their own. They are the millions who possess no tools and can work only by permission of another. In the main, they live miserably, they know not why. They work sore, yet gain nothing. They know the meaning of hunger and the dread of want. They love their wives and children. They try to retain their self-respect. They have some ambition. They give to neighbors in need, yet they are themselves the actual children of poverty. (1904, pp. 4–5)

The total number of people in poverty in the United States fell by nearly 5 million between 1993 and 1998. In 1998, however, with the highest median incomes ever recorded, 12.7% of the overall United States population was poor (Riche, 2000). Slightly more than 11% of families and nearly 19% of children under the age of 18 lived below the poverty line (Seccombe, 2000), which is defined annually by the federal government. (Chapter 5 provides an in-depth discussion of poverty, its causes, and its consequences.)

Federal Support for Families Who Are Poor

At the same time that the United States was experiencing a robust economy in the 1990s, the safety net for poor families was being pulled away. In 1996, the federal Personal Responsibility and Work Opportunity Reconciliation Act (PRWORA) replaced the cash assistance support Aid to Families with Dependent Children (AFDC) with the Temporary Assistance to Needy Families (TANF) (Kalil, Schweingruber, Daniel-Echols, & Breen, 2001). TANF is designed to help families move from welfare to work. It places a 5-year lifetime limit on receipt of welfare benefits and requires that most mothers receiving aid return to work. Each state has created a different approach to implementing PRWORA, and some of the models have been more successful for those involved than others. This legislation, meant to make welfare available on a temporary rather than a continuing basis, has had a profound effect on the numbers receiving welfare. Between the legislation's passage in August 1996 and June 1999, the number of families receiving support dropped by 44% (Children's Defense Fund, 2000). In actual numbers, the TANF caseload dropped from 12.2 million to 6.9 million, eliminating the benefits for 5.3 million men, women, and children (Children's Defense Fund, 2000). Although the full impact of the changes in the nation's welfare system is not known, some follow-up studies are disturbing. Many individuals leaving welfare to enter the workforce have low skills. The jobs that they are able to obtain are low-wage jobs with no benefits and little opportunity for advancement. Data from 1997's American Family Survey, which was the first full year of TANF implementation, showed that 80% of mothers with at least a high school education were working (Children's Defense Fund, 2000). Only 9% of those with more than three barriers to employment such as limited English language skills, a disability, and/or minimal work experience were employed, however (Children's Defense Fund, 2000).

Children in Poverty

Because poverty affects families, it often affects children. In 1998 in the United States, one of every five children was poor; and the child poverty rate was two to three times higher than most of the major industrialized nations (Children's Defense Fund, 2000; National Center for Children in Poverty, 2000). Although each family and each individual living in poverty is unique, some generalizations can inform the thinking about needed changes in policies and programs. Poor and impoverished families tend to

- Be headed by a single parent, typically a mother (Gelles, 1995; Larner & Collins, 1996; Seccombe, 2000)
- Have at least one wage earner whose wages are insufficient to move the family out of poverty (Children's Defense Fund, 2000)
- Live in the central or core area of a city (Gelles, 1995; Larner & Collins, 1996)
- Live in the South (U.S. Bureau of the Census, 1999)
- Be white in terms of absolute numbers, although a considerably larger percentage of Latino and African American families are poor compared with the percentage of white families (Larner & Collins, 1996; U.S. Bureau of the Census, 1999)
- Be undereducated, with the best-educated parent completing less than high school (Larner & Collins, 1996)

Of great concern is the increase in the number of families that are living in extreme poverty—defined as an income that is 50% or less of the federal poverty line. According to the National Center for Children in Poverty, 8% of children in the United States live in extreme poverty which, in 1998, was defined as an annual cash income of $6,502 or less for a family of three. The Children's Defense Fund, as cited by the Institute for Research on Poverty at the University of Wisconsin–Madison (2001), reported that more than 1.8 million children lived in homes with incomes at less than half the poverty level in 1997, representing a 26% increase from 1996.

Poverty and Disability

Among children between 6 and 14 years of age, approximately 1 in 8 have a disability (U.S. Bureau of the Census, 1997). Poverty is frequently associated with developmental risk (Hanson & Carta, 1996). This is because poverty promotes an accumulation of risk factors that compound its hardships. Insufficient food, inadequate housing, lack of health care, nonexistent transportation, homelessness, and neighborhoods plagued by violence interact to reduce resilience. Although many parents and families struggle mightily against the factors that surround poverty, they face many obstacles. Inadequate nutrition, substance abuse, maternal depression, exposure to environmental toxins, trauma, and physical abuse are often part of everyday experience. Children are particularly vulnerable to these frequently co-occurring circumstances. The first years of life contribute significantly to emotional and cognitive development, so the risk factors faced by millions of children living in poverty or extreme poverty place them at considerable risk for negative outcomes including less-than-optimal brain development (Brooks-Gunn, Klebanov, Liaw, & Duncan, 1995; National Center for Children in Poverty, 1997). In a complex statistical analysis of data gathered between 1983 and 1996 from the National Health Interview Survey, poverty emerged as a significant predictor of disability (Fujiura & Yamaki, 2000). In 1983, poverty did not statistically predict disability, but by 1996, the odds of children in poverty having a disability were 86% higher than they were for those children living above the poverty threshold. On reflection, this finding is not surprising given that children living in poverty are more likely to be exposed to conditions that are predictive of disability, such as low birth weight, chronic health problems, limited access to health care, inadequate nutrition, and trauma. As might be predicted, living in a single-parent household was also highly associated with disability because of the correlation between single parenthood and poverty. A correlation also exists between poverty and race; although the likelihood of children of color having a disability is greater than that of white children, when family constellation and income are controlled, the study found no differences (Fujiura & Yamaki, 2000).

Having a disability as an adult is also associated with poverty. Although opportunities for individuals with disabilities have increased substantially in all domains in recent decades, job opportunities for those with and without disabilities remain unequal, making it more difficult for those with disabilities to obtain and retain a job. An analysis of the U.S. Census Bureau's Survey of Income and Program Participation data found that households providing support to a member who has mental retardation or a developmental disability were poorer and received more means-tested, public benefits than the average family household in the United States (Fujiura, 1998).

As the preceding paragraphs suggest, poverty is not an easily understood, unitary problem. It is a series of problems that affect many diverse groups in varying ways, and a single policy or intervention designed to eliminate or significantly reduce poverty is too simplistic (Rodgers, 2000). The same is true for a unitary policy of intervention. Approaches to all families must be tailored to meet their specific preferences and needs.

Affluence in the United States

Despite the alarming statistics on poor families, poverty is not the context in which all families live. The "overclass," as they have been called in the popular press, is a growing population group in this country (Adler, 1995). Difficult to define through statistical measures, members of this group combine both an income and an attitude that set them apart from the middle class. These are not the beneficiaries of family fortunes and wealth that has been accumulated over generations; rather, they have created the wealth that has catapulted them into this group. These individuals tend to be achievement-oriented; they are in the top 20% on income, have a degree from a prestigious university, and are clustered primarily on the East and West coasts but are transnational in perspective. They and their families are emerging as a new elite (Adler, 1995), although *elite* may not be the word that they would choose. With a firm conviction that success flows from merit, it becomes more difficult for many in the overclass to recognize that they have lived a life of privilege. This conviction makes it equally difficult for people in this overclass to understand that failure is often based on societal, rather than personal, shortcomings.

The gap between the overclass and middle class is increasing, and it is becoming clear that there is a chasm between the overclass and the underclass. In 1977, male college graduates out-earned their counterparts who had completed only a high school education by 49%. By 1992, males with college degrees earned 83% more than their counterparts who had only a high school diploma (Reich, 1995). Given that members of the overclass are substantially out-earning those in the middle class, it is not difficult to see that their earnings are dramatically above those of the underclass. The financial trajectory for women who completed college is similar, though not as pronounced. Affluence is more common among families of Anglo-European heritage than families of color—not surprising when one considers the factors that contribute to wealth such as higher education, higher end job opportunities, deeper income pools, and orientation toward personal rather than communal achievement.

With the increase in affluence, two issues especially relevant to this book emerge: The first is involvement in child rearing in some affluent families; the second is the gap between the rich and the poor.

Articles are beginning to appear in the popular media that express concerns over the negative effects of affluence on families and their children. Just as economic strain can prevent parents from giving full attention to parenting (White & Rogers, 2000), so, too, can the strain to earn more, do more, and get ahead faster take parents' attention away from children. As stated by Mack, "Where once maternal engagement was hampered only by the burdens of critical subsistence tasks, today the principal thief of time is a fast-moving market economy offering a cafeteria of ever-changing, often senseless temptations" (2000, p. 11). For many families on the fast track, the temptations become realities as they watch out for the next best thing that will replace today's toys, sport utility vehicles, and exercise gurus. Although the opportunities associated with growing up in a wealthy family cannot be ignored, money does not guarantee success, or even positive outcomes, for children in affluent families. Shootings and other violence in schools have occurred in suburban areas with average and above-average material resources. Material advantages do not outweigh the importance of time with children and instruction and modeling of values that include compassion and social justice.

Concern is mounting over the widening gap between rich and poor within the United States. As the gulf widens, attitudes may become more rigid, and the politics that shape policies related to families who are poor may shift. The shift could take many directions, from paternalistic forms of support to punitive approaches, but it is important for service providers to be aware of the dangers that exist for families who live in the margins. Endorsement of a meritocracy in which rewards are believed to flow fairly to those who work hardest does not take into account the systemic, societal biases in many policies, programs, and services that favor those who are already on top. Service providers are in a position to consider the context of each family's life. What opportunities have been unavailable to the family because of their socioeconomic status, race, educational level, or primary language? And, most important, how can service providers help families overcome these barriers?

RACIAL, CULTURAL, ETHNIC, AND LINGUISTIC DIVERSITY

No aspects of diversity have received more attention in the past decade than cross-cultural diversity in terms of race, culture, ethnicity, and primary language. With the transformation of the United States from a country with a majority group to one in which there is no majority, the emphasis on cross-cultural issues is critical. A first step in understanding the racial, cultural, ethnic, and linguistic dimensions of diversity is considering the terms being used.

Defining Racial, Ethnic, Cultural, and Linguistic Differences

For the past 200 years, physical anthropologists have used race as a way to describe people by their physical characteristics (Gollnick & Chinn, 1997). Early racial categories included the Caucasoid, Mongoloid, and Negroid. When there was little interaction or commerce among peoples of the world, these racial distinctions may have had some descriptive function. Because the classification system was developed by people in the Caucasoid group, however, the descriptions typically involved comparisons among the races that favored the lighter skinned people. With intermixing and intermarrying across all geographic boundaries, the original

racial groups have blended. And, as the Human Genome Project has confirmed, race is not biologically meaningful. No significant difference exists
in genetic makeup among the world's human population (Olson, 2001;
Smith & Sapp, 1996). Why then, is race still important to many in today's
world? It continues to be important because the undeniable scientific
evidence of our similarities does not erase the centuries-old racial stereo-
typing that attributes beliefs and behaviors to skin color and physical
features. Nor does it eradicate the centuries of white privilege that have
enabled some at the expense of others (McIntosh, 1990). The construct
of race affects people every day whether they are aware of it or not,
because personal identity and racial identify are inextricably linked. Even
though race is not scientifically relevant, it is very socially relevant. Ladson-
Billings (1996) argued that grappling with race, racism, and one's own
racial identity are central to reducing oppression. Likewise, understanding
race, racial identity, and racism are essential to working successfully
with families.

Ethnicity or ethnic group has traditionally been defined to include
one's national origin, religion, and race (Gordon, 1964). Racial groups
include many ethnic groups. For example, families with Asian heritage
may have distant or recent origins in India, Indonesia, China, Japan,
Korea, the Philippines, and many other Asian countries. People from each
of these origins may speak a different language or dialect; participate in
one of many different religions; and observe different traditions around
birth, child rearing, death, and healing (Klein & Chen, 2001). Likewise,
ethnic groups include members of different races. For example, Latinos
as an ethnic group are composed of Native peoples, those of African
descent, those of European ancestry, and individuals with Asian heritage.

Although most families can trace their ancestry and may think of themselves as Cuban, Mexican, African American, American Indian, Irish, Italian, or Chinese, others may identify more closely with "just being American." Many individuals identify with more than one ethnic group; others identify with only one; and some consider their ethnic identity to be less relevant. They may identify more closely with their gender, sexual preference, or another characteristic; for example, some individuals within the Deaf community focus on hearing and deafness as the most salient characteristics. Among some families, religion is the most potent force in ethnic identity. For example, Orthodox Jews from Israel, Brazil, the United States, and Russia may have more in common with each other than they have with compatriots in their countries of origin. The search for an integrated theory of racial and ethnic identity development and its measurement is an area of interest for many researchers and advocates. As research in this area continues, the understanding of ethnicity and identity will increase. (Those wishing to read more about ethnic identity development are referred to works by Bernal & Knight, 1993; Cross, 1978; Helms, 1995; and Phinney, 1990.)

Culture, often used interchangeably with ethnicity, has been defined in various ways. Benedict spoke of culture as customs, institutions, and ways of thinking:

> No man ever looks at the world with pristine eyes. He sees it edited by a definite set of customs and institutions and ways of thinking. Even in his philosophical probings he cannot go behind these stereotypes; his very concepts of the true and the false will still have reference to particular traditional customs. (1934, p. 2)

Hall put forth one of the most inclusive and most compelling definitions of culture in 1976:

> Culture is man's medium; there is not one aspect of human life that is not touched and altered by culture. This means personality, how people express themselves (including shows of emotion), the way they think, how they move, how problems are solved, how their cities are planned and laid out, how transportation systems function and are organized, as well as how economic and government systems are put together and function. (pp. 16–17)

Some definitions focus on what is known and shared by a group; others emphasize customs or what is important and meaningful to a group of people (Green, 1982). Regardless of the definition that one chooses to use, family service providers should keep several important points in mind:

1. *Culture is not static; it is dynamic and ever-changing. The cultural practices that individuals remember and practice from their country or place of origin are often different from the practices that are occurring in that same place today.*

2. *Culture, language, ethnicity, and race are not the only determinants of one's values, beliefs, and behaviors. Socioeconomic status, educational level, occupation, personal experience, and personality all exert a powerful influence over how individuals view themselves and how families*

function. Culture is only one of many elements that family members use to define themselves.

3. *In describing any culture or cultural practice,* within-group differences are as great as across-group *differences. In other words, no cultural, ethnic, linguistic, or racial group is monolithic. There are wide variations in attitudes, beliefs, and behaviors. To assume that people who share a common culture or language are alike is to make a dangerous mistake (Lynch, 1998a, p. 27).*

To begin to understand and serve families effectively, determining, acknowledging, and working from their cultural identity and preferences are important first steps.

How Diverse Is the United States?

Data from the 2000 Census present a picture of increasing diversity within the United States. Words such as "majority" are no longer meaningful when the population statistics are examined. In California, for example, no cultural or ethnic group constitutes a majority, with 46.7% of the population white, 32.4% Latino, 10.8% Asian and Pacific Islander, and 6.4% African American ("Diverse, Yet Distinct," 2001). Although the changes may be less dramatic in other parts of the country, the whole nation is growing and being enriched by increased diversity.

Between 1990 and 2000, the U.S. population grew by 13.2%, the largest increase in history (Perry & Mackun, 2001). Regionally, the West and South had the highest growth rates, but all states grew for the first time in a century (Perry & Mackun, 2001). Urban areas also grew between 1990 and 2000. More than 80% of U.S. residents live in metropolitan areas, and the 10 most-populous states, already highly diverse, are home to 50% of the nation's population (Perry & Mackun, 2001).

At the time this book was published, complete data were scheduled to be released on the racial/ethnic breakdown of the U.S. population through 2003. Consequently, only partial data are available for this book. The first release related to the Latino population demonstrates dramatically changing demographics. The Latino population (referred to as Hispanic in U.S. Census Bureau reports), excluding those living in Puerto Rico and the trust territories, grew by 57.9% to 35.3 million between 1990 and 2000—nearly 3 million more than estimated (Schmitt, 2001). Based on these figures, Latinos now make up 12.5% of the population (Guzmán, 2001). This percentage makes the number of Latino Americans and the number of African Americans in the United States close to equal (Schmitt, 2001). These figures also emphasize the diversity of the Latino/Hispanic group. Although the fastest rate of growth within the Latino population was among those from Central America, Mexican Americans are by far the largest group with Latino ancestry. With a continuing influx of individuals and families from Mexico seeking the opportunities they believe to be available in the United States and the population's high birth rate, the number of Mexican Americans is expected to grow steadily in the coming years (Schmitt, 2001). Nearly 60% are of Mexican ancestry, with the remaining ancestries made up of 10% Puerto Rican, 5% Central American, 4% Cuban, 4% South American, 2% Dominican, and less than 1% Spanish. Seventeen percent were described as "other" because detailed information was not provided (Guzmán, 2001). The surge in the Latino population accounts in large measure for another of the census statistics: 1 in 10 Americans is foreign born (Schmitt, 2001). The last time that this was true was in the 1930s.

Diverse Languages

The diversity of the United States can also be described in terms of the languages spoken. In both large cities and smaller communities, it is not uncommon to hear a mélange of languages. In some school districts in California, there are as many as 90 home languages. The 10 most common languages among English language learners in the state in 1998–1999 were Spanish, Vietnamese, Hmong, Mandarin, Tagalog, Khmer, Korean, Armenian, Cantonese, Russian, and Lao (California Department of Education, 2001). California is not the only state in which language diversity is an increasingly important feature; Georgia's Department of Education reported that 8,000 children in its public schools were English language learners in 1994. By 1998, that number had doubled (Myers & Boothe, 2000). States such as Texas, New Mexico, New York, Florida, and Alaska have both immigrants and long-time residents whose first language is not English. Acknowledgment of the nation's language diversity is becoming more evident as billboards, television stations, and radio stations broadcast their messages in Spanish, Chinese, Vietnamese, and a host of other languages.

The Impact of Diversity on Families

The impact of cultural, ethnic, and linguistic diversity is a topic about which there are few generalizations because diversity affects each family and each family member differently. The culture or cultures on which identity is based, the language(s) spoken, and physical characteristics influence each individual's attitudes, beliefs, and behaviors. Cultural norms, traditions, and expectations shape each life from before birth until death in subtle and not-so-subtle ways. At a superficial level, events such as holiday celebrations and sometimes the foods that are served and the clothing that is worn are all influenced by culture. At more profound levels, child rearing, views about the meaning of life and death, and the values related to family, success, social interaction, and social justice are shaped in large measure by deep cultural roots. Within families, children's socialization, the way decisions are made, and who makes those decisions as well as the way in which power is used or shared have a profound impact on daily life, aspirations, and opportunities.

Lynch (1998b) described several cultural continua—value sets that are common across cultures—that are important to consider when providing services to families (see Table 1.1). These continua, such as interdependence—independence, nurturance of young children—independence of young children, time given—time measured, ownership defined in broad terms—ownership defined as individual and specific, harmony—control, and many others exist in all known cultures. Cultural groups and members of cultural groups vary in their beliefs and behaviors associated with each of the continua, however. For example, one of the authors learned by living in Indonesia that the concept of time was viewed differently there than it is in the United States. Time was freely given rather than parceled out in a predetermined way. Interactions were more often based on the time needed rather than the time allocated. This way of viewing time is in complete opposition to the author's life in the United States, where calendars, personal digital assistants, meeting dates, and appointments predominate. Neither approach to time is better than the other; they are simply different. When two people fall at opposite ends of the time continuum, there is likely to be conflict. The same is true in relation to each of the other continua. Professionals who focus on helping a child achieve independence may find themselves in conflict with families or family members who emphasize interdependence. This kind of conflict may manifest itself when an early childhood professional/interventionist is encouraging a mother to wean and toilet train her toddler on a set schedule, for example. It may also come into play in later life when family members are being encouraged to "let go" of their young adult by letting him or her live independently or attend college in another city or state.

Thus, the differences in each family's beliefs and behaviors related to these and other continua influence the impact of diversity on the family. The more closely aligned the family's beliefs and behaviors are to those with whom they associate, the less the impact. But as differences between family beliefs and values and the beliefs and values of others increase, the dissonance and opportunity for conflict become greater. These differences are most likely to occur when families and systems interact. The procedures, emphasis on timeliness, and bureaucracy that are inherent in systems may be at odds with many families' ways of living.

Table 1.1.   Cultural continua common across cultures

Extended family and kinship networks	Small unit families with little reliance on the extended family
Interdependence	Individuality
Nurturance of young children	Independence of young children
Time is given	Time is measured
Respect for age, ritual, and tradition	Emphasis on youth, future, and technology
Ownership defined in broad terms	Ownership, individual and specific
Differentiated rights and responsibilities	Equal rights and responsibilities
Harmony	Control

From Lynch, E.W. (1998b), Developing cross-cultural competence. In E.W. Lynch & M.J. Hanson (Eds.), *Developing cross-cultural competence: A guide for working with children and their families* (p. 58). Baltimore: Paul H. Brookes Publishing Co.; adapted by permission.

Language differences may profoundly affect a family's access to a community and its services. "Language is the primary means of access to understanding, relationships, and services" (Lynch, 1998a, p. 36). In the United States, families whose members are English language learners have fewer opportunities than those who are fluent in English. Imagine that you are just beginning to learn English. Consider how difficult it would be if you had to have an interpreter every time you spoke to your child's teacher, saw a physician, or tried to apply for services. Even for families whose language is English, the language of systems is often highly technical and peppered with abbreviations. Thus, linguistic diversity may have a significant impact on a family's daily life and opportunity.

Diversity and the Socialization of Children

The way in which children are socialized is, to some degree in every family, influenced by cultural and sociocultural norms and traditions. Whether children are encouraged to be curious or compliant, talkative or quiet, assertive or passive, and reflective or reactive are influenced, in part, by cultural beliefs and traditions. Consider the following examples:

AMY AND MARTA

Amy and Marta are two newborns who are leaving the hospital with their families for the first time. Amy will go home to a room of her own with a nightlight and teddy bear wallpaper. When she cries, her parents will be attentive up to a point, but may decide within the first year that sometimes she "just has to cry herself out." Her parents believe in helping children become independent and in developing their ability to comfort themselves at an early age.

Marta will eventually have a room of her own, but for the first 2-3 years of her life she will sleep in her parents' room, often in the bed with them. Whenever she whimpers, cries, or shows any fussiness, she will be held, cuddled, walked, or fed. Her parents are less concerned about independence than interdependence and focus more on nurturance than self-comforting during infancy and early childhood.

Though these very early experiences are mediated by a number of other factors, they will influence each child's behavior. Amy may appear to be more curious and willing to engage with objects as well as people that she is less familiar with. Marta may prefer being close to people she knows well and less interested in amusing herself with toys and objects than with being near an adult that she knows.

These differences in upbringing are further illustrated in the story of Fernando and Kyle, two boys in the same classroom.

FERNANDO AND KYLE

Fernando's family strongly emphasizes cooperation and the good of the group. Fernando has been taught to think of the group before he thinks of himself, and his home life reflects this value. Kyle's family places a very high value on personal achievement, and he has been raised to be competitive. In their classroom, Fernando and Kyle behave quite differently. Fernando is uncomfortable raising his hand when he knows the answer and he is embarrassed by praise. From his teacher's point of view, Fernando is shy and nonparticipatory. Kyle appears just the opposite, eager to demonstrate his knowledge and reinforced by praise. Whether the boys or their teachers are aware of it, the difference in the boys' socialization has shaped their behavior, others' opinions of them, and the opportunities that may come their way.

CARMEN AND TANYA

Carmen's father had left the family by the time she was born. Her mother spent most of Carmen's early years struggling with addiction to alcohol and methamphetamines. Her own needs were so strong that she had trouble meeting Carmen's. Although she could be a loving mother, these times were short-lived. More often, she was psychologically unavailable and sometimes physically abusive. When Carmen was 8 years old, she was removed from her mother's care and placed in a series of foster homes—some wonderful, some not. Carmen is now in her early twenties. She dropped out of high school in her sophomore year, has two children whose fathers are unknown, and is on probation for several counts of petty theft. At this point, she is in danger of having her children removed from her care and placed in foster care.

Tanya's early years with her mother were similar to Carmen's, but Tanya was adopted by an aunt when she was 10. Her aunt, though poor in material resources, provided consistency, love, attention, direction, and support. Tanya completed high school, took a job as a teacher's assistant, and is now working on her bachelor's degree in the evenings. She is the first one in the family to attend college, and she has set her sights on becoming a teacher.

Although early experiences have a dramatic impact on children's later outcomes, supportive adults and children's resilience can reverse even the most negative situations.

LINDA AND ELANA

Linda was raised to believe that she could do or be anything she wanted to be. Her family encouraged her to play with dolls and trucks, to participate in sports and choir, to attend math camp, and to run for office in various organizations. As an adult she is running for State Senate after 6 successful years in the State Assembly.

Elana lived next door to Linda. Her parents were very protective of their daughter. They made sure that her time was spent within the family or with other girls. She studied piano and harp, learned how to manage a home and family with skill and grace, and deferred to her brothers and father in all decisions. Elana has two lovely children, takes care of her mother-in-law, sings in the church choir, and contributes her time and talent to her husband's career as a clergyman. Both Linda and Elana feel lucky that their lives have turned out as they had hoped, and both have lives that were dramatically influenced by their socialization.

MARK AND PHILIP

Mark was brought up in a small town by two parents who loved him and valued his achievements, sense of humor, and ability to get along with others. They were surprised that he was not particularly interested in dating, but saw no need to push him into it. During college Mark studied and got good grades, but he had several bouts of depression that his parents did not understand. They continued to provide love and emotional support, however, and Mark graduated with a degree in business. After college, he took a job, moved to a larger city, and seemed to blossom. He was happy, successful, and socially active. The following year, Mark brought a partner home and told his parents that he was gay and that he was finally comfortable with himself as a gay man. His parents' love and support continued, and they welcomed Mark's partner as another member of the family.

Philip lived in the same town as Mark. Philip's parents loved Philip but they had a very absolute vision about his future. They hoped that he would follow in his father's footsteps and become an evangelical minister. After achieving success as a high school football star and attending college on an athletic scholarship, Philip entered seminary. Like Mark, Philip suffered from depression. When he told his parents that he was considering another career and planned to leave the seminary, his father was furious and forbade him to leave. Several months later, Philip attempted suicide, leaving a note that said he was gay. The way in which Mark and Philip were socialized and their families' beliefs and values had a tremendous impact on their outcomes.

AARON AND GREG

Aaron was born 3 months premature and has significant physical disabilities. Soon after his birth, Aaron's parents divorced. From the beginning, Aaron's mother decided to treat Aaron like a typical child. She advocated for Aaron with every school and agency and sought out allies who shared her passion for including Aaron in inclusive environments. Last June, Aaron graduated from high school, attended graduation parties, and is preparing to attend a university approximately 100 miles from home.

Greg also has significant physical disabilities and was brought up by a devoted single mother. Greg's mother sought services that he needed and felt fortunate that he attended a school for children with similar disabilities and participated in activities such as Special Olympics. Since he graduated from high school 2 years ago, Greg has continued to live at home, taking university online courses now and then. Although a good community college is nearby and Greg has the cognitive ability and the financial resources to attend, Greg and his mother are afraid for him to venture into that world.

Like the story of Mark and Philip, the way in which Aaron and Greg were socialized has had a profound impact on their lives and their opportunities.

These examples illustrate a wide range of socialization experiences influenced by cultural and sociocultural experiences. Each example is designed to help readers think about the beliefs, values, and experiences that have shaped them and those that shape the families and children with whom they work.

How Diversity Affects Daily Life

Although it is difficult to generalize about the impact of diversity on a family or family member, one generalization can be made. When a family's diversity—their culture, color, race, ethnicity, language, or sexual preferences—puts them in danger or deprives them of equal access and opportunity, the well-being of the family and its members is in jeopardy. For most individuals and families in the United States, the impact of their culture, ethnicity, and home language appears to be minimal. They go about the tasks of everyday living without thinking about these characteristics or the ways in which they are touched by each of them. For others, these characteristics define who they are and profoundly affect daily interactions with others. More specifically, being white and speaking English significantly enhances the likelihood that individuals will be treated with respect, have their basic needs met, and have opportunities for material success and advancement.

Diversity and School Success

According to the Children's Defense Fund, "Nearly a half-century after *Brown v. Board of Education* [the U.S. Supreme Court decision that desegregated schools], a student who is Black, Latino, or Native American remains much less likely to succeed in school" (2000, p. 64). Many factors contribute to this disparity. Schools that predominantly serve low-income students often spend less per capita for materials, supplies, and books. These low-income schools tend to serve larger populations of students of color. An analysis by the U.S. Department of Education (1997) suggested that the richest school districts in the nation spend 56% more per student than do the poorest districts. Teachers with less experience or inadequate preparation are also more likely to be found in poorer schools or those that serve children from African American, Latino, or American Indian backgrounds. Family issues interact with systems issues. Poor families and families of color are more likely to live in poor urban or rural communities where schools are less adequate. They may move often, disrupting students' educational continuity. Parents from these poor urban or rural communities are typically less able to help their children with schoolwork because of their own limited education (Children's Defense Fund, 1998).

Even more insidious than the effect of poverty on achievement is the finding of the College Board National Task Force on Minority High Achievement (1999) that a growing number of teachers have lower expectations for African American, Latino, and American Indian students. School failure frequently leads to dropping out and a continuation of the conditions that lead to poverty. Conversely, the higher the education level attained, the greater the earnings. For example, men with a bachelor's degree earned 50% more than men with a high school education or GED equivalency, and women in the workforce with bachelor's degrees earned 91% more than their counterparts with a high school education (Children's Defense Fund, 2000). Considering that the high school completion rate for Latino students in 1998 was 62.8%, improvement in educational outcomes and life circumstances is not promising.

These issues cannot be relegated to the problems of poverty alone or the existence of a permanent underclass. The College Board National Task Force on Minority High Achievement (1999) reported another startling finding: Although the number of middle-class African American and Latino students is growing, they are not performing nearly as well academically as their Anglo-European and Asian American middle-class peers. These achievement disparities continue through college, where African American, Latino, and American Indian students earn significantly lower grades than Anglo-European and Asian American students with similar college admissions test scores (College Board's National Task Force on Minority High Achievement, 1999).

Other Areas of Life Affected by Income and Diversity

Education is not the only arena in which income disparities may positively or negatively affect daily life. Inadequate housing, lack of access to health care, problems with drug and alcohol addiction, and violent neighborhoods severely undermine the lives of many families. These challenges touch families in all cultural, ethnic, and racial groups; however, people of color, particularly African Americans, Latinos, and American Indians, are disproportionately affected.

Housing

As housing costs soar in many areas of the country and income disparities between educated and uneducated adults increase, unemployment and lack of affordable housing leads to homelessness. Families are the fastest growing homeless group in the United States, among which are 1.1 million children (Nunez & Fox, 1999). From their study, Nunez and Fox concluded that the causes of homelessness are complex and vary by community. In their study of 777 families in 10 U.S. cities, however, low educational and income levels, spotty or nonexistent work histories, and dependence on welfare were common themes. Of particular concern was the overrepresentation of African Americans among families who were homeless. Although research on the outcomes of children who are homeless has yielded inconsistent findings (Danseco & Holden, 1998), most agree that homelessness does not support optimal growth and development.

Health Care

In a country with the most technologically advanced health care system, access to affordable health care is a challenge faced by many families. The United States continues to be the only developed nation without a national health care system.

> To a large extent, health status is still determined by race, language, culture, geography, and economics. For example, immunization rates are higher for white children than for black and Hispanic children. Infant mortality rates are twice as high for black infants as for white infants, and black children are 1.7 times more likely to die from an accidental injury than are white children. (Children's Defense Fund, 2000, p. 26)

Health concerns continue to be disproportionately distributed by race and ethnicity in adulthood. In the United States, 33% of Latino and 20% of African American children are uninsured compared with 11% of European American children (Children's Defense Fund, 2000). Although death from coronary heart disease was reduced across all racial and ethnic groups between 1990 and 1998, African American non-Latinos have a considerably higher death rate from heart disease than all other groups—136 per 100,000 compared with the next highest group, which is European Americans at 95 per 100,000 (Office of Minority Health, n.d.-a). Death from strokes is also highest among African American non-Latinos—at 42.5 per 100,000, it is nearly double the rate of the next highest group—23.3 per 100,000 among European Americans (Office of Minority Health, n.d.-b). Diabetes and end-stage renal disease are highest among people of color, with American Indian and Alaska Native death rates at 482 per million, African Americans at 329 per million, followed by Asian and Pacific Islanders at 156 per million. For European Americans, the death rate is 79 per million (Office of Minority Health, 1996). AIDS case rates are highest among African American non-Latinos at 84.2 per 100,000 in 1999—more than double that of Latinos, the next highest group at 34.6 per 100,000 (Office of Minority Health, n.d.-c). When one considers that people of color have less access to affordable and appropriate heath care, these statistics are even more discouraging. It appears that those who may have the greatest need for care are not receiving it.

Drug and alcohol addiction as well as exposure to violent neighborhoods are also more likely for families of color. Issues surrounding these challenges to family functioning and service delivery are discussed in depth in Chapter 6.

Civil Rights and Equality

As long as basic civil rights, equal access, and equal opportunity are not part of each individual's daily experience, some families will continue to be vulnerable. The challenges addressed in the previous section cannot be assumed to be the failures of the families affected. They are, instead, the failures of society. Prejudice, both individual and systemic, is at the root of inequality. Until prejudice is no longer a part of the human vocabulary, families and their members will suffer.

THE IMPACT OF DIVERSITY ON SERVICE SYSTEMS

Most service systems were not designed to accommodate the diversity that is common among today's families. Like most businesses, service systems rely on the "typical" consumer and economies of scale to ensure that their already-heavy workloads can be managed. Although making service delivery and systems of care culturally competent has been the goal of educational, health, and counseling services for more than a decade (e.g., Gibbs & Huang, 1989; Hanson, Lynch, & Wayman, 1990; Kalyanpur & Harry, 1999; Lynch & Hanson, 1992, 1998; Olds, London, & Wieland Ladewig, 1996; Ponterotto, Casas, Suzuki, & Alexander, 1995; Wayman, Lynch, & Hanson, 1990), the goal has been difficult to achieve. In some instances procedures designed to be individualized and responsive to family diversity have become routine in the interests of time. In other situations administrators and staff do not have the training required to create and maintain culturally competent services that build on family strengths. In still others, culturally competent services are not recognized as foundational to effective service delivery.

As diversity increases throughout the nation, the need for services for families from diverse cultures, languages, sociocultural backgrounds,

and sexual orientations also increases. A mismatch between the number of service providers from diverse backgrounds and the number of families exists. The majority of professional-level service providers are European American (Hanson, 1998). Many of the families with whom they work are not. Although the shortage of human services personnel is great throughout the nation, the shortage of human services professionals from diverse cultural and linguistic backgrounds is even greater. Far more effort needs to be placed on the training, education, recruitment, and retention of professionals from diverse groups. This is not to suggest that service providers and those receiving services must be paired by race, language, culture, socioeconomic status, and sexual orientation. It does suggest that all service providers should enhance their cross-cultural sensitivity and skills and that service systems should work to ensure that their staff members reflect the demographics of the population.

Differences in service utilization between various cultural and racial groups are frequently cited in the professional literature (Jackson, 1999). It is not uncommon to find that families of color are less likely to use health, dental, and early intervention services than their European American counterparts. In health services, the disparity is often attributed to lack of insurance and economic resources. Uninsured families may put off medical care because they cannot afford the costs. Families with limited resources may also find it difficult to get to services. Those in remote, rural areas who lack transportation or those in any area with poor public transportation systems may find it too difficult to gain access to services. Both cost and lack of transportation present significant barriers. One of the criteria that many use in seeking and using services, however, has to do with rapport with the provider and comfort with the environment and the bureaucratic procedures associated with the service. The accessibility of the professional selected by the individual, the individual and professional's ability to communicate in a shared language, the availability of information in the preferred language, and the understanding and respect that the professional demonstrates for personal preferences and life circumstances contribute to an individual's willingness to use services. For many families of color, those who are poor, or those who are English language learners, services may not seem welcoming; and few go where they do not feel welcome.

Implications for Service Delivery

The increase in family diversity has significant implications for services and service delivery systems in education, health, and social services. Just as businesses assess consumer needs and preferences and alter their marketing and merchandise to meet evolving needs, so should public service agencies continue to reevaluate their work and audience. Each agency and each individual within it has a different level of knowledge, understanding, and competence in relation to culturally competent service delivery, so no single recommendation would be appropriate. A number of service components should be considered when determining where

Table 1.2.　Questions and activities to help determine and assess culturally competent service delivery

Staffing

- Do the existing staff (including administration) mirror the diversity of the families served in culture, race, and language?
- Have *all* staff members participated in staff development focused on cultural diversity and cultural competence?
- What positive changes have been made as a result of the training?

Activity: Identify and list five behaviors of staff that demonstrate cultural sensitivity and attention to culturally competent services.

Service delivery

- Is information about the agency available in multiple languages? Is it given in multiple locations to reach diverse groups? Is the information provided in multiple formats?
- Are trained interpreters available whenever needed?
- Is there flexibility in times of service and service locations to meet family needs?
- Are different models of service delivery available to match family needs and preferences?
- Are services available to meet the unique needs of grandparents, fathers, foster parents, and others in the parenting role?
- Where are sites where services are provided? Are they accessible to everyone, including those with special needs?
- How do sites where services are provided look? Are they clean and well maintained? Do they appear safe? Are there provisions for waiting comfortably, having privacy, and entertaining young children? Do they appear welcoming to diverse groups of families and individuals?

Activity: Identify and list five aspects of the environment that make it welcoming to families with different backgrounds and languages.

Input and evaluation

- Does the agency have an advisory group that is representative of the families served?
- Does the agency routinely evaluate its services using multiple methods that gather data from diverse groups?
- In the past year, what changes have been made in direct response to the advisory group's input? Family input? Community input?

changes may be needed, however. These components, and questions and activities to help determine the efficacy of the service delivery being provided, are listed in Table 1.2. They represent a sample of the kinds of questions that agencies, administrators, and staff members can use to evaluate their own system.

SUMMARY

Family diversity is increasing throughout the United States along many dimensions. Families vary in membership, socioeconomic status, culture, race, ethnicity, and language. Many families have a single parent who is responsible for providing for children's financial and emotional well-being. Other families may appear to have a single parent responsible for all aspects of family life but in reality they have a wide range of family and kinship support available. Divorce is no longer unusual among families, and many children will live in homes with stepparents, stepbrothers, and stepsisters. More often than one would hope, children of divorced parents will experience a second divorce. Grandparents often become primary parents as an increasing number of children live in homes without either biological parent. It can no longer be assumed that two-parent families are composed of male and female parents. Gay men and lesbian women are forming strong family units and adopting and having their own children.

Families' financial circumstances vary dramatically, with a growing gap between those with resources and those without. At the same time that the two-career family demands more and better services, many other families struggle to obtain any services at all. The sociocultural differences among families and the differences between the sociocultural experiences of the majority of providers and many of the families that they serve provide other challenges.

In addition to the diversity of family membership, the cultural, ethnic, racial, and linguistic diversity among families is on the increase. The nation's demographics paint a colorful picture. The way in which families are organized; their values, beliefs, and behaviors; and what they find meaningful in their lives demand attention as well as new skills from professionals.

If families are to benefit from professional skills and knowledge, it is incumbent on professionals to understand each family's context and to develop interventions that fit those contexts. One size does not fit all when working with families. Instead, both programs and services need to be tailored to fit. When the match between family needs, perspectives, and resources can be made by a service provider, outcomes for children and families will be improved—the ultimate goal of intervention.

ACTIVITIES TO EXTEND THE DISCUSSION

1. **Join a group within your class and discuss the following questions.** When you have answered the questions, compare the responses of group members to develop a profile of the diversity of the families that are represented within the group.

    *   How many members are part of your family?

    *   How is each one related to you (e.g., biological father, step-mother, maternal aunt, half-brother)?

    *   What is the age range within your family? Who is the youngest? Who is the oldest?

    *   What languages are spoken in your home?

    *   Where is your place of origin (e.g., region of the country, state, another country)?

    *   Describe any other characteristic that you are comfortable sharing about your family's diversity.

2. **Investigate the family diversity within your own community.** Find statistics on the racial, ethnic, and linguistic composition; on income; and on age. Develop a profile of the community that can be shared with other class participants.

3. **From this week's newspapers and/or magazines, clip at least one article that addresses some issue that affects families.** Prepare a synopsis of the article and be prepared to discuss which families may be most affected.

REFERENCES

Adler, J. (1995, July 31). The rise of the overclass. *Newsweek, 126*(5), 32–46.

Ahmann, E. (1999). Working with families having parents who are gay or lesbian. *Pediatric Nursing, 25,* 531–536.

Baranowski, M.D., & Schilmoeller, G.L. (1999). Grandparents in the lives of grandchildren with disabilities: Mothers' perceptions. *Education and Treatment of Children, 22,* 427–446.

Benedict, R. (1934). *Patterns of culture.* Boston: Houghton Mifflin.

Bengston, V.L. (2001). Beyond the nuclear family: The increasing importance of multigenerational bonds. *Journal of Marriage and the Family, 63,* 1–16.

Bernal, M.A., & Knight, G.P. (1993). *Ethnic identity: Formation and transmission among Hispanics and other minorities.* Albany: State University of New York Press.

Boyden, J. (1993). *Families: Celebration and hope in a world of change.* London: Gaia Books.

Brooks-Gunn, J., Klebanov, P., Liaw, F., & Duncan, G. (1995). Toward an understanding of the effects of poverty upon children. In H.E. Fitzgerald, B.M. Lester, & B. Zuckerman (Eds.), *Children of poverty: Research, health, and policy issues* (pp. 3–37). New York: Garland Science Publishing.

Brown v. Board of Education, 347 U.S. 483 (USSC+, 1954)

Bryson, K., & Casper, L.M. (1999). *Coresident grandparents and grandchildren.* Retrieved June 11, 2001, from http://www.census.gov/population/www/socdemo/hh-fam.html

California Department of Education. (2001). *California student trends: Top 10 languages of English learner students in public schools.* Retrieved April 20, 2001, from http://www.ed-data.k12.ca.us/dev/County.asp

Casper, L., & Bryson, K. (1998). *Household and family characteristics: March 1998 update.* Retrieved April 20, 2001, from http://www.census.gov/population/www/socdemo/hh-fam.html

Children's Defense Fund. (1998). *The state of America's children: Yearbook 1998.* Washington, DC: Author.

Children's Defense Fund. (2000). *The state of America's children: Yearbook 2000.* Washington, DC: Author.

ChildStats.gov. (1999). *America's children 1999.* Retrieved June 22, 2000, from http://www.childstats.gov/ac1999/poptxt.asp

Christensen, H.T. (1964). *Handbook of marriage and the family.* Chicago: Rand McNally.

College Board National Task Force on Minority High Achievement. (1999). *Reaching the top: A report of the national task force on minority high achievement executive summary.* Retrieved June 11, 2001, from http://www.collegeboard.org/research/html/991017r.html

Coontz, S. (1995). The American family and the nostalgia trap. *Kappan Special Report, 76,* K1–K20.

Crawford, J. (1999). Co-parent adoptions by same-sex couples: From loophole to law. *Families in Society, 80,* 271–278.

Cross, W.E., Jr. (1978). The Thomas and Cross models of psychological Nigrescence: A literature review. *Journal of Black Psychology, 4,* 13–31.

Danseco, E.R., & Holden, E.W. (1998). Are there different types of homeless families? A typology of homeless families based on cluster analysis. *Family Relations, 47,* 159–166.

Daragahi, B. (2001, May–June). Let's trade checks. *Money for Women,* 16.

Diverse, yet distinct. (2001, April 1). *The Union Tribune,* p. A21.

Fujiura, G.T. (1998). Demography of family households. *American Journal on Mental Retardation, 103,* 225–235.

Fujiura, G.T., & Yamaki, K. (2000). Trends in demography of childhood poverty and disability. *Exceptional Children, 66,* 187–199.

Gelles, R.J. (1995). *Contemporary families: A sociological view.* Thousand Oaks, CA: Sage.

Gibbs, J.T., & Huang, L.N. (1989). *Children of color: Psychological interventions with minority youth.* San Francisco: Jossey-Bass.

Gollnick, D.M., & Chinn, P.C. (1997). *Multicultural education in a pluralistic society* (4th ed.). Upper Saddle River, NJ: Prentice Hall.

Gordon, M.M. (1964). *Assimilation in American life: The role of race, religion, and national origins.* New York: Oxford University Press.

Green, J.W. (1982). *Cultural awareness in the human services.* Upper Saddle River, NJ: Prentice-Hall.

Guzmán, B. (2001). Census brief 2000: *The Hispanic population 2000.* Washington, DC: U.S. Census Bureau.

Hall, E.T. (1976). *Beyond culture.* Garden City, NY: Anchor Books.

Hanson, M.J. (1998). Ethnic, cultural, and language diversity in intervention settings.

In E.W. Lynch & M.J. Hanson (Eds.), *Developing cross-cultural competence: A guide for working with children and their families* (2nd ed., pp. 3–22). Baltimore: Paul H. Brookes Publishing Co.

Hanson, M.J., & Carta, J.J. (1996). Addressing the challenges of families with multiple risks. *Exceptional Children, 62,* 201–212.

Hanson, M.J., & Lynch, E.W. (1992). Family diversity: Implications for policy and practice. *Topics in Early Childhood Special Education, 12,* 283–306.

Hanson, M.J., Lynch, E.W., & Wayman, K.I. (1990). Honoring the cultural diversity of families when gathering data. *Topics in Early Childhood Special Education, 10,* 112–131.

Helms, J.A. (1995). An update of Helms' white and people of color racial identity models. In J.G. Ponterotto, J.M. Casas, L.A. Suzuki, & C.M. Alexander (Eds.), *Handbook of multicultural counseling* (pp. 181–198). Thousand Oaks, CA: Sage Publications.

Hunter, R. (1904). *Poverty.* New York: Macmillan.

Institute for Research on Poverty at the University of Wisconsin–Madison. (2001). *How many children are poor?* Retrieved May 7, 2001, from http://www.ssc.wisc.edu/irp/faqs/faq6.htm

Jackson, P. (1999). Health insurance, race, and emergency room utilization. *Review of Black Political Economy, 27*(2), 63–77.

Kalil, A., Schweingruber, H., Daniel-Echols, M., & Breen, A. (2001). Mother, worker, welfare recipient: Welfare reform and the multiple roles of low-income women. In S. Danziger & A.C. Lin (Eds.), *Coping with poverty: The social contexts of neighborhood, work, and family in the African-American community* (pp. 201–223). Ann Arbor: The University of Michigan Press.

Kalyanpur, M., & Harry, B. (1999). *Culture in special education: Building reciprocal family–professional relationships.* Baltimore: Paul H. Brookes Publishing Co.

King, R.K. (1999). Time spent in parenthood status among adults in the United States. *Demography, 3,* 377–385.

Klein, M.D., & Chen, D. (2001). *Working with children from culturally diverse backgrounds.* Albany, NY: Delmar Learning.

Ladson-Billings, G. (1996). "Your blues ain't like mine": Keeping issues of race and racism on the multicultural agenda. *Theory Into Practice, 35*(4), 248–256.

Larner, M., & Collins, A. (1996). Poverty in the lives of young children. In E.J. Erwin (Ed.), *Putting children first: Visions for a brighter future for young children and their families* (pp. 55–75). Baltimore: Paul H. Brookes Publishing Co.

Liao, Y., McGee, D.L., Cao, G., & Cooper, R.S. (2000). Quality of the last year of life of older adults: 1986 vs. 1993. *The Journal of the American Medical Association, 283,* 512–518.

Lynch, E.W. (1998a). Conceptual framework: From culture shock to cultural learning. In E.W. Lynch & M.J. Hanson (Eds.), *Developing cross-cultural competence: A guide for working with children and their families* (2nd ed., pp. 23–45). Baltimore: Paul H. Brookes Publishing Co.

Lynch, E.W. (1998b). Developing cross-cultural competence. In E.W. Lynch & M.J. Hanson (Eds.), *Developing cross-cultural competence: A guide for working with children and their families* (2nd ed., pp. 47–86). Baltimore: Paul H. Brookes Publishing Co.

Lynch, E.W., & Hanson, M.J. (Eds.). (1992). *Developing cross-cultural competence: A guide for working with young children and their families.* Baltimore: Paul H. Brookes Publishing Co.

Lynch, E.W., & Hanson, M.J. (Eds.). (1998). *Developing cross-cultural competence: A guide for working with children and their families* (2nd ed.). Baltimore: Paul H. Brookes Publishing Co.

Mack, D. (2000, June 12). Valuing family time over wealth. *Christian Science Monitor,* 11.

Manton, K.G., Corder, L., & Stallard, E. (1997). Chronic disability in elderly United States populations: 1982–94. *Proceedings of the National Academy of Sciences 94,* 2593–2598.

McCombs, B. (2001, January 8). Demands on boomer bloom: Need of kids, and parents squeeze sandwich generation. *The Denver Post,* p. B–1.

McIntosh, P. (1990, Winter). White privilege: Unpacking the invisible knapsack. *Independent School, 49,* 31–36.

Morton, D.D. (2000). Beyond parent education: The impact of extended family dynamics in deaf education. *American Annals of the Deaf, 145,* 359–365.

Myers, J., & Boothe, D. (2000). Cultural and language diversity in the middle grades. *Clearing House, 73*(4), 230–232.

National Center for Children in Poverty. (1997). *Poverty and brain development in early childhood.* Retrieved May 7, 2001, from http://cpmcnet.columbia.edu/dept/nccp/brain.html

National Center for Children in Poverty. (2000). Child poverty fact sheet July 2000: Child poverty in the United States.

Retrieved May 7, 2001, from http://cpmcnet.columbia.edu/dept/nccp/ycpf.html

Nunez, R., & Fox, C. (1999). A snapshot of family homelessness across America, *Political Science Quarterly, 114,* 289–308.

Office of Minority Health. (1996). *Persons with diabetes and end-stage renal disease.* Retrieved May 7, 2001, from http://www.omhrc.gov/rah/3rdpgBlue/Diabetes/k16.gif

Office of Minority Health. (n.d.-a). *Coronary heart disease death rates* (age adjusted to the year 1940 standard population). Retrieved May 7, 2001, from http://www.omhrc.gov/rah/3rdpgBlue/Cardio/k12.gif

Office of Minority Health (n.d.-b). *Stroke death rates* (age adjusted to the year 1940 standard population). Retrieved May 7, 2001, from http://www.omhrc.gov/rah/3rdpgBlue/Cardio/k14.gif

Office of Minority Health. (n.d.-c). *AIDS case rates among persons 13 years of age and older.* Retrieved May 7, 2001, from http://www.omhrc.gov/rah3rdpgBlue/HIV/k18.gif

Olds, S.B., London, M.L., & Wieland Ladewig, P. (1996). *Maternal–newborn nursing: A family centered approach* (5th ed.). Boston: Addison-Wesley.

Olson, S. (2001, April). The genetic archaeology of race. *The Atlantic Monthly,* 69–80.

Patterson, C.J. (2000). Family relationships of lesbians and gay men. *Journal of Marriage and the Family, 62,* 1052–1069.

Perry, M.J., & Mackun, P.J. (2001, April). *Census 2000 brief: Population change and distribution 1990 to 2000.* Washington, DC: U.S. Census Bureau.

Personal Responsibility and Work Opportunity Reconciliation Act of 1996, PL 104-193. (110 Stat. 2105; Date: 8/21/96). Text from: *United States Public Laws.* Available from: *LexisNexis Congressional* (Online Service).

Phinney, J. (1990). Ethnic identity in adolescents and adults: Review of research. *Psychological Bulletin, 108,* 499–514.

Ponterotto, J.G., Casas, J.M., Suzuki, L.A., & Alexander, C.M. (Eds.). (1995). *Handbook of multicultural counseling.* Thousand Oaks, CA: Sage Publications.

Reich, R. (1995). America's anxious class. *NPQ: New Perspectives Quarterly, 12*(1), 28–30.

Riche, M.F. (2000). America's diversity and growth: Signposts for the 21st century. *Population Bulletin, 55*(2). Washington, DC: Population Reference Bureau.

Rodgers, Jr., H.R. (2000). *American poverty in a new era of reform.* Armonk, NY: M E Sharpe.

Schmitt, E. (2001, May 10). Mexican-American surge. *The Union Tribune,* pp. A1, A23.

Seccombe, K. (2000). Families of poverty in the 1990s: Trends, causes, consequences, and lessons learned. *Journal of Marriage and the Family, 62,* 1094–1113.

Seibert, M.T., & Willetts, M.C. (2000). Changing family forms. *Social Education, 64,* 42–47.

Smith, E., & Sapp, W. (Eds.). (1996). *Plain talk about the Human Genome Project: A Tuskegee University conference on its promise and perils . . . and matters of race.* Tuskegee, AL: Tuskegee University Publications Office.

Teachman, J.D., Tedrow, L.M., & Crowder, K.D. (2000). The changing demography of America's families. *Journal of Marriage and the Family, 62,* 1234–1247.

U.S. Bureau of the Census. (1997, December). *Disabilities affect one-fifth of all Americans. Census brief.* Retrieved May 20, 2003: from www.census.gov/prod/www/abs/briefs.html

U.S. Bureau of the Census. (1999). Poverty 1999. Retrieved May 7, 2001, from http://www.census.gov/hhes/poverty/poverty99/pv99est1.html

U.S. Bureau of the Census. (2000). Money income in the United States. Retrieved May 7, 2001, from http://www.census.gov/hhes/www/income.html

U.S. Department of Education, National Center for Educational Statistics (1997). *The condition of education 1997: The social context of education.* Washington, DC: U.S. Government Printing Office.

Wayman, K.I., Lynch, E.W., & Hanson, M.J. (1990). Home-based early childhood services: Cultural sensitivity in a family systems approach. *Topics in Early Childhood Special Education, 10,* 56–75.

Weiss, R.S. (1979). *Marital separation.* New York: Basic Books.

White, L., & Rogers, S.J. (2000). Economic circumstances and family outcomes: A review of the 1990s. *Journal of Marriage and the Family, 62,* 1035–1052.

CHAPTER 2

THEORETICAL PERSPECTIVES FOR UNDERSTANDING FAMILIES

A family is a circle of caring.
—ANONYMOUS

The family structure...reminds me
of the days of diagramming sentences.
Each clause has its own nouns and verbs,
but they all connect to form a complete sentence.
What makes this family a complete sentence is the
fact that they consider and define themselves as a family.
—N. DREXEL (PERSONAL COMMUNICATION, MAY 2002)

When one of the authors asked a class of graduate students to define *family*, responses varied and represented the panoply of individuals enrolled in the class. In these definitions the number of people composing the family varied, the types of family arrangements differed, and, in some cases, the formal relationships (e.g., marriage, cohabitation, stepparenting) among the family members were dissimilar. The definitions contained these common elements, however: 1) a set of individuals bound together and 2) a shared understanding or commitment to one another among family members.

The chapter-opening comment comparing a family with a diagrammed sentence was made by a graduate student in response to an assignment to portray the family with whom she was working. In her assignment, she went on to describe this family as including a husband and wife, their children (both from their marriage to each other and from previous marriages), the grandmother (the wife's mother), the grandmother's brother, and the wife's sister and her fiancé. The whole family lived with the grandmother with the exception of the wife's sister and fiancé, who had recently moved out of the home but were considered part of the household. The affiliations among these family members came from blood ties, bonds of marriage, and a shared commitment.

Many theoreticians and researchers have attempted to define the core concepts that demarcate *family*. Klein and White (1996) identified four features that differentiate families from other groups:

1. Families usually last for a longer period of time than other groups.
2. Families are intergenerational.
3. Relationships among family members include both biological and affinal relationships (e.g., legal).
4. Family relationships are linked to a larger kinship network.

Children typically enter family units at birth and the family members in these units constitute the children's caregivers. As Klein and White (1996) discussed, entering into and belonging to the family is involuntary and these ties remain in some form over time and link children to a larger network of people (relatives) and family history and traditions. These features serve to distinguish families from other types of social groups, such as friendship networks. Thus, families may include married partners with children, nonmarried partners with children, single parents with children, adults bound by marriage or other contractual commitments, groups of adults and children living communally, and so forth. Even when a child and his or her parents have all died, relatives such as the child's grandparents may remain bound together in some fashion as a family.

This exercise of attempting to define family underscores the breadth of family possibilities and the range of issues that must be considered by service providers when working with families. Just as the many variations among families must be appreciated, the various contexts in which families reside must be recognized. The functioning and development of the family can be understood only in this broader social context.

Several prominent theories and conceptual frameworks have aided the understanding of these influences. They are described in this chapter and include the family systems model and the ecological systems framework. Both have been applied to the study of families of children with disabilities and risk conditions and have been useful in identifying the effect of disability or risk on the family as a whole. Following this discussion, theoretical models of human development and the effects of risk are presented in an effort to examine the influence of the family context on the developing child. Finally, intervention frameworks are introduced for supporting families. The frameworks selected for discussion focus on emphasizing family strengths and resilience.

THEORETICAL MODELS FOR STUDYING FAMILIES

A number of theories have been advanced in the study of families (Klein & White, 1996). Several are highlighted in this text for purposes of explaining and interpreting the effects of disability and/or risk on the developing child within the family. Insights for structuring policies and interventions to support families are derived from these theoretical perspectives. Two theoretical models or frameworks are selected for review: the family systems model and the ecological systems framework.

Family Systems Model

The family systems model is one of the predominant theoretical perspectives in family studies and family therapy (Broderick, 1993; Klein & White, 1996; Whitchurch & Constantine, 1993). This view of the family as an interactive system of individuals has been advanced as a framework for understanding the roles and relationships among family members as they care for an individual with disabilities or developmental risk (Turnbull, Summers, & Brotherson, 1984; Turnbull & Turnbull, 1990, 1997).

A glimpse at the life of Caitlin and her parents, Barbara and Roger, will help us examine the family systems model in an attempt to appreciate the complexity of family interactions as well as the many factors that influence families.

THE MORGAN FAMILY

Barbara and Roger tried for years to have a child. As time passed and Barbara watched her younger sisters deliver healthy babies, her anxiety about parenthood was amplified. Finally, Barbara and Roger became the parents of a girl. Their devotion to Caitlin was fueled by their intense desire to have children and Barbara's efforts to become pregnant.

Caitlin was born prematurely and experienced a prolonged period of hospitalization after birth. Caitlin's difficult delivery and birth experiences necessitated that Barbara take a leave of absence from her job as a nurse at a local university hospital. The round-the-clock care and frequent medical appointments created by Caitlin's chronic illnesses and developmental delays became a full-time job for Barbara. The loss of Barbara's income became a source of concern to the family as they struggled to maintain their home mortgage and move from a dual-income to a single-income family. The long hours required by Roger's job were only increased by his need to advance.

The birth of their child also altered the lifestyle that Barbara and Roger had come to expect in their 8 years as a married couple. Their exercise routines, concert going, and outside interests were put on hold as they adapted to having a new baby and meeting her medical and caregiving needs. Family members' and friends' responses to the family's altered circumstances varied. Most were supportive and offered to grocery shop, babysit, and assist when needed. Several individuals appeared to feel awkward, though, and quit communicating with Barbara and Roger. One friend even suggested that they consider "out-of-home" care for their baby.

Thus, Caitlin's birth brought Barbara and Roger tremendous joy and relief at their fulfillment of parenthood. It also brought concern, lifestyle changes, and new demands.

The family systems model helps us to understand the dynamics of families such as the Morgans. This family systems approach is based on several fundamental assumptions (Klein & White, 1996). The first assumption is that the parts of the system are interconnected. As such, all family members are integrally linked with one another. Second, the family as a system only can be understood as a whole rather than in terms of its individual parts. Third, the family system both affects and is affected by its environment. The fourth assumption is that the system is not a reality but rather a way of knowing. It is a way of understanding the organization and experiences of families rather than an actual physical phenomenon.

The family systems framework defines a system as a set of units, organized with subsystems and characterized by boundaries and rules for change (Klein & White, 1996). The family, thus, is composed of the individual members who in turn are members of subsystems within the family. For example, Caitlin and her parents are a subsystem (parent–child), Barbara and Roger together are a subsystem (marital), and Barbara and Roger are another subsystem with their parents and other family members (parent–extended family).

Families are characterized as well by their types of boundaries, or in other words, their degree of being open or closed to outside influences. Barbara and Roger, for instance, were open to adjusting to their new responsibilities by altering their work schedules and commitments, as well as their lifestyles.

Families also may be examined in terms of their rules for operation or change. These rules represent relationships between family members, such as how a husband and wife behave toward one another and make decisions. Families differ in these unwritten family rules for change. In the instance of Barbara and Roger, for example, both started their marriage as partners who worked outside of the home and shared equally in family responsibilities. Following Caitlin's birth they were able to adapt (but not without ambivalence and difficulties) by shifting roles and relationships (e.g., Barbara quit her job to care for Caitlin at home). Some families have very rigid rules or codes of behavior for the members (e.g., strict religious beliefs, codes of behavior for how children relate to their elders), whereas others maintain flexible rules and adapt readily to change.

Another concept applicable to the systems approach is the notion of *equilibrium*. Family systems tend to maintain a homeostasis. Like the human body's own internal thermostat, families adjust to inputs or environmental demands to maintain the sense of balance. Caitlin's parents, for instance, rearranged their work schedules and outside interests to support the other needs of the family after her birth. The decreased family income and the increased caregiving demands were counterbalanced by cutbacks in the family's recreational and social activities and expenses. This process is dynamic, with new inputs and family outputs always shifting. This family systems approach, thus, presupposes that families are influenced by feedback from the outside. For example, the family will be influenced to various degrees by social feedback such as societal norms to behave or conform in particular ways. In Barbara and Roger's case, they responded to the expectations of the medical community and their own parents' judgments about the situation as well as to feedback from other sources such as their employers and friends. Thus, important concepts in the family systems model are the dynamic and ever-changing influences on the family and the family's internal structures that bind it together in responding to these influences.

The family systems approach has been synthesized with special education concepts and applied in work with families of children who are at risk for or have disabilities. Turnbull, Summers, and Brotherson (1984) proposed such a framework for examining family systems concepts. This framework consists of four components (see Figure 2.1): 1) family resources, 2) family interaction, 3) family functions, and 4) family life cycle. Briefly, family resources refer to the characteristics that each of the family members brings to the family. These characteristics include personality, values and beliefs, cultural background and perspectives, socioeconomic status, disability, health status, and so forth. These characteristics are viewed in this schema as input variables into family interaction. The relationships among family members and family subsystems are considered through the component of family interaction. Relationships vary in terms of their adaptability to change in response to stressors or outside influences, and also in terms of their cohesiveness (i.e., degree of bonding among members and each member's maintenance of independence within the family). The outputs of family interaction address the fulfillment of family needs through accomplishing family functions. Family functions include meeting economic needs, physical and health care needs, recreation and socialization needs, the need for affection, self-identity needs, and educational/vocational needs. These functions are discussed in detail in Chapter 3. Finally, the *family life cycle* component addresses the developmental and nondevelopmental changes that affect families over time.

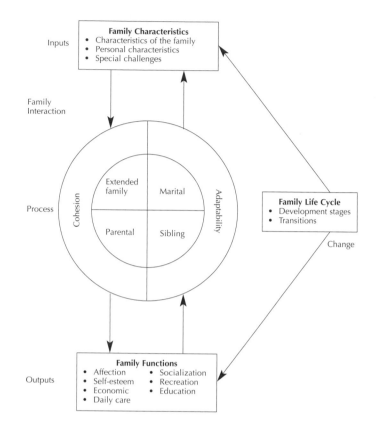

Inputs

Family
Interaction

Process

Outputs

Family Characteristics
• Characteristics of the family
• Personal characteristics
• Special challenges

Cohesion

Extended family

Marital

Parental

Sibling

Adaptability

Family Life Cycle
• Development stages
• Transitions

Change

Family Functions
• Affection   • Socialization
• Self-esteem   • Recreation
• Economic   • Education
• Daily care

Figure 2.1.   Family systems framework. (Turnbull, A.P., Summers, J.A., & Brotherson, M.J. (1984). *Working with families with disabled members: A family systems approach.* Lawrence: The University of Kansas, Kansas University Affiliated Facility; reprinted by permission.)

These life cycle events may include births, deaths, divorce, change in employment, and change in residence, among others.

Returning to the example of the Morgan family, this framework can be used to understand the family's current roles and relationships. With respect to family resources, Barbara and Roger bring to the family their own individual personalities and interests, marital relationship, economic resources and demands, educational backgrounds, and coping styles. Caitlin, too, brings her personal characteristics including her personality, temperament, appearance, and her developmental challenges and needs. These characteristics or inputs influence the family's interaction and the relationships among members within the various subsystems (e.g., husband–wife, parent–child, extrafamilial subsystem–extended family, others). For instance, these variables have had an impact on the relationship Barbara and Roger have with one another and on the relationships they have with their parents, siblings, and their professional colleagues. These relationships or components of family interaction, in turn, have influenced the family's ability to meet basic needs or functions of the family, such as economic provision, recreational, affectional, social, medical, and so forth. Though this family will change as it experiences various transitions and shifts through its family life cycle, this glimpse at life just after Caitlin's birth demonstrates the alterations that already have occurred in response to the infant's birth. The family's resources are changed by the introduction of a new family member and by the needs of that child. The family's functions are altered in that Barbara must go on leave from her job, and the family's economic resources are reduced although economic demands are increased. The ability to meet these family needs or functions will be determined by interaction variables related to Barbara and Roger's relationship and their relationships with others. This brief example demonstrates the complex interconnections of families and the fact that the family is much more than the sum of its parts.

Ecological Systems Model

Families do not exist in a vacuum. Rather, they are situated in their communities and within the broader societal network. The ecology of human development postulated by Bronfenbrenner (1979, 1986) provided a model for understanding the relations between the developing person and the environment. The family is one component or system within the ecological systems described by Bronfenbrenner (1979); however, this ecological systems framework also provides a model for placing families in the broader context of the systems within which they must interact and the broader social environment. This model is particularly appealing for the study of families of children who have disabilities or are at risk in that it enables one to describe the range of influences on families and the interactions among systems over time (e.g., Beckman, 1996; Bernier &

Siegel, 1994; Berry, 1995; Hanson et al., 1998; Kazak, 1989; Odom, 2002; Odom et al., 1996).

Bronfenbrenner (1979) described the ecological environment as a set of structures or systems nested within one another like Russian nesting dolls. This set of structures includes the microsystem, mesosystem, exosystem, and macrosystem (see Figure 2.2). Briefly, the *microsystem* is "a pattern of activities, roles, and interpersonal relations experienced by the developing person in a given setting with particular physical and material characteristics" (p. 22). For the young child, the family is the primary microsystem. Other microsystems may include child care environments and early education programs. The interrelationships among these microsystems are termed the *mesosystem*. For young children, these relationships may occur between the home and child care program, home and school, and home and hospital, to name a few. Thus, the mesosystem is a series of microsystems and encompasses the immediate systems with which families and children may interact. The *exosystem* level is "one or more settings that do not involve the developing person as an active participant, but in which events occur that affect, or are affected by, what happens in the setting containing the developing person" (p. 25). Examples for young children include the policies of the child care and education programs and institutions, neighborhoods, families' social networks, parents' employers and

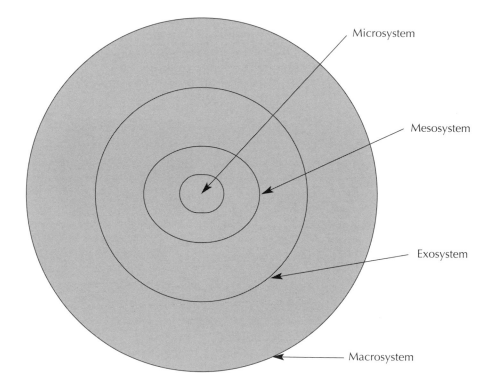

Figure 2.2. Ecological systems framework. (Adapted from Bronfenbrenner, U. [1979]. *The ecology of human development.* Cambridge, MA: Harvard University Press. [ERIC Document Reproduction Service No. ED 128]).

employment policies—all networks outside the family that can have a direct impact on the child and family. At the broader systems level, or *macrosystem*, are societal and cultural beliefs and values that serve to shape and influence the lower order systems. For the young child, societal and cultural views on child-rearing patterns, early education, the meaning of disability, and health and education intervention philosophies and policies (e.g., philosophy of inclusion) all can be found at this macrosystem level.

Bronfenbrenner and colleagues (Bronfenbrenner & Ceci, 1994; Bronfenbrenner & Morris, 1998) have expanded the discussion to more fully describe the impact of the individual's personal characteristics and the influence of time on development. The variable of time can be appreciated both in terms of the effects of the timing of an event on the individual's or family's development and the cumulative effects of an event over time on development. This expanded model has been termed *bioecological.* The ecological systems framework can be illustrated through a discussion of Hwa Hwa and his family.

Hwa Hwa

Hwa Hwa is a 4-year-old boy with Down syndrome who lives with his mother, father, and sister in an urban area with a large Asian population. The family moved to the United States 4 years ago from the People's Republic of China. Both of Hwa Hwa's parents work in blue-collar jobs (one works during the day and one works at night) in order to provide for their family and to meet the high cost of living in this urban area. Hwa Hwa attends a Montessori preschool program, and was one of the children targeted as a good candidate for inclusion because of his friendly personality. One of Hwa Hwa's major developmental needs is speech and language development. Though the program recognizes Hwa Hwa's speech and language needs and these goals are stipulated on his individualized education program (IEP), the one speech-language pathologist available to the preschool speaks only English and Spanish (the languages spoken by the majority of the children in the program).

The primary microsystem in this case is Hwa Hwa's immediate family. Hwa Hwa's family members each bring their own personal characteristics of personality, abilities, values and beliefs, and knowledge and concerns about Hwa Hwa's disability. The other microsystem is Hwa Hwa's preschool program with its particular philosophy and resources.

At the mesosystem level, Hwa Hwa's parents interact with his preschool program, his sister's elementary school, and their employers. For instance, the preschool program not only welcomes—but also in fact, expects—parental involvement. No one on staff at the program speaks Cantonese, however. This has a significant negative impact on the communication and relationships between the family and the preschool staff members.

At the exosystem level, several school and employment policies are used to demonstrate this ecological model. The school system that operates the preschool is a strong advocate for inclusion of children with disabilities.

Hence, Hwa Hwa is given an opportunity to participate in a neighborhood school with his typically developing peers even though he shows marked developmental delays. The school's lack of employee experience with the Cantonese language, however, has a direct effect on Hwa Hwa's ability to participate and learn in that environment. Thus, the school's policies and hiring practices have a direct impact on the ability or inability of the program to address or meet Hwa Hwa's developmental and educational needs.

Exosystem issues are evident for the parents as well. Neither parent is allowed time off from his or her job to attend school functions, thus making it difficult for both parents to stay informed regarding the education program and to participate in school activities.

Examined from the broader macrosystem level, this family lives in a community with a large Asian population, and many supports are available to families from this ethnic and linguistic background. Furthermore, the community is known for its liberal policies and support for diverse populations, including people from non–Anglo-European backgrounds and those with disabilities. Though the values and beliefs espoused in the community provide a supportive environment for this family, however, these beliefs and values have not been enacted for the betterment of the family at the lower systems levels through the use of interpreters for the child and family or through involving the parents through culturally appropriate approaches.

This story of Hwa Hwa and his family allows us to examine the interconnections and influences between layers or systems described in this framework. Like the nesting dolls, Hwa Hwa and his family are nested within multiple contexts that are interrelated and that exert a profound influence upon one another.

The ecological systems framework, although a theoretical framework to explain human development rather than a theory of family development, nevertheless provides a structure for examining and appreciating the broader societal context in which families must function. The family is the primary microsystem for its members. Members are nurtured and cared for in the family home. The family is connected to other microsystems such as schools, community programs, child care programs, and health care systems. These interact with and influence the family and its individual members. These systems, in turn, are influenced by the broader policies and structures of other systems (exosystems) such as the parents' workplace, the medical care system, the education system, insurance programs, and so forth.

At the still broader macrosystem level, societal values and policies influence the other priorities, policies, and resources in other systems. Examples include public policies related to diversity (immigration, language supports) and disabilities (federal legislation pertaining to education and disability rights such as Individual with Disabilities Education Act [IDEA] of 1990 [PL 101-476] and the Americans with Disabilities Act [ADA] of 1990 [PL 101-336]). This ecological systems model or framework, thus, provides a mechanism for examining the multiple and interconnected influences on the family.

TRANSACTIONAL MODELS OF RISK AND RESILIENCE

This section focuses on families with members who have a disability or are at risk for developmental delay. Factors that constitute risks to individual members within the family are examined and the family environment is emphasized as a source of risk or support to the developing individual. The transactional model of human development illuminates these interactions among constitutional and environmental factors. These transactional effects are discussed in terms of the concepts of risk and resilience.

Transactional Models of Development

A seminal article by Sameroff and Chandler (1975) examined developmental outcomes for infants with respect to reproductive and caregiving risks. The extensive literature review on reproductive risks and the "continuum of caretaking casualty" (p. 218) documented the myriad risks to the infant from biological factors including premature delivery and anoxia (i.e., a lack of oxygen delivered to tissue), and factors associated with social conditions such as poor socioeconomic conditions and mothers' physical and mental health. Sameroff and Chandler contrasted developmental models that seek to explain outcomes according to these factors. They described the *main effects model* (often termed *medical model*) that explains development primarily in terms of the individual's constitutional characteristics (e.g., presence of biological damage) or environmental factors (e.g., neglect). In this model a risk condition is causally linked directly to a developmental outcome. The main effects model, which considers a particular variable as an independent determinant of child outcome, was contrasted with models that focus on interactional effects. A transactional model of development was postulated as the optimal model through which to view development. This transactional model recognizes the "continual and progressive interplay between the organism and its environment" (1975, p. 234) and views the contributions of the individual to his or her development. In other words, individuals are seen as actively engaged in constructing their own worlds. For most children (and adults), their primary world is their family. Thus, the family and caregiving environments are both shaped by the individual family members' characteristics and, likewise, serve a primary role in shaping the development of family members.

Viewing child and family development through a transactional perspective allows us to understand the complex interactions and transactions that occur. This perspective also guides notions of early intervention goals and focus (Sameroff & Friese, 1990). Using a main effects or medical model, the birth of a baby with biological risks or a genetic anomaly would lead to linear predictions of developmental risks and characteristics. The implications and predictions when using a transactional lens are different. Take, for example, an individual born with Down syndrome. Prior to the 1960s, physicians often counseled parents to institutionalize a child with Down syndrome, and predicted that the child's developmental prognosis and life expectancy were poor (a viewpoint represented by a medical or main effects model). Today, one sees individuals with Down syndrome going to school, starring in television programs, featured as models in clothing catalogs, working in restaurants and businesses, and writing books. What happened? Down syndrome was not cured, nor have the genetic mysteries that produce Down syndrome been solved. Rather, these children and families have been given early supports that fostered positive transactions. Children now typically begin participating in early intervention regimens in which they are helped to develop more fully and at an advanced rate. This fosters increased skills whereby children can interact with their environment through more competent and complex communication, exploration, and social interactions. This increased child competence also may affect the parental feelings of competence and raise parental expectations for their children's developmental potential. Like an upward spiral, these positive effects lead to positive transactions that, in turn, change the opportunities and expectations in the next phase of development. As individuals with Down syndrome are seen participating in society, the community has more opportunities to develop greater understanding of individuals with Down syndrome and higher expectations for them.

As is evident from this example, educational policies, intervention services, and societal expectations can and do enhance the early developmental potential and opportunities of children and their families. Although opportunities are not without bounds or limits, these transactions do create a dynamic context for the developing child.

These perspectives are further underscored by recent research in neuroscience that documents the impact that early experiences (both positive and negative) or the absence of appropriate stimulation has on brain development (Shore, 1997). Understanding how experience acts on the nervous system to shape early brain growth and development undoubtedly has contributed to increased attention to identifying the most beneficial learning environments for young children (Bruer & Greenough, 2001). Although these findings have documented the dynamic interplay between nature and nurture and increased our understanding of brain plasticity, these findings are only beginning to be translated into policy implications and recommendations (Shonkoff & Phillips, 2000; Young, 2002).

Risk and Resilience

Scarcely a day goes by that the news media does not feature a story about risk—children at risk for school failure, toxins released into the environment that constitute health risks, deviant behavior explained in terms of poor parenting, risks of abuse or neglect encountered in an individual's early years, and risks of physical violence in our communities. To be sure, these factors all constitute major risks to human development. As such, it is tempting to focus attention in education, health care, and the social services on what can and does go wrong. Many things "go right" in human development and in the development and interactions within families, however. This section endeavors to emphasize these positive aspects as well.

What is the meaning of the terms *risk* and *resilience?* Researcher Emmy Werner posited the following:

> *The concepts of* resilience *and* protective factors *are the positive counterparts to the constructs of* vulnerability *(which denotes an individual's susceptibility to a negative outcome) and* risk factors *(which denote biological or psychosocial hazards that increase the likelihood of a negative developmental outcome). (1990, p. 97)*

Variables associated with risk and developmental vulnerability are described in order to examine the challenges faced by families. These issues are considered for the purpose of developing structures to prevent risk or reduce the effects of risk through supportive interventions to children and their families, thus fostering resilience.

In discussing the concept of risk, Rutter (1996, 2000) explained the importance of differentiating between *risk indicators* and *risk mechanisms*. Risk indicators are broadly defined variables statistically associated with risk. Poverty and homelessness are examples of risk indicators. On the one hand, though they are strongly associated with risk, these factors do not necessarily in and of themselves create risk for the individuals. Risk mechanisms, on the other hand, denote how risk works or the risk process itself that results in the disorder; for instance, a child may be born to a family living below the poverty level and in difficult circumstances (risk indicators). Whether those circumstances lead to risks in the child's development will depend on the risk mechanisms, such as the family's access to medical and health care, the family's extended family and friendship resources, the parent's resourcefulness and support networks, and so forth.

According to Rutter (1996, 2000), the risk process also is greatly influenced by the individual's response to stressors. Each individual responds differently. Rutter cautioned that protection from risk might derive, in some cases, from exposure to risk rather than avoidance of the risk if the individual is able to successfully cope with the event. He likened this process to the effects of inoculations used to build resilience to infections. Some experiences can be seen to have a "steeling" effect. For example, observations revealed that in families growing up in the Great Depression, older children who were given early responsibilities and who performed these responsibilities successfully fared better in the long run in their capabilities.

Rutter (1996, 2000) also noted that protection from risk is affected by prior experiences and that different factors may operate differently at different periods during the lifespan. For example, experiencing early malnutrition or subnutrition is associated with developing heart disease in later life; whereas, in mid-life, being overweight increases risk for disease. Rutter (1996, 2000) explained that a particular event might constitute a risk for one person but a protective event for another. He used the example of adoption. In most cases, adoption may protect a child from a poor, non-nurturing environment; in other instances it may constitute a psychological risk.

The transactional nature of development is highlighted in Rutter's work (1996, 2000). In his discussion and analysis of risk, he underscored the need to focus on individualized aspects or experiences rather than broad categories of risk factors. One's personal characteristics such as temperament and coping abilities, and one's attitudes or appraisals of one's abilities, can greatly affect one's resilience to risk factors. The importance of the individual's interaction and contribution to his or her own development is evident from this research. So, too, is the importance of the individual's social context in posing risk or in providing protection and support.

Families clearly are an important social context for all individuals. A risk condition within the family, such as marital discord or parental mental illness, may exert a profound influence and may affect the children within the family differently, depending on each child's ability to cope with the stressors. Societal influences, too, can play a major role in supporting both families and the individuals within them.

Several researchers have examined supportive factors, termed *protective mechanisms* by Rutter (1990, 1996) and *protective factors* by Werner (1990). Rutter (1990, 2000) postulated different types of protective mechanisms that promote resilient responses to potentially stressful factors. First, he described reducing the risk itself. An example is children who are able to distance themselves emotionally from a mentally ill parent or an acrimonious divorce situation. Other examples include parents who avoid drawing a child into a marital conflict and those who provide adequate parental supervision and monitoring to their children to prevent exposure to or continuance of risk from such dangers as the influence of a negative peer group.

A second protective mechanism was termed by Rutter as preventing or reducing "negative chain reactions" (Rutter, 2000, p. 672). For instance,

hostile family exchanges may escalate when hostile comments are made by one of the members. Teaching family members to use humor or other coping strategies to diffuse the situation may lessen the hostility cycles that are likely to occur otherwise. Using effective coping strategies and avoiding damaging coping strategies such as the use of alcohol or drugs are other ways family members can reduce negative chain reactions.

Third, Rutter described the importance of promoting self-esteem and self-efficacy in individuals. Factors that produce self-esteem and self-efficacy include secure and supportive personal relationships, successful accomplishment of tasks or responsibilities, and successful use of coping strategies when encountering stresses.

Fourth, the act of opening up positive opportunities may be protective, such as in the case of when families with teenagers move to a new town or school and away from high-risk peer groups. Other positive opportunities may include educational and career opportunities, broader choices of relationships with others, and even a change in home environment.

Finally, a fifth protective mechanism identified by Rutter is the individual's way of cognitive processing or, in other words, how the individual accepts negative experiences and reframes them around positive concepts. Rather than dwelling in denial or deception, the individual with this protective mechanism in place accepts and focuses on the positive aspects of the situation or the experience.

The work of Werner and colleagues (Werner, 1990; Werner, Bierman, & French, 1971; Werner & Smith, 1977, 1989, 1992) also examined risk and protective factors from a transactional perspective. Their core research is based on a longitudinal study of children in Kauai from the prenatal period to adulthood. Findings from this longitudinal investigation documented that poor developmental outcomes were associated with perinatal assaults (i.e., difficulties or trauma associated with the birth or delivery), particularly when paired with poor environmental conditions. Children who were reared in more favorable environments, however, fared better even if they began life at greater biological risk. Werner and colleagues attempted to identify factors over time that had served as protectors. These general factors (listed from early childhood to later childhood) include the following:

- Birth order (being first born)
- Activity level (having a high activity level)
- Individual characteristics such as absence of distressing habits associated with eating and sleeping
- Responsiveness to people
- Ability to display affectionate or cuddly behaviors
- Autonomy
- Positive social orientation
- Advanced self-help skills
- Adequate motor and communication skills
- Strong problem-solving abilities and achievement scores
- Ability to focus attention and control impulses
- Positive self-concept
- High regard for school and future expectations

In addition to individual characteristics, family variables were examined in the Kauai study. Those factors that serve a protective function were parent's educational level, attention paid to the infant, positive early parent–child relationships, care by other kin, adult coping styles, family coherence demonstrated through shared values, and adult structuring and rule setting at home. Factors outside of the family also served as protective influences, such as the support of other family members, teachers, neighbors, community leaders, and friends.

These studies demonstrate the dynamic interplay between the personal characteristics of individuals and families and the broader environment in which they grow and live. Both the immediate family environment and the communities in which families are nested exert a tremendous influence on the children and families.

This research highlights not only areas of influence but also intervention arenas for fostering resilience. The concepts of risk and resilience apply not only to an examination of child development but also to family development and functioning (Singer & Powers, 1993). Families' resilience in adapting to challenges such as the birth of a child with a disability has received less attention in the literature than have the risks to family functioning posed by such events. Patterson's review of the literature (1991) describing the resilience of families of children with chronic illness, however, sheds some light on resilience and adaptation in families. Patterson noted that resilient families

- Maintained their family boundaries and control over their family decisions in the face of interactions with outside forces such as professionals
- Were able to openly and assertively express feelings and convey communications competently
- Ascribed positive meanings to difficult situations and remained flexible in their roles and tasks
- Demonstrated teamwork within the family and maintained the family as a unit
- Engaged in active problem solving and coping skills
- Maintained social integration through friendships and participation in social networks and activities
- Developed collaborative relationships with professionals

Like service needs related to disability, the demands of a chronic illness require frequent contacts with professionals. Patterson's work points to the importance of a partnership or alliance between family and professionals as the basis for supportive interventions.

FAMILY SUPPORT: MODELS OF INTERVENTION

The family support movement has received increased attention both nationally and internationally from policy makers and clinicians over the past several decades. Family initiatives also have been brought to the forefront of disability rights and services. These initiatives have raised awareness of the importance of the family as the primary context for children's development and the family unit is now viewed as the major focus of intervention and support services.

Contemporary approaches to supporting families center on recognizing family strengths and resources. These notions are often in sharp contrast to more traditional approaches. Singer and Powers reviewed traditional models of supports for families and described them as often characterized by "residualism, professional dominance, and pathology" (1993, p. 4). In other words, supports were traditionally given to a small, residual number of families who were viewed as unable to function without such services (e.g., the traditional welfare system in the United States). Second, approaches were professionally driven so that families were fitted to the services rather than the reverse. Third, services were developed around a pathological or problem-oriented approach and interventions were focused on "fixing" families.

This shift in perspective to family support has been applied and expanded to families of children with disabilities (Dunst, Trivette, & Deal, 1988; Singer & Irvin, 1989). Family support is construed in a broader social context and the family unit is recognized as embedded in other social networks in the ecological framework. Family competencies and capabilities are stressed and the role of professionals has shifted to support, rather than control, over family goals and decisions.

Using a social systems perspective, Dunst, Trivette, and Deal (1994) outlined six principles that reflect this family support philosophy based on family competency:

1. Enhancement of a sense of community
2. Mobilization of resources and support
3. Shared responsibility and collaboration
4. Protection of family integrity
5. Strengthening of family functioning
6. Proactive practices in the human services

In this perspective, interventions build on the family's interactions within its community and focus on the resources and informal supports, such as family members and friends, inherent in that family. Interventions are conducted in a manner that enhances families' competencies, recognizes families' values and life ways, and maximizes families' control over decision making and services. This approach allows for a more individualized and flexible system of service delivery that is responsive to the particular needs of families and their cultural and linguistic heritage and preferences. Collaborative partnerships between family members and professionals are at the heart of all interventions delivered in this manner.

This consumer- or family-driven approach to services has been termed a family-centered approach. Dunst, Trivette, and Deal (1988) suggested four essential intervention principles associated with this approach:

1. To promote positive family functioning, intervention efforts are focused on "family-identified needs, aspirations, and personal projects." (p. 48)

2. To meet the needs identified by the family, capitalize on family strengths and capabilities as they mobilize their needed resources.

3. To ensure that the family obtains resources to meet their needs, emphasize strengthening existing social support networks and identifying other potential sources of information and assistance.

4. To enhance the family's ability to become self-sustaining in meeting their needs, use helping behaviors that promote the family's ability to gain and use its own competencies and skills to obtain needed resources.

These principles not only provide the nexus of a philosophy of service delivery but they also offer direct benchmarks for practice. Service providers can evaluate their own methods and approaches to serving children and families by reflecting on these principles. The story of Kasheen and his family illustrates these principles of family support.

KASHEEN

Kasheen was adopted when he was 6 months old, and his parents later discovered that he had been born prematurely and prenatally addicted to drugs. The first years were difficult for his parents as they adapted their home to provide a calming and consistent environment for Kasheen, who was easily excited and difficult to console. At first they were barely able to leave home without him crying intensely, but over time they were able to participate in neighborhood and family events. Kasheen was able to attend a preschool program at their church when he turned 3. A special education consultant for the school district provided on-site consultation for children with developmental delays. Given his delays in communication and in meeting cognitive developmental milestones, Kasheen qualified for services. Then, suddenly, when Kasheen was only 3½ years old, his father died of a heart attack. At that point Nonda and Kasheen moved in with Nonda's mother to save money on rent and so that Nonda would have supportive child care when she was at work during the day.

Kasheen's grandmother became a tremendous source of support for both Nonda and Kasheen. Nonda's two sisters, her brother, and their families also lived in nearby communities, and the whole family and neighbors chipped in to provide child care and to take Kasheen to and from school and other appointments.

Now, Kasheen is 6 years old. He attends his neighborhood kindergarten. During the early months of the school year, his teachers requested that Kasheen be tested for learning disabilities because of his inability to master early literacy concepts and to follow directions and focus his attention. His teachers reported that even during recess, Kasheen shifted from activity to activity and playmate to playmate without sustaining attention in any one place. The kindergarten teachers are convinced that Kasheen "has learning problems." Nonda followed through with these recommendations, at which point Kasheen was identified as having attention-deficit/hyperactivity disorder (ADHD). The teachers believe that their suspicions were confirmed by the educational psychologist's diagnosis.

Although Nonda welcomed the assessment to learn more about Kasheen's needs, she has found it demoralizing to be told that Kasheen will always have "problems" and that she should ensure that he has a male role model integrally involved in his life. She feels like she is doing the best that she can. This diagnosis came as a blow to Nonda on top of the previous disappointments and challenges that she has experienced.

What types of support have Nonda and Kasheen needed throughout Kasheen's lifetime? What service approaches have and have not been helpful? First, when Nonda and her husband adopted Kasheen, they were faced with caregiving challenges (e.g., crying, inconsolability) that they had not anticipated. Nonda reported that their strong marital foundation and the support of their own families helped them to meet the needs that Kasheen presented. The teachers and other service providers in the preschool early intervention program and preschool helped Nonda by providing her with practical tips and educational information for supporting Kasheen's development at home. They made home visits as well, and actively included Kasheen's grandmother in all planning and delivery of services.

The family also benefited from participating in early intervention services during which teachers and an occupational therapist provided them with information on how to hold and feed Kasheen and how to structure their home environment so that it would be less likely to overtax his senses. Nonda felt less supported when Kasheen was in kindergarten, however.

If this family is viewed through the lens of the service provider as "the expert" and dispenser of services to individuals in need, one may see a single parent, a child without a father, a child with learning difficulties, and other risk conditions. If one views the family through a different lens, however, one that is based on a family-centered approach, very different phenomena may become apparent. Through this lens, one can see that Nonda and Kasheen have many strengths and resources. Kasheen is able to participate in his local school program and make friends. Nonda is employed and able to support her family. She is also quite capable of gaining access to community resources and services for Kasheen. Furthermore, the family has a tremendously close network of family and friends who are an active and integral part of their lives. Nonda also relies on spiritual guidance from her faith and her faith community. She is confident in that guidance and in her own abilities to see the family through whatever challenges they may encounter. Those teachers, therapists, and other service providers who acknowledged these strengths were able to provide the most support for Nonda and Kasheen. They answered Nonda's questions, provided the specific technical information that she requested in order to manage and address Kasheen's needs, and helped her to obtain information on school programs in her area. They also told Nonda about a parent-to-parent support network in her community for parents of children with similar needs (see Santelli, Poyadue, & Young, 2001, for resources). Nonda has found this to be another valuable resource for child-rearing tips as well as an avenue to broaden her own friendship relationships.

SUMMARY

In contemplating the perspective from which families should be viewed, the choice is not unlike that posed in the old cliché of viewing the cup as either half empty or half full. Each view leads to a different approach to our lives and/or our work. The approach advocated in this text is to examine the many possibilities for supporting families to fulfill their roles as primary contexts for growth and nurturance for each individual within the family.

The transactional and ecological system frameworks for understanding families illuminate the complex nature of human development and the ever-changing nature of the environments in which the individuals and families reside. This approach presents a complex array of service needs and collaborative challenges. The dynamic and complex nature of families also presents a wealth of opportunities for change and growth through supportive environments.

ACTIVITIES TO EXTEND THE DISCUSSION

1. **Describe your family system.** What are the subsystems within your family? What are the roles played by family members within these subsystems? Are some roles preferred or easier to play than others? Do these roles ever conflict or seem out of balance?

2. **Draw an ecological map of your family.** Describe the major influences at the microsystem, mesosystem, exosystem, and macrosystem levels? Around what individual or family issues do these systems connect or overlap?

3. **Think of a character in a book or in a movie or television program that you would describe as "resilient."** What are the characteristics of that individual that led you to that conclusion?

REFERENCES

Americans with Disabilities Act (ADA) of 1990, PL 101-336, 42 U.S.C. §§ 12101 *et seq.*

Beckman, P. (Ed.). (1996). *Strategies for working with families of young children with disabilities.* Baltimore: Paul H. Brookes Publishing Co.

Bernier, J.C., & Siegel, D.H. (1994). Attention-deficit hyperactive disorder: A family and ecological systems perspective. *Families in Society, 75,* 142, 150.

Berry, J.O. (1995). Families and deinstitutionalization: An application of Bronfenbrenner's social ecology model. *Journal of Counseling and Development, 73,* 379–383.

Broderick, C.B. (1993). *Understanding family process: Basics of family systems theory.* Thousand Oaks, CA: Sage Publications.

Bronfenbrenner, U. (1979). *The ecology of human development.* Cambridge, MA: Harvard University Press. (ERIC Document Reproduction Service No. ED 128).

Bronfenbrenner, U. (1986). Ecology of the family as a context for human development research perspectives. *Developmental Psychology, 22,* 723–742.

Bronfenbrenner, U., & Ceci, S. (1994). Nature–nurture reconceptualized: A bioecological model. *Psychological Review, 101,* 568–586.

Bronfenbrenner, U., & Morris, P. (1998). The ecology of developmental processes. In R. Lerner (Ed.), *Handbook of child psychology (5th ed.): Vol. I: Theoretical models of human development* (pp. 993–1028). New York: John Wiley & Sons.

Bruer, J.T., & Greenough, W.T. (2001). The subtle science of how experience affects the brain. In D.B. Bailey, Jr., J.T. Bruer, F.J. Symons, & J.W. Lichtman (Eds.), *Critical thinking about critical periods* (pp. 209–232). Baltimore: Paul H. Brookes Publishing Co.

Dunst, C.J., Trivette, C.M., & Deal, A.G. (1988). *Enabling and empowering families: Principles and guidelines for practice.* Cambridge, MA: Brookline Books.

Dunst, C.J., Trivette, C.M., & Deal, A.G. (1994). *Supporting and strengthening families: Methods, strategies and practices* (Vol. 1). Cambridge, MA: Brookline Books.

Hanson, M.J., Wolfberg, P., Zercher, C., Morgan, M., Gutierrez, S., Barnwell, D., & Beckman, P.J. (1998). The culture of inclusion: Recognizing diversity at multiple levels. *Early Childhood Research Quarterly, 13*(1), 185–209.

Individuals with Disabilities Education Act (IDEA) of 1990, PL 101-476, 20 U.S.C. §§ 1400 *et seq.*

Kazak, A. (1989). Families of chronically ill children: A systems and social-ecological model of adaptation and challenge. *Journal of Consulting and Clinical Psychology, 57,* 25–30.

Klein, D.M., & White, J.M. (1996). *Family theories: An introduction.* Thousand Oaks, CA: Sage Publications.

Odom, S.L. (Ed.). (2002). *Widening the circle: Including the child with disabilities in preschool programs.* New York: Teachers College Press.

Odom, S.L., Peck, C.A., Hanson, M.J., Beckman, P.J., Kaiser, A.P., Lieber, J., Brown, W.H., Horn, E.M., & Schwartz, I.S. (1996). Inclusion at the preschool level: An ecological systems analysis. *Social Policy Report: Society for Research in Child Development, 10*(2 & 3), 18–30.

Patterson, J.M. (1991). Family resilience to the challenge of a child's disability. *Pediatric Annals, 20,* 491–499.

Rutter, M. (1990). Psychosocial resilience and protective mechanisms. In J. Rolf, A. Masten, D. Cicchetti, D. Nuechterlein, & S. Weintraub (Eds.), *Risk and protective factors in the development of psychopathology* (pp. 181–214). New York: Cambridge University Press.

Rutter, M. (1996). Psychosocial adversity: Risk, resilience, and recovery. In *Conference proceedings, Making a difference for children, families and communities: Partnerships among researchers, practitioners and policymakers,* for Head Start's Third National Research Conference, June 20–23, 1996. Washington DC: The Administration on Children, Youth and Families, Department of Health and Human Services.

Rutter, M. (2000). Resilience reconsidered: Conceptual considerations, empirical findings, and policy implications. In J.P. Shonkoff & S.J. Meisels (Eds.), *Handbook of early intervention* (2nd ed., pp. 651–682). New York: Cambridge University Press.

Sameroff, A.J., & Chandler, M. (1975). Reproductive risk and the continuum of caretaking casualty. In F.D. Horowitz (Ed.), *Review of child development research: Vol. 4* (pp. 187–244). Chicago: University of Chicago Press.

Sameroff, A.J., & Friese, B.H. (1990). Transactional regulation and early intervention. In

S.J. Meisels & J.P. Shonkoff (Eds.), *Handbook of early childhood intervention* (pp. 119–149). New York: Cambridge University Press.

Santelli, B., Poyadue, F.S., & Young, J.L. (2001). *The parent to parent handbook: Connecting families of children with special needs.* Baltimore: Paul H. Brookes Publishing Co.

Shonkoff, J.P., & Phillips, D.A. (Eds.). (2000). *From neurons to neighborhoods: The science of early childhood development.* Washington DC: National Academy Press.

Shore, R. (1997). *Rethinking the brain: New insights into early development.* New York: Families and Work Institute.

Singer, G.H.S., & Irvin, L.K. (1989). *Support for caregiving families: Enabling positive adaptation to disability.* Baltimore: Paul H. Brookes Publishing Co.

Singer, G.H.S., & Powers, L.E. (Eds.). (1993). *Families, disability, and empowerment: Active coping skills and strategies for family intervention.* Baltimore: Paul H. Brookes Publishing Co.

Turnbull, A.P., Summers, J.A., & Brotherson, M.J. (1984). *Working with families with disabled members: A family systems approach.* Lawrence: The University of Kansas, Kansas University Affiliated Facility.

Turnbull, A.P., & Turnbull, H.R. (1990). *Families, professionals, and exceptionality: A special partnership* (2nd ed.). Columbus, OH: Charles E. Merrill.

Turnbull, A.P., & Turnbull, H.R. (1997). *Families, professionals, and exceptionality: A special partnership* (3rd ed.). Columbus, OH: Charles E. Merrill.

Werner, E.E. (1990). Protective factors and individual resilience. In S.J. Meisels & J.P. Shonkoff (Eds.), *Handbook of early childhood intervention* (pp. 97–116). New York: Cambridge University Press.

Werner, E.E., Bierman, J.M., & French, F.E. (1971). *The children of Kauai: A longitudinal study from the prenatal period to age ten.* Honolulu: University of Hawaii Press.

Werner, E.E., & Smith, R.S. (1977). *Kauai's children come of age.* Honolulu: University of Hawaii Press.

Werner, E.E., & Smith, R.S. (1989). *Vulnerable but invincible: A longitudinal study of resilient children and youth.* New York: McGraw-Hill.

Werner, E.E., & Smith, R.S. (1992). *Overcoming the odds: High risk children from birth to adulthood.* Ithaca, NY: Cornell University Press.

Whitchurch, G., & Constantine, L. (1993). Systems theory. In P. Boss, W. Doherty, R. LaRossa, W. Schumm, & S. Steinmetz (Eds.), *Sourcebook of family theories and methods: A contextual approach* (pp. 32–352). New York: Plenum.

Young, M.E. (Ed.). (2002). *From early child development to human development: Investing in our children's future.* Washington, DC: The World Bank.

CHAPTER 3

TRADITIONAL AND EVOLVING FAMILY ROLES AND FUNCTIONS

Things hold. Lines connect in ways
that last and last and lives become
generations made out of pictures and words just kept.
—Lucille Clifton (as Quoted by Deirdre Mullane, 1995, p. 85)

The family is resilient, flexible, a survivor. It
could probably flourish (and has certainly shown
in the past that it can) without the wider society. But if we
erode the role of the family, can the wider society flourish?
—Jo Boyden (1993, p. 23)

What do families do? How have the roles and responsibilities of families changed over time? Why are families important? These are complex questions with no short answers, but this chapter provides a discussion of these issues as well as their implications for service delivery. Readers of this chapter may want to think of their own family or families as a backdrop to the discussion. Did the family you grew up with differ from the family you live with today? How was it different? Do family members have different roles, different responsibilities? How did these changes occur? Were they planned, or did they just happen? Reflecting on the individual, political, and societal influences that have shaped our own families provides a perspective for considering the challenges and changes that families have encountered.

FAMILY ROLES AND RESPONSIBILITIES: WHAT DO FAMILIES DO?

This chapter first poses the question, "What do families do?" The short answer is that they do a lot. Consider all of the things that family members do to survive economically; support one another psychologically; ensure that basic needs for food, shelter, health, and nurturance are met; and find meaning in life. It is no wonder that families feel stressed. In the United States and around the world, families are responsible for providing for their members in a variety of ways and serve multiple functions.

Throughout the world, family roles and functions are evolving. Occupational, social, political, and economic changes have contributed to this evolution, as have industrialization and technological advances. For example, in 1940, only 25% of U.S. women worked outside the home (Riche, 2000). This figure has greatly increased; in 1997, 71.9% of women with children younger than age 18 were in the labor force, and 64.8% had children younger than age 6 (AFL-CIO, 2001). As women enter or advance in the workforce, their roles and responsibilities increase, and the whole family may need to change to accommodate work hours, travel, and new child care arrangements. Fathers may expand their roles to include more time for working in the home or running more errands.

As family roles have evolved from men working and women staying at home to care for children, social mores have also changed. The social stigma attached to women who work, especially mothers, is no longer a significant deterrent. Unlike the 1950s, when many people viewed working women as abandoning their children and demonstrating that their husbands were unable to provide adequately, today it is assumed that many women will be in the workforce. The women's liberation movement beginning in the 1960s dramatically changed the political landscape by providing opportunities and equal rights for women. Economic conditions have also had a significant influence on the number of women in the workforce. As consumer goods and costs increase, so does the need for additional income, making women's salaries and wages a necessity in many families. Industrialization and technology have had an impact on the number of women working, as well. Although women throughout the world have always engaged in manual labor, industrialization expanded the availability of less physically demanding work. Technology, especially medical technology that enables women to control their reproduction, has had a profound effect on women's ability to become economically independent and pursue a career.

These changes have altered the functions in some families. For example, families may have less time to provide for their children's daily care and recreation and entrust more of those functions to child care providers, after-school programs, organized sports, or camps.

Roles and functions in families with children with disabilities have also evolved as society has changed. Society's attitudes toward individuals with disabilities have changed dramatically over the years. Formerly institutionalized or otherwise hidden from society, people with disabilities are now included as valued brothers, sisters, colleagues, and friends. The political capital of the Civil Rights movement and the women's movement provided a launching pad for advocacy groups that sought equal rights and opportunities for individuals with disabilities. Political action resulted in a series of precedent-setting laws such as the Education for All Handicapped Children Act of 1975 (EHA; PL 94-142), which, for the first time, mandated a free and appropriate public education for *all* children and youth regardless of their disabilities. This enabled families to send their children with disabilities to public schools, reducing the educational, economic, and caregiving demands that these families had traditionally borne exclusively. The EHA was reauthorized in 1990 as the Individuals with Disabilities Education Act (IDEA; PL 101-476) and amended in 1991 (PL 102-119), 1997 (PL 105-17), and was set to be reauthorized in 2003 (HR 1350). The new laws have not eliminated the need for advocacy efforts on the part of families to ensure that their children receive appropriate programs and services, however. Nor have they reduced the time that is required of families to participate with teachers, therapists, physicians, and others as members of the team.

Subsequent legislation such as Section 504 of the Rehabilitation Act of 1973 (PL 93-112) and the Americans with Disabilities Act (ADA) of 1990 (PL 101-336) increased rights and opportunities through adulthood and across areas unrelated to education. This enabled families to think and plan differently for the life needs of their sons and daughters with disabilities. Supported apartments, group homes, and other living options for individuals with disabilities enabled many parents to contemplate an "empty nest" rather than lifelong responsibilities for their son's or daughter's direct care. These laws made it possible for individuals with disabilities to anticipate fair hiring practices, accommodations in the workplace, and independence as adults.

Technology has also provided a real boon for individuals with disabilities. New technologies have made communication and mobility possible for people whose physical disabilities challenged both of these areas. New knowledge has prevented some disabilities and reduced the consequences of others, significantly improving the quality of life for many individuals with disabilities and their families. The information age of technology has also provided a new array of job opportunities for individuals with disabilities, increasing their vocational and career opportunities.

Frameworks for Understanding Family Systems

Chapter 2 provides an overview of the theoretical frameworks that have been used to study and understand families. This chapter presents an overview of several theoretical approaches that incorporate family functions in their conceptualization; then it narrows the focus to a detailed discussion of the family systems framework described by Turnbull, Summers, and Brotherson (1984) and Summers, Brotherson, and Turnbull (1988). Their framework addresses family functions as one component of the family system and describes the roles and functions that are expected of families in the contemporary Western world.

One conceptual framework used to understand families is the structural functionalism framework. This framework first emerged in the late 1930s (Malinowski, 1939) and incorporates psychological, sociological, and anthropological traditions. It assumes that structures are designed to provide specific functions. From a macrosocial perspective, the family is one of the structures within the larger social system responsible for supporting the social system and contributing to the maintenance of social order. From a microsocial perspective, the family itself can be viewed as a system in which the positions held by family members (e.g., mother, daughter, grandmother, father) and the roles that they play can be studied (Gelles, 1995). The structural functionalism framework assumes that social order is possible because social structures exist that have responsibility for carrying out various tasks or functions. Like systems theories that have been developed since 1939, the structural functionalism framework assumes that structures are nested in larger systems. It differs in that it has been interpreted from a biological or organic perspective that maintains that when a structure is missing there is no replacement for its function. That interpretation is seldom true in families. In most families, when a structure is no longer present, another assumes its functions. Consider Pablo's family.

PABLO

When Pablo was 3 years old, his mother was killed in an automobile accident. Afterward, Pablo's father and maternal grandmother assumed more responsibility for his daily care and nurturance. Pablo's aunts took care of him when his father had to be out of town on business or just needed time for his own grieving and healing. Over time, Pablo's father was able to adjust his work schedule to be home when Pablo returned from school so that he could take him to soccer practice and be available in general to meet the needs of a growing boy.

From a strict structural functionalism perspective, the roles and responsibilities of Pablo's mother would be lost when she died. This was not the case in Pablo's life, however. Although the original structure provided by his mother was missing, the functions that she provided were not. Other family members assumed those roles and ensured that Pablo was loved and well cared for.

Structural functionalism has been replaced by other theories of family, but this chapter acknowledges the contributions of this theory to underscoring the various functions that families perform daily and throughout an individual's lifespan. For families and their members to survive, certain jobs have to be done—obtaining financial resources, providing daily care, helping family members to stay healthy, and transmitting family values. Each family may accomplish these jobs in different ways, but each family grapples with the jobs by setting priorities and assigning responsibilities or by ignoring or deferring the responsibilities.

Perhaps the best way to understand family functions is to consider them in the broader context of the family systems framework (Summers et al., 1988; Turnbull et al., 1984). Although this framework was developed to enable professionals and families alike to consider the ways in which having a son or daughter with disabilities may affect the family, it is equally helpful in thinking about all families. The framework includes *inputs* made up of the family characteristics such as the size and constellation of the family, family ideology, and cultural identification; *process,* which is characterized by family interactions such as the patterns and style of communication, cohesion, and adaptability; *outputs,* which are made up of the family functions mentioned previously; and *change* through the life cycle as a result of changes within and outside the family (Turnbull et al., 1984). (See Figure 2.1) (For a comprehensive review of this model and its components, see Turnbull & Turnbull, 2001.)

Family Characteristics

One might think of family characteristics as the family's signature—those aspects that make each family unique. The characteristics include the number of individuals in the family and the family constellation. As discussed in the previous chapters, family size and constellation vary dramatically from family to family and over the years as children are born; divorces, remarriages, and blending occur; children leave home and perhaps return; and family members die.

Family members' cultural beliefs, values, and behaviors; their race; the languages that they speak; and the traditions that they follow are also a part of the family's characteristics. Sociocultural aspects of the family such as family members' level of education, socioeconomic status, and geographic locale may contribute significantly to a family's signature. Regardless of a family's culture, race, or ethnicity, the circumstances of having little education, being poor, and living in a remote, rural area result in an individual having very different life experiences than those of someone who is well educated, affluent, and urban, for example.

Personal characteristics of family members also influence families, just as families influence each member's personal characteristics. A demanding, difficult family member who is both alcoholic and abusive has a profound effect on every other member of the family. The effect that such a family member has on individuals within the family may vary dramatically, however. Some family members may gain personal strength and autonomy from learning to cope with and negotiate and/or free themselves from this person's demands and abuse. Other family members may lose all sense of personal control, ambition, and self-esteem; still others will fall somewhere in between. In some families, a member's personal characteristics may include a disability. For example, having a child with autism may bring the entire family together as they love, care for, and advocate for their son, daughter, brother, sister, grandchild, niece, or nephew. In other families, incorporating a child with autism may result in isolation, resentment, or blaming, causing the family to pull apart rather than together. Although every family member's personal characteristics affect every member of the family, the nature of the impact—like the weather—cannot be predicted.

Family Interaction

Family interaction is made up of the complex relationships among and between the various subsystems within and outside of the family. Each subsystem is separated by boundaries that help to define interactions. In some families these boundaries are relatively fluid; in others they are not. Four subsystems are included in the framework proposed by Turnbull and colleagues (1984). They include the marital, sibling, parental, and extended family subsystems. As you think of your own family, you may discover that these subsystems may overlap, are nonexistent, or fail to describe the way in which your family is structured. To a great extent, subsystems are determined by cultural and sociocultural experience. For example, the marital subsystem is traditionally composed of a husband and wife. As discussed in Chapter 1, a wide range of adult partnerships may constitute the marital subsystem. The official sanction of marriage is not available to all couples whose roles are described by this subsystem. The extended family subsystem is equally diverse. For many families, the extended family *is* the family. All members are important participants; no one is considered to be distant or extended as the words suggest. The sibling subsystem exists within families that have more than one child. In blended families, the sibling subsystem may be divided into additional subsystems representing half brothers and sisters from previous marriages in addition to those from the current marriage. The parental subsystem is typically the same as the marital subsystem; however, this is not always the case. For example, in some families, grandparents are fulfilling the parenting role when members of the marital subsystem are unable to assume that role. In other families, an older sister or brother may assume a parenting role to ease the burden. It is not atypical in families with a child with disabilities for brothers and sisters to be involved in some of the parenting tasks, just as older sisters and brothers often participate in parenting a younger sibling.

Regardless of the makeup of the various subsystems, each operates within a range of cohesion and adaptability that is defined by the family.

Culture often plays a significant role in determining both cohesion and adaptability, but each family ultimately plays by its own rules. Cohesion is the extent to which families are emotionally bonded to one another as well as the extent to which they feel that they are independent from the family (Turnbull & Turnbull, 2001). A critical point in any discussion of family cohesion is the cultural identification of the family. No universal norm exists. A family that may seem cohesive to the point of being enmeshed may be typical for the values, beliefs, and behaviors of their culture. Likewise, a family in which members have considerable independence from one another and lead their own lives without ongoing consultation and feedback from the family may be typical for their culture but seem quite unusual to those who come from traditions that are more obviously cohesive. (For a more thorough discussion of theoretical, clinical, and research bases of family cohesion see Olson, Russell, & Sprenkle, 1980; and Minuchin & Fishman, 1981.) For example, a family that is very cohesive—one that depends almost exclusively on family members for social support, recreation, decision making, and so forth—may be less open to intervention from outsiders and see less need for intervention for children or other family members with disabilities. Families whose members have considerable autonomy outside of the family may be more inclined to seek external support and services.

According to Turnbull and Turnbull, adaptability refers to "the family's ability to change in response to situational and developmental stress" (2001, p. 126). Some families are masterful at dealing with stress and adapting to stressful situations when they arise. Other families have considerably more difficulty in changing to reduce stress or dealing with difficult situations such as the birth of a child with a disability, job loss, or a move

to a new community. Families at the extremes in adaptability are those that change so often and so quickly that life is chaotic versus those that have become rigid because they cannot change. As in most areas of life, the extremes are not optimal for family well-being. (For a more thorough discussion of the theoretical underpinnings of family adaptability, see Olson et al., 1980, and Olson, Sprenkle, & Russell, 1979.)

Theories of Family Functions

In its most recent adaptation by Turnbull and Turnbull (2001), the family systems framework describes eight functions that families provide for their members. These include affection, self-esteem, spiritual, economic, daily care, socialization, recreation, and education. Although discussed in relation to families who have children with special needs, these researchers' conceptualization of family functions is relevant to all families. Bristor (1995), whose work has been applied in the field of mental health, listed the following seven responsibilities as functions of families: protection, economic resources, nurturance, mediation, education, adaptation, and continuity. Ronneau (1999) provided another listing of functions in a descriptive study of families who care for children with severe emotional disabilities. The six functions identified for this study included domestic, self-identity, affection, socialization, recreation, and education or vocational needs. Overlap among the models is evident and is highlighted in Table 3.1. Although some individuals and cultures may emphasize the importance of the family's role in certain functions more than in others, the expectation that families will fulfill these functions is nearly universal. The next major section of this chapter discusses each of the family functions in greater detail.

Family Life Cycle

The final component in the family systems framework is the family life cycle—the changes over time that typically cause stress and influence family functioning. The traditional model of family follows this evolution: A couple begins as a family without children, which is followed by years

Table 3.1.   Family functions as identified by researchers

Turnbull, Summers, and Brotherson (1984)	Bristor (1995)	Ronneau (1999)	Hanson and Lynch
Affection	Protection	Domestic	Love and affection
Self-esteem	Economic resources	Self-identity	Daily care and health maintenance
Spiritual	Nurturance	Affection	
Economic	Mediation	Socialization	Economic support
Daily care	Education	Recreation	Identity development
Socialization	Adaptation	Education or vocational needs	Socialization and guidance
Recreation	Continuity		
Education			Educational and vocational development
			Recreation, rest, and recuperation

devoted to child rearing and launching children into their own lives, after which the couple become empty nesters, enter old age, and lose a partner through death. Needless to say, it does not work that way for all families. Many families begin with one or more children. Partners may change over time. Some children are never launched. Empty nesters may take on the parental role again with their grandchildren, or an individual might experience the death of a spouse prior to old age. These benchmarks are part of the developmental life cycle of many families. Change, such as the large and small transitions within our lives and the lives of families, is stressful. Having a baby, becoming responsible for an elderly parent, getting a new job, or moving to a new community are big changes that are often accompanied by considerable stress. Even small changes take their toll, however. A substitute teacher at school, a change in child care hours, or a parent's need to stay late at work one evening are small changes that can be disruptive for families. The way in which families cope with the stress of change is, in part, determined by the other components of the family systems framework including family members' characteristics— particularly their cultural affiliation and identity, their range of cohesion and adaptability, and their perception of and ability to fulfill family functions during times of added stress. (For a more complete discussion of family life cycle theory, refer to Carter & McGoldrick, 1980, 1989.)

When viewed as a system, the roles, functions, and impact of individual family members becomes more clear. Just as a pebble tossed into a pond creates ripples that magnify its influence, each family member affects every other. As you read the next section about specific family functions, consider the ways in which individual family members, the characteristics of the family, their cohesion and adaptability, and their place in the life cycle may affect their ability to fulfill each function.

FAMILY FUNCTIONS

As described previously, authors provide different but overlapping lists of family functions (Bristor, 1995; Onaga, McKinney, & Pfaff, 2000; Ronneau, 1999; Turnbull et al., 1984). This chapter takes a broad view of family functions and combines and adapts functions listed by several authors. We include seven functions: 1) love and affection; 2) daily care and health maintenance; 3) economic support; 4) identity development; 5) socialization and guidance; 6) educational and vocational development; and 7) recreation, rest, and recuperation. Each is described in the sections that follow, with an emphasis on the ways in which having a child with a disability and family diversity may influence the ways in which functions are performed.

Love and Affection

Perhaps the most basic function of families is to love and show affection for one another. The bond that links family members is often thought to be the strongest among all human interactions, and the axiom that "blood is thicker than water" underscores this belief. Many aspects of love and

affection fall within this function, such as the love and intimacy between adult partners in the family, the nurturing and unconditional love given by parents to children, and the special support and caring for older family members or those who have special needs.

Families and family members demonstrate their love and affection for one another in a variety of ways. Some families exhibit considerable physical contact—hugs, kisses, pats, and snuggles. Other families may be less demonstrative but show their love and affection in other ways, from specially prepared meals to fond looks to making remarkable sacrifices to support and care for another family member. Culture, gender, situational variables, and personal preferences all influence the ways in which families show their love and affection.

In all families sometimes and in a few families most of the time, love and affection seem to be absent. An abusive spouse, a demanding grandparent, or an angry teen is difficult to love when he or she is engaging in these behaviors. Family members may find it more difficult to express love and affection when a child's autism makes him or her not want to be touched, or when a conduct disorder causes him or her to be combative and destructive. It may take considerable time for members of blended families to love each other and find comfortable ways of showing affection. For some, caring and respect may be the ultimate, and most appropriate, outcome. Family members who are not psychologically available because of their own mental health problems or addictions have difficulty fulfilling this family function because they cannot engage in the reciprocal interactions that love and affection require (Seifer & Dickstein, 1993). Maternal depression has been studied for its potential for causing psychological unavailability. As emphasized by Clark and Fenichel (2001), when a woman is diagnosed with maternal depression, it does not tell us how that mother is caring for her child. She may be sensitive and responsive, but maternal depression may also cause her to be unable to respond to her child's physical and emotional needs. The extent of maternal depression and the ways in which it is manifested are critical elements in determining the type and intensity of intervention for the mother and other family members. Well-publicized incidents, including one in which a mother allowed her car to roll into a lake with the children inside and another in which a mother drowned her children in the bathtub, illustrate the tragic consequences of ignoring maternal depression.

Regardless of how one perceives a family as an outsider, family bonds are often much stronger than they appear. One can never assume that love and affection are not present.

Daily Care and Health Maintenance

Every family has its daily chores that keep individuals and the household running. Shopping for groceries, preparing meals, getting dressed, cleaning, transporting family members, managing home maintenance, and obtaining health care consume major portions of the day. Few individuals who work and have families feel that they have adequate time for these routine but necessary activities—this is one of the reasons why so many products and strategies have been developed that are devoted to saving time. Fast food, shoes that use Velcro instead of shoelaces, drive-through banks and ATMs, washing machines and dryers, dishwashers, microwaves, personal digital assistants, and cellular phones are all designed to reduce the time spent in daily care. For two-career families, single parents, and those families who care for their own children as well as their aging parents, daily responsibilities can be daunting.

Families from collectivist cultures may be more effective at mobilizing resources for daily care because of a greater pool of people from which to draw (Lynch & Hanson, 1998). Likewise, families with many brothers and sisters, aunts and uncles, grandparents, and cousins nearby may find it far easier to manage the demands of daily life than a single parent struggling in isolation.

The complexities of daily care and health maintenance and the time they require may be even greater in families in which a member has a disability. In Knoll's (1996) study of 48 families in New York State who had children with low incidence disorders and complex medical histories, families reported that their son or daughter needed complete supervision throughout large portions of the day. In addition to the extra time required for daily routines such as bathing, dressing, eating, and sleeping, many children required time-consuming medical procedures as well as scheduled administration of medications. Other disabilities also add time and complexity to a family's daily demands. Children who need considerable structure to accomplish tasks and maintain their behavior require pre-planning and support through the most routine tasks. Greenfeld described childhood with his brother Noah, who has autism, in a popular press piece:

> *Noah, who can't speak, dress or go to the bathroom completely unassisted,
> will always be the center of our family. He never earned that role; his needs
> dictated it. . . . I accepted the fact that Noah and his problems could fill a
> battleship of parental duty and obligation, leaving my mother and father too
> spent to worry about the more banal problems of their normal son. (2002,
> p. 54)*

Other children with disabilities may require frequent occupational, physical, speech-language, or psychotherapy with the attendant issues of scheduling, time, and transportation. And many will require additional time to
participate in every activity because of motor problems or cognitive delays
that interfere with their understanding and responding. In some instances
the family member with a disability may be a young adult or an aging
parent whose needs are equally demanding physically and psychologically.
Regardless of family constellation, culture, language, ethnicity, and socioeconomic circumstances, families are responsible for many chores that
keep family members healthy and well cared for. Having a child or other
family member with a disability often adds to the tasks that must be
accomplished and the time that it takes.

Economic Support

Although the standard of living across families in the United States and
throughout the world varies markedly, families in the United States are
expected to be financially independent. The welfare reform legislation
discussed in Chapter 1 underscores this value, or at least the value that
individuals should not be lifelong dependents on government support.
Financial independence in this chapter is viewed very conservatively as
a living wage—one that enables a family to live above the poverty level
(Roston, 2002). This is not a generous wage nor one that many would
choose, but it is one that enables individuals and families to pay for
adequate housing, food, and basic health care, with some extra at the end
of the month. Although the American society values financial independence, for many families it has proved unattainable. The number of children living in poverty has not changed since 1981 (Pollard, 1998), and
projections from the Children's Defense Fund (2000) suggest that a third
of the children born in the year 2000 will live in poverty for at least 1
year prior to their 18th birthday. Families in which parents do not have
an education, job skills, or English language competence have far less
access to financial resources. Teen parents often lack both an education
and marketable skills, and many single parents struggle to earn enough
to care for themselves and their children. (See Chapters 1 and 5 for more
information on poverty.)

Families of children with disabilities, especially disabilities such as
mental retardation, autism, cerebral palsy, and complex medical conditions
that require technological support, spend more money on their children
with a disability than on their other children (Turnbull & Turnbull, 2001).
Extra costs combined with a frequent need for one parent to leave the
workforce for a period of time to care for or manage the child's care make

many families of children with disabilities more vulnerable to economic stress. Many people with children with disabilities find it difficult to ask for help, especially financial help. As Knoll concluded from his study of families of children with complex, low-incidence disabilities,

> *Again and again, the families tell of benefits managers, service coordinators, discharge planners, and social workers whose actions indicate that they regard the families as welfare junkies out to milk the system for everything it's worth. An attitude is conveyed, even in dealing with entitlements and plans to which the parents have long contributed, that the families are the beneficiaries of some benevolent charity and should be happy with what they are given. Families struggling to come to terms with their child's disability and the care demands associated with it find themselves stigmatized, impoverished, and degraded. In a society of rugged individualists they are forced to ask for help, which, in itself, is more than some parents can deal with. (1996, p. 220)*

The families whose views Knoll expressed were widely spread across the socioeconomic continuum. They were also culturally, racially, and geographically diverse within the state of New York. But regardless of these differences, they shared a common concern about the ability to provide for their family financially and to support the additional costs associated with their child with a disability.

Identity Development

One of a family's most important responsibilities is to help each member develop his or her own identity. Developing a sense of self, self-esteem, and moral/ethical character that enables one to contribute constructively as a member of a family, a community, and the larger society is one of the most important developmental tasks. Development of one's sense of self begins within the first 12 months of life and is a never-ending process (Roth-Hanania, Busch-Rossnagel, & Higgins-D'Alessandro, 2000). Based on Minuchen's (1974) work, Deason and Randolph suggested that "the family is the laboratory in which the ingredients of belonging and being separate are mixed to produce an identity" (1998, p. 2 of electronic version). Identity development requires opportunities to explore possibilities and try various ways of being and interacting.

Families typically provide the social context that is the most enduring and open to identity exploration (Deason & Randolph, 1998). Identity development occurs as part of overall growth and development. In the majority of families, parents note the qualities, preferences, and characteristics of their children and work to shape those that are consistent with the family's beliefs. For example, a family with strong ties to their church may notice that their daughter enjoys music. To encourage her preferences within the family's beliefs, they may buy her a CD with hymns and spirituals for children, take her to concerts featuring spiritual music, and see that she joins the children's choir at church. Another family may have strong convictions about social justice and human rights. When their son displays a passion for history and geography, they may ensure that he is exposed to documentaries and history books that present multiple perspectives. They may take him along when they volunteer at the migrant community center and encourage him to learn the stories of the children and families that they meet there. In these families, there may be bumps in the road, but identity development occurs rather naturally with only short-term strife. In other families, identity development is fraught with difficulties and poses significant challenges to parents and children alike. In some families, a son or daughter may seem to rebel against all that his or her parents stand for and develop an identity that bears little relationship to other family members. In other families, the adults themselves are still working to develop their self-identity, self-esteem, and moral/ethical character, making it more difficult, if not impossible, to provide the support and guidance that their sons and daughters need in their own search for self.

In research on the outcomes of children of adolescent mothers, low maternal self-esteem and depression have been cited as factors that contribute to negative outcomes in children's behavior and developmental outcomes (Osofsky, Hann, & Peebles, 1993). Personal, cultural, sociocultural, and political issues can also challenge identity development. The experiences of children with disabilities may be dramatically different from the experiences of their peers. For example, having a physical disability in a community in which sports define one's place in the social hierarchy is likely to result in a severe challenge to an individual's healthy identity development. Likewise, having developmental delay and/or mental retardation makes it more difficult to fit into a fast-track world oriented toward achievement.

One's race, culture, and/or ethnicity may also interfere with identity development. In schools, communities, and countries in which prejudice against certain ethnic, racial, religious, or language group flourishes, it is more difficult for those who are discriminated against to develop a healthy self-identity. The same is true when poverty is considered. Being impoverished does not contribute to the development of a positive self-identity. None of the characteristics that interfere with the development of a positive self-identity is all encompassing, nor do any of these characteristics alone define the outcomes. They do, however, make it more difficult for children and families alike to fulfill the function of identity development.

Socialization and Guidance

For most young children, families provide the first opportunities for socialization. Finding a place within the family and interacting with an expanding network of family members lays the groundwork for future social interactions. In large, extended families, children's early socialization may occur as they interact with siblings, grandparents, cousins, aunts, and uncles before they interact with others. In smaller families without a nearby extended family or kinship network, children may meet family friends and their children early in their development. They may also be exposed to children in playgroups or formal child care environments.

Schools, camps, religious activities, and neighborhoods provide opportunities for socializing with others and developing social skills.

As children participate in social situations within and outside of the family, their behavior is typically guided by the values and beliefs of their parents or primary caregivers. Guidance may include helping with problem solving, providing advice and feedback, shaping basic beliefs and values, and transmitting spiritual and/or ethical/moral values (Summers et al., 1988). For example, some families believe in the importance of giving to others in tangible ways, and they transmit this value to their children very concretely. From volunteering as Meals-On-Wheels drivers to inviting international students or away-from-home military personnel over for dinner to helping construct or fix up homes for those in need, these families are guiding their children by modeling basic beliefs and values. Although the guidance provided varies from culture to culture, religion to religion, and place to place, providing guidance to children as they develop is universal. When guidance provided by family members or caregivers conflicts dramatically with that expected within the larger cultural milieu, however, success with this family function is threatened.

Providing guidance to a child with a disability may require different skills and approaches. If the disability interferes with the child's understanding, cognitive ability, or judgment, guidance may be more direct. For example, exploring spiritual or political values different from those of the family may not be possible.

Having a disability often interferes with a child's socialization. The considerable emphasis on inclusion in a natural environment for very young children underscores the need for expanded opportunities for socialization for children with disabilities (e.g., Brault, Ashley, & Gallo, 2001; Dunst & Bruder, 2002; Dunst, Hamby, Trivette, Raab, & Bruder, 2000; English, Goldstein, Shafer, & Kaczmarek, 1997; Guralnick, 2000, 2001; Hanson et al., 2001; Lieber et al., 2000; Mullis, 2002; Odom, 2000). Physical or sensory disabilities that interfere with play, communication disabilities that make it difficult to communicate preferences and/or needs, or social-emotional disabilities that result in challenging behaviors interfere with individuals' capabilities in developing social skills and finding opportunities in which to practice them. Although advocacy efforts and legislation support increased opportunities for inclusive social opportunities, families of children with disabilities are most often responsible for ensuring socialization opportunities (Turnbull & Rueff, 1997).

Educational and Vocational Development

Families are not expected to provide formal education or vocational training; but although it has become somewhat of a cliché, parents are their children's first teachers. Much of what each person knows was first taught and learned at home. Likewise, many of the behaviors that lead to success or failure in our work derived from our families—the ability to accept feedback and get along with others, persistence, thoughtfulness, motivation, and courtesy are a few examples. Adolescents' or young adults' first jobs are often the result of family connections. Although the educational/ vocational function of families is not always direct, it is their responsibility to ensure that their children are educated and have opportunities to prepare for a career or vocation.

Like the other functions described in this chapter, having a child with a disability or departing from the norm in any other sociocultural dimension may make fulfilling this function more difficult. Until 1975, children with disabilities in the United States were not guaranteed a free, public education. Infants and toddlers in the United States were not guaranteed early intervention services until the late 1980s; and the ADA, which made discrimination against individuals with disabilities in the workplace illegal, was not passed until 1990. Clearly, family members have had to play a significant role in obtaining education and vocational opportunities for their sons and daughters over many years.

IDEA and its subsequent amendments mandates a free appropriate education for individuals from birth through age 22. Although this has been a critical and much-needed piece of legislation, it has not always resulted in the intended benefits. For some, the mandated services have not been easy to obtain; and parents and advocates have continued to fight for their children's needs and rights. For others, local districts and state systems have been far too willing to provide services to certain groups, which has resulted in a serious overrepresentation of children of color in programs and services for individuals with disabilities.

Overrepresentation is particularly evident among African American children and youth. Data from the 1998–1999 school year indicate that compared with their white peers, African American students were 2.9 times as likely to be labeled as having mental retardation, 1.9 times as likely to be identified as having an emotional disability, and 1.3 times as likely to be labeled as having a learning disability. The study found that, once placed in special education, African American students were also less likely than white students to return to general education (National Alliance of Black School Educators [NABSE] and the IDEA Local Implementation by Local Administrators [ILIAD] Partnership, 2002). These and similar issues, such as the underrepresentation of African American children and youth in programs for the gifted and talented, suggest that parents need to continue to have a significant role in advocating for the appropriate educational programs and services for their sons and daughters who are exceptional.

Recreation, Rest, and Recuperation

The enormity of tasks required of families indicates that another important family function is creating time and opportunity for its members to recreate, rest, and recuperate. Each family has its own definitions of these terms. For some, recreation may mean participating in active sports; for others, it may be reading, playing the piano, attending concerts and plays, or playing cards. Rest may be taking a nap or simply doing something different from the typical demands of daily living. Recuperation also takes

different forms depending on time, personal preferences, and resources. Regardless of how each family defines this function, it is critical to healthy functioning for all family members over the long term.

Finding time, opportunity, and resources for each of these may be more difficult when a family member has a disability. Issues of access, acceptance, and sometimes behavior may have to be considered. Is it possible to go to the beach with a child who travels by wheelchair? What will it be like to take a child with loud vocalizations to a restaurant? Will it be possible for a child who is extremely active to sit through story time at the local library? Although these things may all be possible, when a family member has a disability, these are the types of issues that may confound a family's ability to have fun together.

Other challenges are lack of time and experience. Caregiving may take more time or skills when a child has a disability, and it may be more difficult to find babysitters who are both competent and comfortable with staying with the child while other family members spend time together. The basic lack of free time is an issue for many families, but especially for families of children with disabilities. Even when well-trained care workers are available, many families could not find the time to go out. Families of children with disabilities may find that rest, recuperation, and recreation are difficult to incorporate into their lives.

Families who are impoverished or those in which mental health problems prevail may also be challenged to fulfill this family function. Lack of financial resources limits the options for free time as well as the options for ways to spend that time. Likewise, families with serious mental health issues may be unable to mobilize themselves to engage in family activities.

IMPACT OF CONTEMPORARY
SOCIETY ON FAMILY ROLES AND FUNCTIONS

Changes in the economy, health care, legislation, and the political climate exert ongoing influences on the roles that families play, the functions they perform, and the ways in which they are supported or deterred in fulfilling those functions. This section illustrates some of the ways in which family functions have been supported or supplanted by the larger societal context.

Federal and enabling state laws have had a profound effect on the support that families receive in performing the functions ascribed to them. Legislation establishing Head Start in 1965 was one of the first federal efforts to support low-income children and their families in a more comprehensive way. In addition to providing preschool experiences for 3- and 4-year-olds from low-income families, the legislation provided physical and mental health care, nutrition, social services, and opportunities for parents to be involved in their children's education and to develop their own leadership skills (Children's Defense Fund, 2000). This support service has assisted families for several decades with the functions of daily care and health maintenance, identity development, socialization, and education. Other federal laws have had a significant impact on families' abilities to perform their expected functions. As mentioned previously, in 1975 IDEA required federal and state support for students with disabilities, which released many parents from the full responsibility of providing education for their sons and daughters with disabilities. Although parents, families, and professionals continue to report inadequacies and injustices within the special education system of services, the guarantee of a free and appropriate public education aids in the education, vocational development, and socialization of children with disabilities. It may also contribute to family members' ability to work outside the home to increase their economic self-sufficiency, and provides a few hours each day that can be used for recuperation or at least attention to tasks other than child care and monitoring.

The home schooling movement has had the opposite effect. Rather than cast parents and family members in the role of overseeing, monitoring, and/or orchestrating their children's education, this phenomenon allows parental education to replace public education. In other words, parents and families take responsibility for the delivery of formal education to their children as a family function. A common rationale is that home schooling is an antidote to public schools that are inadequate. The social and political agenda of home schooling has been questioned and concerns expressed that home schooling may, in fact, threaten the democratic ideals of public education (Apple, 2000). Families who select home schooling may have less time for other family functions, or one parent in a dual-career family may need to leave or substantially alter his or her work hours. Home schooling may affect the family's ability to provide recreation, rest, and recuperation. For some, eliminating school hours and schedules may increase the time that family members have to be together for relaxation and recreation. For others, the role of parent as teacher may interfere with recreation as every activity becomes a lesson. Regardless of the way each family handles the responsibilities involved, other family functions will be affected.

Welfare reform has also influenced families' abilities to fulfill various family functions, but its effects have been argued as both positive and negative. Designed to increase employment opportunities by increasing the skills of welfare recipients, many questions about the long-term effects on families remain. For example, has job training resulted in employment that is sustainable and sufficient for economic independence? Have child care options for parents in job training or newly acquired jobs been adequate to ensure that young children are receiving high-quality daily care, positive opportunities for identity development, and socialization? Has income been sufficient to provide health care and health maintenance, or have health benefits been lost through welfare reform?

Families in which both parents work have also affected the way in which family functions are performed. Second incomes are always welcome and often a necessity in homes across the nation. On the one hand, families with dual wage earners increase the likelihood that they will have adequate financial resources; on the other hand, the demands may reduce their ability to perform other functions effectively. Exhausting schedules may make it more difficult for parents to participate in their sons' or daughters' education; provide opportunities for socialization; and engage in recreation, rest, and recuperation individually or as a family. Conversely, families that are impoverished may be very successful in providing love and affection for their children, but they may have significantly reduced options when fulfilling other family functions.

The availability of information and increased access, especially through electronic media, has also influenced family functioning. Internet access has brought some families resources on health care enabled them to bank and make purchases on line, helped them research educational alternatives, and provided quick access to information about promising vocational pursuits. For some, this may result in additional time spent in such functions as identity development; socialization; love and affection; and recreation, rest, and recuperation. For others, it may simply result in more time spent at the computer.

Medical breakthroughs have also influenced family functions. In 1979, van Eys stated that a number of diseases that were once considered to be terminal are no longer life threatening; rather, they result in chronic illness. That statement continues to be true. As mortality from disease and disability is reduced, morbidity increases. Whether care is provided for a premature infant, a medically fragile child, or an older adult experiencing a host of physical and mental difficulties, chronic illnesses place considerable demands on family members financially and in daily caregiving. These demands often interfere with the performance of other family functions.

The mobility of the population in the United States does not, at first consideration, appear to be related to family functions. But it has had a rather profound effect. When extended family members were closer together, greater opportunities existed to share family functions. Grandparents might assist with daily care, the expression of love and affection, and socialization. Aunts, uncles, and cousins might also contribute to child rearing and to supporting each of the family members. As many families have become more dispersed, support for family functions is not so readily available from other family members. Many single parents and couples are on their own and are expected to fulfill all of the familial functions. Every day, families demonstrate that this can be done; but every day, in families throughout the nation, it takes its toll.

SUMMARY

Families can best be understood as a system that includes the characteristics of the family and its members, their ability to communicate, the way in which they fulfill family functions, and their place in the life cycle. Outside influences have profound effects on families, but families also influence the larger society. Contemporary families are expected to fulfill a wide range of roles and functions. Sometimes these roles and functions are supported by society as a whole—its attitudes, laws, economic structures, and resources. Sometimes the same forces undermine the roles and functions expected of family members. Each family, regardless of its makeup, develops ways to accomplish its work as effectively as possible, but the path is seldom smooth and straight. As circumstances and life situations change, so must families. Strategies for fulfilling family functions often need to change to address changes within and outside of the family. Families throughout time have demonstrated remarkable abilities to change, adapt, and continue to provide the care, love, and support that is foundational to being a family.

ACTIVITIES TO EXTEND THE DISCUSSION

1. **Consider your own family functions.** Make a list of all of the things that the family and its members do to survive economically; support one another psychologically; ensure that basic needs for food, shelter, health, and nurturance are met; and find meaning in life.

2. **Think about your own family and the family functions that this chapter discusses.** Which of the functions is most challenging to fulfill in your family? Which are the easiest? Are there other functions that you would add to the list?

3. **Make a list of all of the things that you do on a typical day.** Review the list and indicate which function each one addresses. Are there any activities that do not fit into one of the functions? Share your responses with others in your group.

4. **On the Internet, find a policy paper on an issue that has implications for families.** You might explore the Children's Defense Fund site, a government site, or a site developed by a professional organization. Read the policy and be prepared to discuss how this policy might affect families of children with disabilities, families who are caring for an ill and aging grandparent, or families who are English language learners.

REFERENCES

AFL-CIO. (2001). *Fact sheet: Facts about working women.* Retrieved June 5, 2003, from http://www.aflcio.org/women/wwfacts.htm

Americans with Disabilities Act (ADA) of 1990, PL 101-336, 42 U.S.C §§ 12101 *et seq.*

Apple, M.W. (2000). The cultural politics of home schooling. *Peabody Journal of Education, 75,* 256–271.

Boyden, J. (1993). *Families: Celebration and hope in a world of change.* London: Gaia Books.

Brault, L.M.J., Ashley, M., & Gallo, J. (2001). One program's journey: Using the change process to implement service in natural environments. *Young Exceptional Children, 5*(1), 11–19.

Bristor, M.W. (1995). *Individuals and family systems in their environments* (2nd ed.). Dubuque, IA: Kendall/Hunt.

Carter, E.A., & McGoldrick, M. (Eds.) (1980). *The family life cycle: A framework for family therapy.* New York: Gardner Press.

Carter, E.A., & McGoldrick, M. (Eds.) (1989). *The changing family life cycle: A framework for family therapy* (2nd ed.) Boston: Allyn & Bacon.

Clark, R., & Fenichel, E. (2001). Mothers, babies, and depression: Questions and answers. *Zero to Three, 22*(1), 48–50.

Children's Defense Fund. (2000). *Yearbook 2000: The state of America's children.* Washington, DC: Author.

Deason, D.M., & Randolph, D.L. (1998). A systematic look at the self: The relationship between family organization. Interpersonal attachment, and identity [Electronic version]. *Journal of Social Behavior & Personality, 13,* 465–479.

Dunst, C.J., & Bruder, M.B. (2002). Valued outcomes of service coordination, early intervention, and natural environments. *Exceptional Children, 68,* 361–375.

Dunst, C.J., Hamby, D., Trivette, C.M., Raab, M., & Bruder, M.B. (2000). Everyday family and community life and children's naturally occurring learning opportunities. *Journal of Early Intervention, 23,* 151–164.

Education for All Handicapped Children Act of 1975 (PL 94-142), 20 U.S.C. §§ 1400 *et seq.*

English, K., Goldstein, H., Shafer, K., & Kaczmarek, L. (1997). Promoting interactions among preschoolers with and without disabilities: Effects of a buddy skills-training program. *Exceptional Children, 63,* 229–243.

Gelles, R.J. (1995). *Contemporary families: A sociological view.* Thousand Oaks, CA: Sage Publications.

Greenfeld, K.T. (2002, May 6). My brother. *Time, 159,* 54.

Guralnick, M.J. (2000). An agenda for change in early childhood inclusion. *Journal of Early Intervention, 23,* 213–222.

Guralnick, M.J. (Ed.) (2001). *Early childhood inclusion: Focus on change.* Baltimore: Paul H. Brookes Publishing Co.

Hanson, M.J., Horn, E., Sandall, S., Beckman, P., Morgan, M., Marquart, J., Barnwell, D., & Chou, H-Y. (2001). After preschool inclusion: Children's educational pathways over the early school years. *Exceptional Children, 68,* 65–84.

Individuals with Disabilities Education Act (IDEA) of 1990, PL 101-476, 20 U.S.C. §§ 1400 *et seq.*

Individuals with Disabilities Education Act Amendments of 1991, PL 102-119, 20 U.S.C. §§ 1400 *et seq.*

Individuals with Disabilities Education Act Amendments of 1997, PL 105-17, 20 U.S.C. §§ 1400 *et seq.*

Knoll, J.A. (1996). Charting unknown territory with families of children with complex medical needs. In G.H.S. Singer, L.E. Powers, & A.L. Olson (Eds.), *Redefining family support: Innovations in public–private partnerships* (pp. 189–220). Baltimore: Paul H. Brookes Publishing Co.

Lieber, J., Hanson, M.J., Beckman, P.J., Odom, S.L., Sandall, S.R., Schwartz, I.S., Horn, E., & Wolery, R. (2000). Key influences on the initiation and implementation of inclusive preschool programs. *Exceptional Children, 67,* 83–99.

Lynch, E.W., & Hanson, M.J. (Eds.). (1998). *Developing cross-cultural competence: A guide to working with children and their families* (2nd ed.). Baltimore: Paul H. Brookes Publishing Co.

Malinowski, B. (1939). The group and the individual in functional analysis. *American Journal of Sociology, 44,* 938–964.

Minuchin, S. (1974). *Families and family therapy.* Cambridge, MA: Harvard University Press.

Minuchin, S., & Fishman, H.C. (1981). *Family therapy techniques.* Cambridge, MA: Harvard University Press.

Mullane, D. (Ed.). (1995). *Words to make my dream children live: A book of African American quotations.* New York: Doubleday.

Mullis, L. (2002). Natural environments: A letter from a mother to friends, families, and professionals. *Young Exceptional Children, 5*(3), 21–24.

National Alliance of Black School Educators (NABSE) and the IDEA Local Implementation by Local Administrators (ILIAD) Partnership. (2002). *Addressing over-representation of African American students in special education: The prereferral intervention process, an administrators guide* [Electronic version]. Retrieved June 19, 2002, from http://www.IDEApractices.org/resources/detail.php?id=22070

Odom, S.L. (2000). Preschool inclusion: What we know and where we go from here. *Topics in Early Childhood Special Education, 20,* 20–27.

Olson, D.H., Russell, C.S., & Sprenkle, D.H. (1980). Circumplex model of marital and family systems II: Empirical studies and clinical intervention. *Advances in Family Intervention Assessment and Theory, 1,* 129–179.

Olson, D.H., Sprenkle, D.H., & Russell, C.S. (1979). Circumplex model of marital and family systems I: Cohesion and adaptability dimensions, family types, and clinical applications. *Family Process, 18,* 3–28.

Onaga, E.E., McKinney, K.G., & Pfaff, J. (2000). Lodge programs serving family functions for people with psychiatric disabilities. *Family Relations, 49,* 207–217.

Osofsky, J.D., Hann, D.M., & Peebles, C. (1993). Adolescent parenthood: Risks and opportunities for mothers and infants. In C.H. Zeanah, Jr. (Ed.), *Handbook of infant mental health* (pp. 106–119). New York: Guilford Press.

Pollard, K.M. (1998). Outlook mixed for America's children. *Population Today, 26*(10), 4–5.

Rehabilitation Act of 1973, PL 93-112, 29 U.S.C. §§ 701 *et seq.*

Riche, M.F. (2000). America's diversity and growth: Signposts for the 21st century. *Population Bulletin, 55*(2). Washington, DC: Population Reference Bureau.

Ronneau, J.P. (1999). Ordinary families—extraordinary caregiving. *Family Preservation Journal, 4*(1), 63–80.

Roston, E. (2002, April 8). How much is a living wage? *Time, 159,* 52–54.

Roth-Hanania, R., Busch-Rossnagel, N., & Higgins-D'Alessandro, A. (2000). Development of self and empathy in early infancy: Implications for atypical development. *Infants and Young Children, 13*(1), 1–14.

Seifer, R., & Dickstein, S. (1993). Parental mental illness and infant development. In C.H. Zeanah, Jr. (Ed.), *Handbook of infant mental health* (pp. 120–142). New York: Guilford Press.

Summers, J.A., Brotherson, M.J., & Turnbull, A.P. (1988). The impact of handicapped children on families (pp. 504–544). In E.W. Lynch & R.B. Lewis (Eds.), *Exceptional Children and Adults: An Introduction to Special Education.* Glenview, IL: Scott Foresman.

Turnbull, A.P., & Rueff, M. (1997). Family perspectives on inclusive lifestyle issues for people with problem behavior. *Exceptional Children, 63,* 211–227.

Turnbull, A.P., Summers, J.A., & Brotherson, M.J. (1984). *Working with families with disabled members: A family systems approach.* Lawrence: University of Kansas, Kansas Affiliated Facility.

Turnbull, A.P., & Turnbull, H.R. (2001). *Families, professionals, and exceptionalities: Collaborating for empowerment* (4th ed.). Upper Saddle River, NJ: Merrill-Prentice Hall.

van Eys, J. (1979). The normally sick child. In J. van Eys (Ed.), *The normally sick child* (pp. 11–27). Baltimore: University Park Press.

SECTION II

RISK
AND
RESILIENCE

CHAPTER 4

THE EFFECTS OF DISABILITY ON FAMILY LIFE

He's definitely been a blessing over
and over and over again. He's always had a
positive attitude. He's taught me what unconditional love is.
—PARENT (AS CITED IN HANSON, 2003b)

Having [a child with a disability] has taught me not to judge
others who are different...rather find their strengths.
—PARENT (AS CITED IN HANSON, 2003b)

M ost expectant parents have developed a picture in their minds of the child they will have. Wrapped up in these mental images are all the hopes and dreams, cultural values and expectations, family histories, and personal likes and dislikes of each parent. When a child is born with or subsequently acquires a disability or disorder, all of these images, hopes, and expectations must be revisited and adjusted.

This chapter explores the challenges faced by families and describes models that help us to understand families' adjustment and adaptation to these altered family circumstances. Implications and recommendations for service providers who work with these families also are offered. Options for service delivery reflect a shift since the 1980s from service models that are primarily professionally driven to service systems that are more family centered and designed to support and enable families to function effectively.

In order to fully appreciate the circumstances faced by families as they adjust to challenges posed by a disabling condition, it is useful to reflect on the family systems and ecological models of development in Chapter 2. The experiences of families and the options that are available to them in rearing and supporting a family member with disabilities or risks is deeply embedded in the values and culture of the society within which the family resides. Likewise, the way that families interact with the various systems in which they are nested (e.g., neighborhood; community; health, education, and social service agencies; government) can play pivotal roles in how they adapt.

Societal attitudes and perspectives on the meaning of disability have varied over the years and across cultures (Berry & Hardman, 1998; Safford & Safford, 1996). In ancient times, individuals with disabilities often were rejected and even killed or cast out of societies as burdens or nonproductive members of that society. Though the industrial age gave rise to more humanitarian perspectives and reforms, disability typically was viewed as a disease. Although greater focus was given to intervention through medical and/or education regimens, attempts to "cure" the disability were generally unsuccessful. Societies that placed high value on the economic contributions of its citizenry showed a lack of acceptance toward individuals with disabilities because they doubted the productivity of these individuals. In time, most cultures have embraced social and educational programs for individuals with disabilities. The participation or self-determination of those individuals and their families in defining their own needs and supports has increasingly become the priority.

The perspectives and experiences of families in rearing children with disabilities has been the subject of reflection and study by clinicians and researchers. Here, too, societal values and mores have dictated the values and approaches taken in examining this topic. For many years, parents, particularly mothers, were blamed for their children's disabilities such as mental retardation, emotional disturbances, and health problems. For instance, mothers of children with autism were characterized as cold and unresponsive and, thus, were seen as responsible for their children's disorders (Bettelheim, 1950). Notions promulgated during the eugenics movement (1880–1930) undoubtedly fueled this view of parents as causing their children's disabilities (Turnbull & Turnbull, 1990). Certainly, some disorders are linked to parental abuse and/or neglect or to genetic causes; however, the contemporary viewpoint has led to a less linear, more transactional approach to understanding the nature of human development and to promoting models that support more optimal outcomes. The dynamic nature of the interplay between the child and the family, between the family and the larger world or community, and the interactions among family members allow us to identify points of support and intervention that more closely meet family needs.

INITIAL EXPERIENCES WITH DISABILITY

Parents who give birth to a child with a disability or disabilities often describe their initial reaction as one of feeling "shattered," "overwhelmed," or "devastated." These adjectives underscore the shock, the suddenness, and the comprehensive impact of this event on the family. They also highlight the sadness and the violation of expectations that the event precipitates. Families may experience trauma when this discrepancy occurs between the ideal or fantasized child and birth experience and the actual child and less optimal birth situation (Bruce & Schultz, 2001; Solnit & Stark, 1961). When the reality of the circumstances does not match parents' fantasies, hopes, and expectations, parents are faced with an altered course for their family.

Clinicians have likened parents' responses to those of people who experience the terminal illness or death of a loved one. Parental response has been described as mourning the loss of the "expected" child. Using stage models, typically based on the work of Elisabeth Kübler-Ross (1969), clinicians have speculated that parents go through a series of responses to the traumatic event that begins with shock and disorganization or disequilibrium (including feelings of denial, anxiety, guilt, anger, depression, fear, blame, and bargaining or shopping for another option or cure) and is followed by acceptance and reorganization.

One hypothetical model for understanding parental adaptation was developed from parental interviews conducted by Drotar, Baskiewicz, Irvin, Kennell, and Klaus (1975), who outlined the following similar stages of adaptation: shock, denial or disbelief, sadness and anger, and adaptation and reorganization. Although such models can be useful for understanding the range of emotions and feeling states that family members may experience as they grapple with the new knowledge of the child's disability, caveats are in order. Some family members may experience these feeling states whereas others may not. Some may pass through these states, but in a different order. Some individuals may experience these states, but each may take varying amounts of time to go from state to state; for example, individuals may dwell in an emotional state for a long time or for a day. Categorizing family members as being lodged in a particular stage based on a limited interaction can be disrespectful, overly simplistic, and poor clinical practice. Rather, one must appreciate the tremendous variation in parental reactions as well as the other stresses, strains, and supports that are brought to bear on the situation.

Furthermore, cultural backgrounds and values play a significant role in defining the meaning families place on having children with disabilities (Hanson, Lynch, & Wayman, 1990; Lynch & Hanson, 2004). Just as different cultures stress different child-rearing practices, roles for family members, and family values, so too does the meaning and causation ascribed to disability or risk vary according to cultural history and background. In some cultures, disability may be attributed to chance, whereas in others it may be seen as a punishment for a sin committed or a taboo violated by one of the parents (e.g., eating the wrong food) or an ancestor (e.g., committing a wrongdoing or crime). In some cultures the individual with a disability may be seen as virtually possessed by an evil spirit, whereas in other cultures the individual with a disability may be seen as a gift from God and as imbued with special powers or perceptions. The interaction of disability and gender may play a role, as well. In some cultures the birth of a male child is more highly prized than that of a female; in these cultures, if the boy is born with a deformity or disability the reaction may be particularly adverse. Given the diversity among the families and the variability of cultural responses to the meaning of disability, care must be taken by family service professionals not to jump to rapid conclusions about the family's interpretation or behavior with respect to the meaning of the birth event or disability. Until service providers can say that they have "walked a mile in the shoes" of the family, they cannot make assumptions about their responses or the stages that the family will encounter. Stage theories simply do not account for diversity among families and do not acknowledge the transactional nature of family responses and adjustment.

STRESS, ADAPTATION, AND COPING

The addition of *any* new member to the family usually brings not only joy and hope but also some trepidation and stress. Although stress is a part of human existence for all individuals and families, families of individuals with disabilities may be subject to additional stressors created by the risk or disabling conditions (Singer & Irvin, 1989). Families are typically thrust into new interactions with a myriad of professionals in the medical and health care fields, education, and social services. Some of these interactions may relate to highly emotional and draining life and death decisions. Families also are met with increased bills and financial burdens for these services. Parental employment and child care arrangements often are affected by the child's disorder, and the family's routines and activities may be dramatically altered in response to the child's needs. The challenges of caregiving may be overwhelming to primary caregivers, not to mention their impact on interactions with other family members, friends, and acquaintances. The disability, like a rock thrown into a pond, has repercussions that reverberate throughout the elements and routines of the family's life. As one father related, "Adam's our cruise, our new home, our boat. You know over the years, we laugh because every time we would get a down payment, it would go for Adam" (cited in Hanson, 2003b). Though this family realistically appraised their situation and lamented some of their sacrifices, they also added that they "wouldn't have had it any other way."

A number of research studies have examined stress in relationship to families of children with disabilities. In general, findings comparing these families with those of children who are typically developing find increased stress and greater caregiving demands for families with children with disabilities (Beckman, 1991; Dyson, 1991, 1993; Palfrey, Walker, Butler, & Singer, 1989; Winkler, 1988). The type of disability also has been linked to amount of stress. Greater stress has been associated with severe physical disabilities (Sloper & Turner, 1993), autism, conduct disorders and behavior problems (Noh, Dumas, Wolf, & Fishman, 1989; Orr, Cameron, Dobson, & Day, 1993), and neurological disorders (Hanson & Hanline, 1990). Some studies have noted different predominant types of stress for mothers (e.g., caregiving) and fathers (e.g., financial), as well as the effect of family structure (e.g., being a single parent versus having a partner) on stress levels (Bailey, Blasco, & Simeonsson, 1992; Beckman, 1991; Trute & Hauch, 1988). Thus, it is likely that most families of children with disabilities will encounter additional stressors or demands necessitating changes and reorganization in families' expectations for their children, in the roles and relationships among family members, and in the routines and priorities of the family.

Frameworks for Understanding Families' Experiences and Outcomes

Frameworks or models have been developed to understand the meaning of stress and how it operates in families' lives. Psychological stress has been defined as "a particular relationship between the person and the environment that is appraised by the person as taxing or exceeding his or her resources and endangering his or her well-being" (Lazurus & Folkman, 1984, p. 19). This definition underscores the interaction between *personal* variables and *environmental* variables in defining stressors and their impact.

ABCX Model

A useful conceptual model designed to study the impact of stressful events is the *ABCX model* advanced by Hill (1949, 1958) (see Figure 4.1). In this model, Factor *A* refers to the stressor event. Factor *A* can include both *normative* stressors (e.g., family adding a new member through the birth of child) and *nonnormative* stressors (e.g., birth trauma, specialized medical needs). Factor *B* refers to the family resources to meet the stressor, and Factor *C* to the family's appraisal or definition and interpretation of the event. According to this model, *C* interacts with *A* and *B* to produce *X*, the family's response to the crisis. To see how this model operates, take the example of Trudy, Kevin, and their daughter, Samantha.

TRUDY AND KEVIN

Trudy and Kevin's second child, Samantha, was born 12 weeks prematurely with the cord wrapped around her neck. Samantha experienced anoxia and was rushed to the neonatal intensive care unit (NICU) shortly after her birth. Trudy and Kevin went home but continued to visit Samantha daily. Trudy was able to express milk to bring to her baby and got to hold Samantha in the NICU. Though terrified and saddened by their baby's trauma, Trudy and Kevin relied on the support of the professionals and their friends and hoped for the day when they could bring baby Samantha home. This support enabled them to remain confident of Samantha's recovery. The information that they received from professionals also gave them options for services and supports that they could use in the future as needed.

In this case, *A* refers to the premature and high-risk birth and includes both normative and nonnormative stress factors. *B*, the families' resources, includes the support Trudy and Kevin provided each other as well as that given by friends and family who lived close by, good medical care in a facility with a NICU, and sufficient health insurance. *C*, which is the primary emphasis in this model, is the family's appraisal or interpretation of the stressor event. Due to the supportive resources of the care institutions and family and friends, Trudy and Kevin were optimistic about Samantha's future.

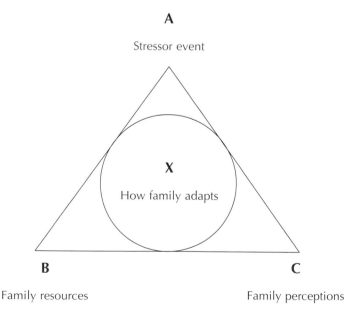

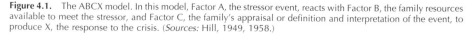

Figure 4.1. The ABCX model. In this model, Factor A, the stressor event, reacts with Factor B, the family resources available to meet the stressor, and Factor C, the family's appraisal or definition and interpretation of the event, to produce X, the response to the crisis. (*Sources:* Hill, 1949, 1958.)

Double ABCX Model

McCubbin and Patterson (1982, 1983a, 1983b) expanded the ABCX model in their work with families of children with disabilities and chronic illness. This expanded model is typically called the *double ABCX model*. In this model more emphasis is placed on the family's appraisal of the event (the C factor) and also the *interactive* and *additive* nature of events. In this expanded model, *aA* refers to the original stressor and to the pile up of other stresses and strains, and *bB* denotes the perception of resources. Factor *cC* alludes to the family's perception of the original stressor event and their appraisal of the demands and their own capacity for managing or meeting these challenges. This model also introduced the concept of "sense of coherence" (based on Antonovosky, 1979), which refers to the family's ability to balance trust and control (i.e., their ability to know when to trust other authority figures versus when to take charge with their own resources). Consider this model as it relates to the story of Trudy and Kevin.

TRUDY AND KEVIN

Right before Samantha's birth, Kevin was laid off his job in construction. Trudy anticipated that she would not return to her job as a teacher until the children were older. Now she had to consider going back to work to make ends meet for the family, but she worried about Samantha's caregiving because she realized that her daughter may have special needs. The couple's other child, 3-year-old Joshua, had recently been diagnosed with asthma and that had produced new challenges for the family in terms of procuring health services and modifying their home environment to support Joshua's health needs. Thus, Samantha was born into a family that was already grappling with some stressors. Her traumatic birth situation multiplied the concerns of the family (*aA*).

Trudy and Kevin sat down and analyzed their situation. They decided that they had enough health insurance to get by and that they could borrow some money from Trudy's parents if needed. They also felt comfortable with the medical care and regimen for Joshua. He seemed to have adjusted well to medication and his condition was under control. Kevin met with a friend who promised to help him get a job with another construction company. Both parents recognized the resources they had (*bB*) and planned for how to deploy these resources. They were confident that although times would be tough, they would get through this together and provide the needed care for their children (*cC*). They felt that they had the abilities and resources to meet the challenges that Samantha's condition might produce.

Family Adjustment and Adaptation Response Model

A related model that is useful in understanding families' adjustment to stressors is the *Family Adjustment and Adaptation Response Model* (FAAR) (Patterson, 1988, 1989). This model represents an expansion over the previous models in that it examines the family's adaptation and adjustment over time. Thus, the emphasis is placed on the adaptation rather than the stress. Emphasis also is placed on positive, or salutogenic, outcomes. The term *salutogenesis* was coined by Antonovsky (1979, 1993) in his analysis of the study of disease. This term is intended to capture a more constructive orientation to developing healthful (as opposed to disease) states and contrasts with more traditional approaches with a pathogenic orientation to the study of disease.

Like the previous models discussed, the FAAR model stresses the cognitive appraisal or the role of the meanings families give to events as they shape their responses and adaptation to the crisis. Two different levels of meaning used by families in the adaptation process are considered: situational meanings and global meanings (Patterson, 1988, 1989). *Situational meanings* refer to the immediate situation and how a family defines the demands and assesses their capacity to meet them. For instance, the family may have a child who is very sick. Their expectations for how to care for the child, what the child's needs necessitate, and what their resources are all fall into this category. The family's cognitive coping strategies can be used to meet the situational demands. When demands supersede the family's capability to manage them, the family will experience stress. Examples of cognitive coping include recognition of one's self-esteem or efficacy (i.e., knowledge and confidence that one can handle the situation), knowledge that physical resources exist to alleviate the demand (e.g., money, insurance, caregivers), and awareness of characteristics of the individual child and/or parents that may be helpful, such as a responsive or warm personality, assertiveness or perseverance, or the family's ability to work together.

Global meanings, however, transcend the specific situation and refer to a more stable set of beliefs and values. Patterson referred to this as the "family schema" (1993, p. 227). The family schema can be characterized by five dimensions based on the beliefs and meanings reported in research with families of children who were medically fragile (Patterson & Leonard, 1993):

1. *Shared purpose.* The family has reordered priorities with a greater focus on people and commitment to life.
2. *Collectivity.* The family focuses on working closely together and with others such as doctors in meeting the demands of the child.
3. *Frameability.* The family has a new, more optimistic focus or outlook on the characteristics of the child or family as a whole, such as being grateful for what they do have.
4. *Relativism.* Family members feel more tolerant, flexible, and less judgmental.
5. *Shared control.* Parents realize that they have less control over life than they previously thought and often acknowledge a "higher power" in their lives.

The FAAR model includes both the adjustment and the adaptation phases of response. It is in the adjustment phase that the family makes first-order changes in response to the demands (e.g., mother or father takes time off of work, couple hires a new caregiver). When the "crisis" continues, second-order changes are required. During this adaptation phase the family system is restructured and changes may occur in family roles, functions, or boundaries. For instance, the mother or father may decide to quit employment outside of the home in order to care for the child. Clearly, this signals a change in family roles and resources.

As families are able to adapt, they may attain a positive perspective of the situation (salutogenesis). Research with families of children who were medically fragile revealed that parents often reported positive aspects of raising their children that included 1) the child's warmth and responsiveness; 2) the tenacity and perseverance of the child, which made the parents want to invest more effort; 3) the family's closeness in pulling together as a unit; 4) the assertiveness skills parents developed and the ability to deal with multiple providers and third-party payors, and 5) the empathy and growth witnessed in their other children (Patterson & Leonard, 1993). These perceptions relate to the situational meanings. At the global meanings level, family members may believe themselves better able to draw from their previous experiences in managing a situation, have confidence in their abilities to be assertive and communicate effectively with other care providers, and be able to amass their resources and supports quickly and effectively (e.g., calling on a neighbor or family member).

The changes that families make in their beliefs and in their behaviors to manage the demands of a disability or illness occur within the "social context of relationships" (Patterson, 1993, p. 235). One can debate whether behavior changes cognitive meanings or cognitive meanings change behavior, or both. Regardless, it is clear that families of children with disabilities or other special needs are faced with increased stressors and demands in their lives. These demands by definition do create the need for changes or adjustments. The capacity to change varies across individuals and from family to family, of course. Clearly, not all families have the same resources or the abilities to change and thrive. Real limits exist in the degree to which families can change the world in which they live. The emotional reactions of individuals, the behaviors of family members, family members' cognitive beliefs, and the family's external or physical resources all play a role. We can only conclude and appreciate that, in the words of Patterson, "Families are complex social units and they vary widely in their adaptive capacities" (1993, p. 236).

SERVICES AND SUPPORT FOR
FAMILIES OF CHILDREN WITH DISABILITIES

All service delivery systems in the fields of health care, education, and social services are challenged to appropriately support families as they adjust to the different or increased demands associated with raising a child with a disability or conditions that place the child at developmental risk. Since the 1990s, many service systems for families of individuals with disabilities have reflected a more positive approach to service delivery. As discussed throughout this text, service delivery philosophies have shifted away from linear or medical models that directly link the individual's outcome to a pathology or disorder to more dynamic approaches aimed at capitalizing on the resources and strengths that individuals and families bring to their situations. It is likely that families have not suddenly developed new strengths and resources. Rather, service providers are making a transition into new roles and relationships with families. As witnesses to these service and policy shifts, one is reminded of Robert Frost's poem, "The Black Cottage," written in 1914 (1987, p. 62).

> *Most of the change we think we see in life*
> *Is due to truths being in and out of favor.*

These philosophical shifts and concomitant changes in service delivery models are directly linked to societal values and mores and to beliefs about families. As service providers travel this road of working with families in various capacities, it is important to remember that these values and philosophies drive services. Service providers have personal choices to make along this path with respect to how they behave with families.

Historically, when a child was diagnosed with a disability, parents and other family members were given a prescribed set of activities or directives for where and how to care for their child. Specialists in the various helping professions (i.e., health, education, and social services) functioned as experts and, like orchestra conductors, they assessed the child's difficulties and needs and provided guidance and direction to families.

The importance of parents' involvement in the care and education of their children with disabilities has long been understood, and the roles and relationships of family members in their children's intervention regimens have been paramount. Over the years, parents of children with disabilities have functioned as their children's advocates, political advocates, organization members, teachers, assistant staff members in intervention programs, and program catalysts. Many parents still actively participate in their children's services through these roles. Although parents historically have been seen as crucial to their children's development, they have often been relegated to the role of recipients of services rather than decision makers. These service philosophies can be contrasted with more contemporary program philosophies that emphasize parent–professional partnerships and relationships and place the family at the core of the decision making process (Sandall, McLean, & Smith, 2000).

Family-Centered and Relationship-Based Approaches

Two terms have entered the early intervention service delivery lexicon and best describe the goals of contemporary service philosophy. These terms are *family-centered* and *relationship-based* interventions or service delivery models. Both stress the importance of acknowledging the child as living within the context of the family, the family members as the primary decision makers for the child, and the relationships among family members and among family members and professionals as being essential to the intervention and support processes.

Family-centered (also referred to as *family-focused* or *family-based*) approaches place emphasis on the following:

- Helping the family to care for and raise their child with a disability and cope with unique needs
- Helping the family understand the development and needs of the child both as an individual and as a family member
- Promoting parent–child interactions that are sensitive and warm, mutually enjoyable, and appropriate to the child's developmental level
- Preserving and reinforcing the dignity of the family by responding to their needs and desires in all phases of service—assessment, planning, and evaluation (Bailey et al., 1986)

Family-centered models can be contrasted with more traditional approaches in that the focus is on the child within the context of the family, not just on the child. The child's and family's strengths and resources are highlighted and form the basis for the intervention. Again, this is in contrast to previous approaches that focused on the disability as a pathology or difficulty. Families are placed in the role of decision makers rather than merely as the recipients of decisions made by experts or specialists. This orientation represents a shift in power in the relationship.

The implementation of family-centered services often involves new roles and relationships and "ways of doing business" for professionals who have been trained as experts. Professionals must continue to maintain and update their knowledge and special expertise and share this information with families. The goals, styles, and methods they use in their delivery of services may be modified somewhat from traditional approaches, however. The following nine key elements or guidelines for professional behavior have been suggested as essential to the implementation of family-centered services (Edelman, Greenland, & Mills, 1992):

1. Recognizing the family as the constant in the child's life whereas other caregivers and service systems may come and go
2. Facilitating collaboration at all service levels between parents and professionals
3. Honoring and respecting family diversity in all dimensions—cultural, racial, ethnic, linguistic, spiritual, and socioeconomic
4. Recognizing family strengths and the different approaches that families may use in coping
5. Sharing unbiased and honest information with family members on an ongoing basis
6. Encouraging family-to-family support and networking
7. Acknowledging and incorporating the developmental needs of the child and other family members into the service

8. Implementing policies and services that promote emotional and financial support for families

9. Designing and implementing services that are accessible, culturally and linguistically respectful and responsive, flexible, and based on family-identified needs

The centrality of the relationship between parent and child is emphasized in the expanded concept of "relationship-based" service approaches. Although typically applied to clinical approaches in infant mental health and early intervention, the "relationship-based" model underscores the crucial importance of services aimed at supporting and nurturing sensitive and satisfying parent–child interactions and relationships (Weston, Ivins, Heffron, & Sweet, 1997). Similarly, this approach advocates and incorporates partnerships between parents and professionals in the planning and implementation of appropriate services for the child and family.

Enabling and Empowering Families

The family-centered and relationship-based approaches focus on the child within the context of the family, rather than on the child alone. As Dunst, Trivette, and Deal (1988) reminded us, the family is part of a social system and all parts of the system are interconnected. They use the perspective of *empowerment* as a helpful concept for guiding service practices with families. They operationalized empowerment to include the person's access to and control over needed resources, decision-making and problem-solving abilities, and abilities to interact effectively with others to gain the resources they need (p. 3). In examining the early intervention context and analyzing the roles of help seekers and help givers, they highlighted the importance of service providers (help givers) in creating opportunities for families (in this case, help seekers) to experience and display their competence. They referred to these experiences as *enabling.* Thus, the major thrust of these family-centered services is to help families become more competent and mobilize their resources.

The assessment and intervention model advocated by Dunst, Trivette, and Deal (1988) describes four components. The first component is the identification of family needs and aspirations (i.e., what the family's priorities are; where the family wants to expend their efforts and resources). Second, the family's style and functioning or, in other words, the unique ways in which that family operates, are considered. Third, the family's social network is "mapped" to identify resources for meeting the family's needs. Fourth, the help-giving behavior of the professionals facilitates families' aligning their needs and resources to implement their goals.

Support for families comes from many sources. Both formal and informal networks may provide important support. Formal networks typically include professionals and helping agencies (i.e., education, health, and social service) that are formed to provide assistance to families needing services. Informal networks refer to family members, friends, neighbors, social groups, spiritual leaders, and so forth. Although these informal networks are not formed to provide assistance, they often serve that purpose. For many years, these informal sources of support were often overlooked or underrated. As services have been implemented with a social systems perspective in mind, the importance and power of these informal social support resources to family well-being has come to be recognized (Dunst, Trivette, Gordon, & Pletcher, 1989).

Family Services and Outcomes

Families of children with disabilities, like all families, face an inordinate number of daily demands. When the child (or any family member) has extra or extraordinary needs for care, the family may be faced with even more demands. The discussion that follows highlights some of the resources and personal characteristics that have been described by families as useful or as outcomes of their experiences in parenting a child with a disability. These issues are directly, forcefully, and eloquently described by parents themselves in a number of publications (e.g., Naseef, 2001; Spiegle & van den Pol, 1993; Turnbull et al., 1993; Turnbull & Turnbull, 1985).

Growing Personally

Families often describe their own personal growth and that of their immediate family members as a result of raising a child with disabilities. It is common for parents to describe increases in their abilities to advocate for their children and their own sense of self-reliance and self-esteem. They often take great pride in the challenges they have effectively met and

express confidence in their abilities to continue to address the needs of their child and family. Family members also mention the growth they have experienced in terms of helping others and being more receptive to other people who may be different. One mother of a (now adult) child with Down syndrome described her experience of returning to study at a community college. She related with pride that she went out of her way to help foreign students find their way around the college because she understood what it was like to be treated as different and what it was like to be fearful of new challenges. These experiences do not minimize the many difficulties that families may encounter, but they do illustrate the opportunities for personal growth and satisfaction that many family members report.

Developing New Skills and Resources

Families of children with disabilities may need and receive a variety of services from formal networks. Caring for a child with a disability typically demands that the parents develop a certain degree of expertise in complex medical jargon and procedures, therapy techniques, and educational protocol. A major goal of most helping agencies is to provide information, education, and training in caring for and educating children with disabilities. Through the use of these informational and education/training resources, family members often become quite knowledgeable in and adept at working with children with that particular disability. They use these skills to help other families of children with similar challenges. Increasingly, parents and other family members have become teaching partners in inservice and preservice training programs for professionals in the helping fields. Parents' input and perspectives are highly valuable to new and continuing professionals in training.

Supporting Parent–Child Interactions and Relationships

A child with a disability may present many caregiving challenges. Some young children, for example, are hard to soothe. Others, due to their physical disabilities, may remain in rigid postures or fail to make eye contact with their parents. All of these characteristics can affect the way that parents feel about their children and can hamper parents' feelings of competence and enjoyment when interacting with them. Professionals can assist parents to more effectively read and understand their children's signals or cues and respond in a fashion that will enhance interaction and their children's development (Hanson, 1996).

Reducing Stress

Family services may be aimed at reducing the family's stress and demands. This may be as simple as a professional being more attentive to the stress of a family and showing care not to pile on programs, services, or appointment demands. It may come in the form of helping parents procure needed services such as respite care, child care, or community programs that will include the child with special needs. In some cases, formal counseling or stress reduction workshops may be useful for the parent, and the professional can assist him or her in finding such services.

Linking to Parent-to-Parent and Community Resources

Some families may choose the opportunity to get to know other parents in similar circumstances or parents who have "gone before" them and have experiences to share. Numerous parent-to-parent networks and family resource centers are found throughout the nation, and professionals may help families to link to these networks in their communities (Santelli, Poyadue, & Young, 2001). Similarly, a variety of national, state, and local organizations that range from disability rights organizations to city recreational programs may be useful to families. Again, the role of the professional is to provide parents with the information they need to be able to gain access to these services. Some parents desire active participation in parent networks and/or other community organizations and others prefer to remain more contained within their immediate family or ethnic, cultural, or spiritual communities. Although information and service options should be made available and accessible to all families in the modality and language of their choice, professionals must respect families' decisions regarding whether or to what degree they wish to participate in these organizations.

Focusing Services on Family Priorities and Strengths

Services that are truly family centered are culturally sensitive and respectful. Implementing these services typically requires a shift in perspective or point of view for most service providers. Rather than starting with professional assumptions about what the family needs or should have based on the challenges posed by the disability, professionals must begin with identifying the family's priorities and concerns. This focus precludes an a priori view of what impact the disability may have or what services the family may need or desire. Working with families in mapping or creating a strategy for their resources puts the family in the position of power and responsibility. This perspective, thus, emphasizes the strengths and resources that families bring to the table rather than the problems created by the child's disability. Consider the story of Thomasina and Demiko.

THOMASINA AND DEMIKO

Thomasina is 19 years old and is a high school dropout and single mother raising her 3-year-old son, Demiko. Demiko was born prematurely and hospitalized for a prolonged period of time at birth. Medical personnel suspect that the premature delivery was related to Thomasina's lack of prenatal care and drug use during pregnancy. Demiko has multiple disabilities including cerebral palsy, speech delays, and visual impairments. Thomasina lives in a large urban area on very little income from her part-time job.

If the story ended here, it would be easy to predict that the outcome for Demiko and Thomasina will not be a very happy one. Many professionals would be tempted to blame Thomasina for Demiko's poor developmental prognosis and prescribe an intensive regimen of therapy and education outside of the home. But the story does not stop here. Thomasina lives with her mother and her grandmother in her mother's home. All three women love Demiko dearly and spend countless hours tending to him. A home-based early intervention teacher visits their home weekly to help teach them strategies for caring for Demiko and enhancing his development. Together, these women are looking for preschool programs in their local community so that he can begin school. Furthermore, Thomasina no longer uses drugs and has been "clean" since Demiko's birth. She is also working on her GED so that she can get a better job. To be sure, Thomasina and Demiko face many challenges, but they have many resources and strengths even though they are poor and Demiko has severe disabilities.

How different are the outlooks and options available to families depending on whether the focus is on their difficulties and what they lack or on the strengths and resources that they bring to meet their challenges.

POLICIES FOR CHILDREN WITH DISABILITIES AND THEIR FAMILIES[1]

The following section provides an overview of primary special education policies in the United States that are designed to address the needs of children with disabilities like Demiko. These laws and policies have their foundation in years of experience and advocacy by professionals and parents of children with disabilities.

Prior to the 1970s, some children in the United States were denied a public school education because they had disabilities. These children were considered unable to learn, and many schools did not have adequate or appropriate programs for children with disabilities, particularly those children with severe disabilities. Family and advocate-initiated litigation, court decisions, national legislation, research studies, and family grassroots advocacy efforts all served to change this perspective dramatically. The 14th Amendment to the U.S. Constitution guarantees equal protection for all citizens under the law and establishes the right to not be discriminated against for an unjustifiable reason such as race or handicap. This amendment was central to establishing a legal remedy for this inequity in educational opportunities for children with disabilities. As parent-initiated

---

[1]A portion of the discussion in this section on disability policy is adapted from Hanson (2003a). Minor alterations have been made throughout from the original text.

movements and significant court cases were heard in the 1950s and 1960s, the shifts in policies began to occur.

Key Legislative Initiatives

Several key laws were passed that have provided far-reaching guarantees and rights for children with disabilities. This legislation charted new policies and services to ensure that children with disabilities received equal protection under the law and public education and that families were active participants.

Americans with Disabilities Act (ADA)

The American with Disabilities Act (ADA) of 1990 (PL 101-336) is a landmark piece of legislation with crucial implications for access and education for children with disabilities. The ADA is a federal civil rights law that ensures that people with disabilities have access to all facets of life, including child care for young children. It gives individuals with disabilities civil rights protection like those provided to people on the basis of race, sex, national origin, and religion, and it requires that reasonable accommodations be made to allow everyone to participate in the services and opportunities offered.

Individuals with Disabilities Education Act (IDEA) of 1990 and Amendments of 1997

Access to public education and special education services and supports were realized for school-age children through another piece of landmark legislation, the Education for All Handicapped Children Act of 1975 (PL 94-142). (See Braddock, 1987, and Turnbull, 1986 for reviews of federal policies and the development of this law in the United States.) This law subsequently was modified to apply to all preschool-age children with disabilities and, through state discretionary programs, to children with disabilities from birth through 2 years. This legislation has been retitled as the Individuals with Disabilities Education Act (IDEA) of 1990 (PL 101-476) and Amendments of 1997 (PL 105-17).[2]

IDEA provides the framework for educational policies and services for children with disabilities and their families. Six principles are core to this framework.

1. *Free and appropriate public education (FAPE)*. This provision requires that special education and related services be provided to children at public expense and that these services meet the standards of the state educational agency. A policy of "zero reject" is inherent in this law

---

[2]In 2003, this act was reauthorized as the Improving Education Results for Children with Disabilities Act, but had not been implemented by the time this book was published.

that precludes public schools from excluding children with disabilities. Furthermore, services are to be "appropriate" to the individual needs of each child.

2. *Appropriate evaluation.* This law stipulates many conditions related to evaluation: a "full and individual initial evaluation," the requirement of parental consent for the initial evaluation, evaluation by a team of professionals, assessment in the child's native language or mode of communication, the use of multiple measures rather than a single instrument to determine eligibility, and the provision for reevaluations. Furthermore, evaluation activities are to include data gathering information pertinent to the child's involvement and progress in the core general education curriculum, and evaluation procedures must be nondiscriminatory.

3. *Development of an individualized education program (IEP).* IDEA requires that an individualized education program (IEP) be developed for each child with a disability. IEPs must state the child's current level of educational performance; measurable annual goals and short-term objectives; specified special education and related services; the dates, frequency, location, and duration of services; and transition services to the next educational environment. The IEP is developed through a team approach that includes the child's parents and professionals. The child's strengths and the parents' concerns for enhancing the child's education are taken into consideration. For children from birth through 2 years of age, the individualized plan is termed the individualized family service plan (IFSP). These plans are described in greater detail in a subsequent discussion.

4. *Education provided in the least restrictive environment (LRE).* Children with disabilities must be provided an appropriate education designed to meet their individual needs in environments in which the children are educated with their peers without disabilities to the maximum extent possible. The intention of the law is to maximize the opportunities for children with disabilities to be educated with their peers and in their neighborhood communities. The emphasis is on creating services and supports that allow young children to have access to and participate in the general education curriculum.

5. *Parent and student participation in decision making.* Parents have the right to review their child's educational records, and parental informed consent is required for children's initial evaluation and placement. Parents can actively participate in all aspects of the evaluation, placement, and education process, and they have the right to challenge or appeal any decision related to the identification, evaluation, or placement of their child.

6. *Procedural safeguards to protect the rights of parents and their child with a disability.* IDEA outlines safeguards to ensure that the rights of children with disabilities and their parents are protected, including parents' access to educational records, right to request a due process hearing, and right to appeal the hearing decision and bring civil action to appeal

a hearing decision. Rights and requirements related to discipline are specified in the law as well.

Family Roles and Services for Children

IDEA essentially establishes a national policy and infrastructure for a system of service delivery across the United States. Central to this service system is the recognition of the unique role that families play in children's development.

Because of their focus on parental involvement, two primary components or parts of IDEA that pertain to young children are reviewed: the Early Intervention Program for Infants and Toddlers with Disabilities, Part C of IDEA, which covers services to children from birth through age 2, and the Preschool Grants Program (Section 619), Part B of IDEA, which covers services to children from ages 3 through 5 years.

Early Intervention Program for Infants and Toddlers with Disabilities

In 1986, the U.S. Congress established the Early Intervention Program for Infants and Toddlers with Disabilities in recognition of "an urgent and substantial need" to enhance the development of infants and toddlers with disabilities, reduce education costs by minimizing the need for special education through early intervention, minimize the likelihood of institutionalization of individuals with disabilities and maximize independent living, and enhance the capacity of families to meet their children's needs.

The Program for Infants and Toddlers with Disabilities (Part C of IDEA) is a federal discretionary grant program that assists states in planning, developing, and implementing a statewide system of early intervention services for infants and toddlers with disabilities, ages birth through 2 years, and their families. The statute and regulations for Part C stipulate state requirements for implementing this comprehensive, coordinated, multidisciplinary, and interagency service delivery program.

In order for states to participate in the program they must ensure that early intervention will be available to every eligible child. The law defines an eligible infant or toddler with a disability as

> An individual under 3 years of age who needs early intervention services because the individual (i) is experiencing developmental delays, as measured by appropriate diagnostic instruments and procedures in one or more of the areas of cognitive development, physical development, communication development, social or emotional development and adaptive development; or (ii) has a diagnosed physical or mental condition which has a high probability of resulting in developmental delay. (20 U.S.C. §1432[5][A])

States may, at their discretion, also serve children who are at risk as defined by that state, and approximately 20% of the states have elected to do so. Thus, definitions of eligibility vary considerably across states.

In implementing the program, the governor of each state designates a lead state agency to administer the program. A variety of agencies may function as the lead agency including education, health, human services, social services, developmental disabilities, and rehabilitation service agencies. The governor also appoints an Interagency Coordinating Council (ICC), including parents of young children with disabilities, to advise and assist the lead agency. Currently, all states and eligible territories of the United States are participating in the Part C program. Annual funding to each is based on census figures of the number of children.

Despite potential state differences with respect to child eligibility criteria and the state's lead agency of administration, several elements must be stipulated in each state's plan. These common elements are the minimum components required of a statewide comprehensive system for early intervention for infants and toddlers with special needs:

- Definition of developmental delay
- Timetable for ensuring appropriate services to all eligible children
- Timely and comprehensive multidisciplinary evaluation of needs of children and family-directed identification of the needs of each family
- Individualized family service plan and service coordination
- Comprehensive child find and referral system
- Public awareness program
- Central directory of services, resources, and research and demonstration projects
- Comprehensive system of personnel development
- Policies and procedures for personnel standards
- Single line of authority in a lead agency designated or established by the governor for carrying out a) general administration and supervision; b) identification and coordination of all available resources; c) assignment of financial responsibility to the appropriate agencies; d) development of procedures to ensure that services are provided in a timely manner pending resolution of any disputes; e) resolution of intra- and interagency disputes; and f) development of formal interagency agreements
- Policy pertaining to contracting or otherwise arranging for services
- Procedure for securing timely reimbursement of funds
- Procedural safeguards
- System for compiling data on the early intervention system
- State interagency coordinating council
- Policies and procedures to ensure that to the maximum extent appropriate, early intervention services are provided in natural environments (20 U.S.C. §1435[a], as cited in National Early Childhood Technical Assistance System, 1998)

The range and types of services that are funded through this program are varied and represent services from many different disciplines. Services may include the following:

(i) Family training, counseling, and home visits; (ii) special instruction; (iii) speech-language pathology and audiology services; (iv) occupational therapy; (v) physical therapy; (vi) psychological services; (vii) service coordination services; (viii) medical services only for diagnostic or evaluation purposes; (ix) early identification, screening, and assessment services; (x) health services necessary to enable the infant or toddler to benefit from the other early intervention services; (xi) social work services; (xii) vision services; (xiii) assistive technology devices and assistive technology services; and (xiv) transportation and related costs that are necessary to enable an infant or toddler and the infant's or toddler's family to receive another service [from this service list]. (20 U.S.C. §1432 [E])

The law also stipulates the types of personnel that may be considered qualified to provide these services. Again, a range of disciplines are reflected and they may include special educators, speech-language pathologists and audiologists, occupational therapists, physical therapists, social workers, nurses, nutritionists, family therapists, orientation and mobility specialists, and pediatricians and other physicians. These services also may be provided in a range of environments that include the child's home and community, such as a child care or infant/toddler program.

Preschool Grants Program

Services for preschool-age children are administered through state education agencies under this provision of the law. Thus, this section of the law extends the provisions of IDEA down to children from 3 to 6 years of age. The provisions of due process, nondiscriminatory testing and evaluation, IEP, and placement in LREs that were reviewed earlier are applied to educational services for preschool-age children. Important provisions of the law also acknowledge the role of parent involvement, particularly in programs for young children with disabilities, and highlight strengthening the role of parents and ensuring "meaningful opportunities" for parents to participate in their child's education at school and home.

Eligibility criteria for a child with a disability under Section 619 of Part B of IDEA include the following conditions: mental retardation, hearing impairments including deafness, speech or language impairments, visual impairments including blindness, serious emotional disturbance, orthopedic impairments, autism, traumatic brain injury, other health impairments, or specific learning disabilities. For children from ages 3 to 9 years, the state and local educational agency may, at their discretion, also serve children who are "experiencing developmental delays" as defined by that state and may include delays in the areas of physical, cognitive, communication, social or emotional, or adaptive development. In the majority of states that use quantitative criteria to determine eligibility under developmental delay, they use 2.0 SD (standard deviations) below the mean in one developmental area and/or 1.5 SD below the mean in two or more developmental areas (range 1.0 SD in one area–3.0 SD in one area) as the "cutoff" criteria for eligibility. In other states a percentage of delay (i.e., range of 20%–33%) in one or more developmental areas is specified to determine eligibility. In still other states, eligibility is determined through professional team consensus, professional judgment, or informed clinical opinion in lieu of quantitative criteria.

Educational Environments

Educational and related services are provided in a range of service environments. Generally, educational environments are classified as one of the following:

- *General class.* Children receive services in programs designed primarily for children without disabilities.

- *Resource room.* Children receive services in programs designed for children without disabilities, but children with disabilities are in a separate program 21%–60% of time.

- *Separate class.* Children receive services in separate programs more than 60% of time.

- *Separate school (public or private).* Children receive services in a separate public or private facility for children with disabilities 61%–100% of the time.

- *Residential facility.* Children receive care 24 hours per day through a public or private residential facility such as a public nursing care facility or a residential school.

- *Homebound/hospital environments.* Children receive services either at home (may include services from a regular home visitor) or in a hospital environment.

A wide range of services may be considered in special education service delivery systems. These types of services include assistive technology devices and services, audiology, counseling services, early identification and assessment, medical services of diagnosis or evaluation, occupational therapy, parent counseling and training, physical therapy, psychological services, recreation, rehabilitation counseling services, school health services, social work services in schools, special education, speech pathology, and transportation.

Educational environments are typically more broadly construed for young children than they are for school-age children. For children younger than kindergarten age, educational environments may include child care and Head Start programs as well as school programs. Head Start is a key environment for services. The Head Start program was established in 1965 through provisions in the Economic Opportunity Act of 1964 (PL 88-452). A primary focus was to provide early educational and social services for young children from low-income families in an effort to provide them with a head start and to break the cycle of poverty. The Economic Opportunity Act subsequently was amended to require that at least 10% of the enrollments in Head Start be children with disabilities and that their specialized services be provided in these programs. As such, these Head Start service options have had a major impact in expanding inclusive services.

Head Start also has had, from its inception, a strong family and community focus, and it has emphasized multidisciplinary service provision and coordination. These are important components of services for children with disabilities, as well. Early Head Start programs for pregnant mothers and infants and toddlers have been added and are included in the range of service options under Part C Programs for Infants and Toddlers.

In the past decade, general education classrooms have become the most common service environment for children with disabilities. In 1997–1998, for instance, those states that reported environments indicated that more than 92% of preschoolers with disabilities received special education or related services in a general public school environment (U.S. Department of Education, 2000). The majority of these children (52.5%) were served in classrooms with children without disabilities for at least 80% of the day.

KEY EDUCATION SERVICE DELIVERY CONCEPTS

IDEA addresses a number of key concepts and components. The primary elements are outlined and briefly discussed.

Individualized Education Programs for Children

Under the law all children with disabilities are required to have IEPs. The requirements differ somewhat on this component for infant/toddlers as contrasted with children who are preschool and school age. The IEP pertains to preschool-age children with disabilities (whose services are stipulated under Part B, Section 619 of the law) and to school-age children. The IEP consists of a written statement that includes 1) the child's present level of educational performance; 2) measurable annual goals and objectives to meet the child's educational needs; 3) special education and related services, supplementary aids and services, and program modifications or supports needed to enable the child to meet educational goals and participate with other children; 4) an explanation of the extent, if any, to which the child will not be involved in a general education class; 5) needed modification in the administration of state or school district assessments of student achievement in order for the child to participate; 6) the date for beginning services and the frequency, location, and duration of those services and modifications; and 7) the system for measurement of the child's progress toward goals. An IEP team includes the child's parents, general education teacher, special education teacher, representative of the local educational agency, and other individuals who may have knowledge of or expertise regarding the child.

Under Part C, infants and toddlers and their families receive an IFSP. The IFSP is viewed as a logical precursor to the IEP. The IFSP includes written statements of 1) the infant's or toddler's present levels of physical, cognitive, communication, social or emotional, and adaptive development; 2) the family's resources, priorities, and concerns relating to enhancing the development of the infant or toddler with a disability; 3) the major outcomes expected to be achieved for the infant or toddler and the family; and the criteria, procedures, and timelines used to determine the degree to which progress toward achieving the outcomes is being made and whether modifications or revisions of the outcomes or services are necessary; 4) specific early intervention services necessary to meet the unique needs of the infant or toddler and the family, including the frequency, intensity, and method of delivering services; 5) the natural environments in which early intervention services will be provided, including a justification if services will not be provided in a natural environment; 6) the projected dates for initiation of services and the anticipated duration of services; 7) the identification of the service coordinator from the profession most immediately relevant to the infant's, toddler's, or family's needs who will be responsible for the implementation of the plan and coordination with other agencies and people; and 8) the steps to be taken to support the transition of the toddler to preschool or other appropriate services.

These individualized plans are fundamental to services for children with disabilities. Education plans and the delivery of services, thus, are designed to meet each child's unique needs, and systems of accountability are stipulated. Challenges have centered around the provision of appropriate and meaningful assessments, establishing parent–professional partnerships for planning and implementation, ensuring parents' meaningful roles while individualizing for each family's cultural and linguistic background and preferences, and exercising professional teamwork in developing and providing services.

Family-Centered Service Delivery Models

In family-centered service delivery models the full and active participation of parents and family members is encouraged, particularly in early intervention service delivery systems for infants, toddlers, and preschoolers. This national law and its regulatory procedures formalized due process procedures and requirements for involving families in decisions regarding their child's assessment, placement, and education program planning and implementation.

The roles of families and the many ways in which families can be involved in their children's education programs have taken various forms and shifted over the years. At times, emphasis has been placed on notions of parents as teachers, parents as advocates, and parents as assistants in classrooms. Of course, one size does not fit all. Families differ in terms of their family membership or structure, family roles, culture and linguistic background, faith backgrounds, values and belief systems, resources, and the family's priorities and concerns for their children. So too do they differ in the roles and preferences for their involvement.

Family-centered or family-focused services refer not only to a philosophy of services, but also to a set of standard practices often considered recommended practices in the field of early intervention (Bruder, 2000; Sandall, McLean, & Smith, 2000; Shelton, Jeppson, & Johnson, 1987).

These services describe a cluster of practices including providing respectful and culturally sensitive family services, identifying families' concerns and priorities for their children, obtaining families' informed consent and participation in the decision-making process regarding service decisions for their children, and implementing practices that empower families and support and enhance families' development and competencies.

Inclusion/
Least Restrictive Environment/
Natural Environment

The law specifies that services should be provided to the maximum extent possible in educational environments in which children with disabilities are educated with children who do not have disabilities. It further stipulates that children should be removed from such an environment only when the nature or severity of the child's disability is such that the education cannot be achieved adequately in the general education environment with supplemental aids or services. This provision is often referred to as education in the *least restrictive environment*. Different terms, such as *mainstreaming* and *integration*, have been used over the years to describe the participation of children with disabilities in educational environments with their typically developing peers. Today the practice is termed *inclusion*.

The intent is similar for infants and toddlers, though the language of the law differs somewhat. The Part C program for infants and toddlers states that services should be provided to the maximum extent appropriate in natural environments. Such environments include the child's home and community environments in which children without disabilities participate.

The provision of the children's individualized and specialized services within their homes and community and school programs requires careful planning, teamwork, administrative support, flexibility, and family involvement. Learning opportunities abound in daily routines and family and community activities. Particularly in the early years, interventionists are challenged to adapt activities, curricula, and environments and forge new working relationships in order to meet the needs of children with disabilities in a range of environments (Bruder & Dunst, 2000; Guralnick, 2001; Hanson & Beckman, 2001; Odom, 2002; Sandall, McLean, & Smith, 2000; Sandall & Schwartz, 2002).

Transitions

A child's life is characterized by crucial transitions, particularly for children born at risk. These transitions are defined as "points of change in services and personnel who coordinate and provide services" (Rice & O'Brien, 1990, p. 2). The first transition may occur as the child moves from care in the hospital to the family's home. Subsequent transitions for children with disabilities include the transitions from home into infant/toddler services, from infant/toddler services into preschool, and from preschool to kindergarten to elementary school, and so forth. Transitions can be stressful for families under the best of circumstances. Because in many states different agencies are responsible for early intervention services for infants/toddlers than for preschool/school-age education services, these transitions may be particularly challenging. Interagency agreements and transition procedures, support for families from key personnel, preparation of children for the transition, information exchange procedures between the sending and receiving services and personnel, and staff training and preparation for transition are but a few of the areas targeted for careful planning and support in order to ease transitions for children and their families (Hanson, in press; Rosenkoetter, Hains, & Fowler, 1994).

Personnel Preparation and Interdisciplinary Team Models

Professional standards and personnel licensure, certification, and credentialing requirements may differ by state and also across professions based on the standards set by each professional discipline. Thus, considerable variability can be found across states, although all must adhere to provisions for a comprehensive system for professional development as stipulated in the law.

Most professional groups have expanded curricula at both the preservice and inservice levels to address competencies related to serving young children and their families, and many have separate certification or add-on training programs in pediatric or early care. Creative and cross-disciplinary approaches are needed, however, for personnel development across health, education, and social service fields (Winton, McCollum, & Catlett, 1997).

The range of service needs experienced by children with disabilities and their families bridge professional disciplines. Only through collaborative team models can these service needs be fully addressed. In early intervention, the transdisciplinary team model is considered the most optimal for service delivery. The transdisciplinary team model highlights a team approach through which "role release" is practiced, in that one or a few professionals are the primary individuals responsible for implementing a child's program with assistance, consultation, and continuous skill training and development from the full spectrum of team members representing various disciplines (McGonigel, Woodruff, & Roszmann-Millican, 1994). This team approach requires careful collaboration across professional service providers and requires time and resource allocation for training and planning, as well as commitments and effective working relationships among professionals (Hanson & Bruder, 2001).

Parents and other family members are crucial members of any intervention/education team. Including families in a respectful, culturally sensitive, and family-centered way has necessitated adaptations and shifts in preservice and inservice personnel preparation for professionals. Most programs now actively seek and involve families in these training regimens.

Service Coordination and Interagency Collaboration

Service coordination is a mandated service under Part C of IDEA, and it is to be provided at no cost to families. It is defined as an "active, ongoing process that assists and enables families to access services and assures their rights and procedural safeguards" (NECTAS, 2001). Early intervention team members must jointly provide assessment, intervention, and evaluation activities in a partnership with the child's family and enable families to obtain the various services they need (Bruder & Bologna, 1993). Active and collaborative cross-disciplinary working relationships and interagency coordination are needed regardless of the child's age and special needs. Such collaboration forms an important element in providing support to families.

Benefits of the Laws

The passage of IDEA has provided an unprecedented opportunity in the United States to establish a unified service delivery system to address the complex needs of children with disabilities and their families. A child's individualized service needs and goals and the active inclusion and participation of the child's family are at the core of policies and procedures. The legislation has provided the necessary infrastructure for developing a system that spans the United States and incorporates the full range of service delivery agencies, structures, and professional disciplines that deliver education services. It has afforded the means to cross boundaries of agencies and professions in order to serve the diverse needs of children and their families. By the same token, the comprehensive nature of this legislation also has produced tremendous challenges related to interagency coordination, teaming and collaboration, and the provision of full and meaningful participation options for families in a manner that is congruent with family priorities and needs.

SUMMARY

Although having a family member with a disabling condition may have a great impact on a family, many of the challenges these families face are the same or similar to those of other families. In other words, parents of children with disabilities should be viewed as parents first, just as their children with disabilities should be viewed as children first. When the child has a disability, however, it may create the need for more supports or specialized services to enable the child and family to participate in normative family events and routines.

As service providers continue to explore their views on families and families' perspectives on parenting children with disabilities, they must be vigilant and keep in mind the impact of cultural and societal values in shaping these service priorities and approaches. Families are nested within the contexts of their neighborhoods and communities as well as the larger society in which they live. The policies, laws, values, and priorities of these communities help shape the experiences that families will have and the services and supports that will be available to them and desired by them.

Most individuals and families readjust and adapt to the new challenges presented to them by the presence of a disability. As the literature previously reviewed has suggested, families who have a member with a disability are often even inspired to reach out to others, and develop a sense of their roles in the "greater good" of their communities. For instance, as one mother reflected, "I guess the hardest part has been to figure out what his little niche is. And I think maybe it's just that he's a teacher [of others]" (as cited in Hanson, 2003b). Regardless of a family's goals, professionals can best help families by engaging in practices that facilitate the family's sense of competence and confidence and the family's abilities to determine the services and resources that they will need throughout their journey.

> *Once we got over the dismay and shock at the hospital and picked up our shattered dreams and hopes, we began the slow process of reorienting and reorganizing those dreams and hope into a different set of rules, a different lifestyle. No, maybe our little Down syndrome boy wouldn't be able to realize some of those high dreams we had composed before his birth, but with a little reshuffling (and a lot of hard work) he will be able to realize other dreams that we are composing day by day. So the song will have different words and a different melody, but will still be a masterpiece. (Timothy & Marilyn Sullivan, parents; as cited in Hanson & Harris, 1986, p. 8)*

ACTIVITIES TO EXTEND THE DISCUSSION

1. **Imagine how it feels.** To envision the experience for families as they encounter new stresses, try this activity with a friend or colleague. Have your partner make a list of all the stressors the family may encounter. With each stressor or demand, have your partner place a balloon in your arms. Before long you will find it difficult to manage or juggle the many balloon "stressors." Suddenly the balloons will start to drop or pop creating even more chaos and instability for you as you struggle to keep them in order and afloat. While this task graphically displays the juggling act, it cannot possibly do justice to the emotional experience of coping with these issues, especially with a loved one such as one's child.

2. **Mapping supports.** Identify a difficulty or issue of significance with which you or a family member is grappling. Develop a map or outline of the resources and supports that you have for addressing this concern. Try to consider the broad range of resources and supports that are available to you and the ways in which they are interconnected. Try to sketch out or display your "map" of these resources and supports much as you would an organizational chart for a business or corporation.

REFERENCES

Americans with Disabilities Act (ADA) of 1990, PL 101-336, 42 U.S.C. §§ 12101 *et seq.*

Antonovsky, A. (1979). *Health, stress and coping.* San Francisco: Jossey-Bass.

Antonovsky, A. (1993). The implications of salutogenesis: An outsider's view. In A.P. Turnbull, J.M. Patterson, S.K. Behr, D.L. Murphy, J.G. Marquis, & M.J. Blue-Banning (Eds.), *Cognitive coping, families, and disability* (pp. 111–122). Baltimore: Paul H. Brookes Publishing Co.

Bailey, D., Blasco, P.M., & Simeonsson, R.J. (1992). Needs expressed by mothers and fathers of young children with disabilities. *American Journal on Mental Retardation, 97,* 1–10.

Bailey, D., Simeonsson, R., Winton, P., Huntington, G., Comfort, M., Isbell, P., O'Donnell, K.J., & Helm, J.M. (1986). Family-focused intervention: A functional model for planning, implementing, and evaluating individualized family services in early intervention. *Journal of the Division for Early Childhood, 10,* 156–171.

Beckman, P.J. (1991). Comparison of mothers' and fathers' perceptions of the effect of young children with and without disabilities. *American Journal on Mental Retardation, 95,* 585–595.

Berry, J.O., & Hardman, M.L. (1998). *Lifespan perspectives on the family and disability.* Boston: Allyn & Bacon.

Bettelheim, B. (1950). *Love is not enough.* Glencoe, NY: Free Press.

Braddock, D. (1987). *Federal policy toward mental retardation and developmental disabilities.* Baltimore: Paul H. Brookes Publishing Co.

Bruce, E.J., & Schultz, C.L. (2001). *Nonfinite loss and grief: A psychoeducational approach.* Baltimore: Paul H. Brookes Publishing Co.

Bruder, M.B. (2000). Family-centered early intervention: Clarifying our values for the new millennium. *Topics in Early Childhood Special Education, 20,* 105–115, 122.

Bruder, M.B., & Bologna T.M. (1993). Collaboration and service coordination for effective early intervention. In W. Brown, S.K. Thurman, & L. Pearl (Eds.), *Family-centered early intervention with infants and toddlers: Innovative cross-disciplinary approaches* (pp. 103–127). Baltimore: Paul H. Brookes Publishing Co.

Bruder, M.B., & Dunst, C.J. (2000). Expanding learning opportunities for infants and toddlers in natural environments: A chance to reconceptualize early intervention. *Zero to Three, 20*(3), 34–36.

Drotar, D., Baskiewicz, A., Irvin, N., Kennell, J., & Klaus, M. (1975). The adaptation of parents to the birth an infant with a congenital malformation: A hypothetical model. *Pediatrics, 56,* 710–716.

Dunst, C.J., Trivette, C.M., & Deal, A.G. (1988). *Enabling and empowering families: Principles and guidelines for practice.* Cambridge, MA: Brookline Books.

Dunst, C.J., Trivette, C.M., & Deal, A.G. (1994). *Supporting and strengthening families: Methods, strategies and practices* (Vol. 1). Cambridge, MA: Brookline Books.

Dunst, C.J., Trivette, C.M., Gordon, N.J., & Pletcher, L.L. (1989). Building and mobilizing informal family support networks. In G.H.S. Singer & L.K. Irvin (Eds.), *Support for caregiving families: Enabling positive adaptation to disability* (pp. 121–141). Baltimore: Paul H. Brookes Publishing Co.

Dyson, L.L. (1991). Families of young children with handicaps: Parental stress and functioning. *American Journal on Mental Retardation, 95,* 623–629.

Dyson, L.L. (1993). Response to the presence of a child with disabilities: Parental stress and family functioning over time. *American Journal on Mental Retardation, 98,* 207–218.

Economic Opportunity Act of 1964, PL 88-452, 42 U.S.C. §§ 2701 *et seq.*

Edelman, L., Greenland, B., & Mills, B.L. (1992). *Family-centered communication skills: Facilitator's guide* (Project Copernicus, Kennedy Krieger Institute). St. Paul, MN: Pathfinder Resources.

Education for All Handicapped Children Act of 1975 (PL 94–142), 20 U.S.C. §§ 1400 *et seq.*

Frost, R. (1987). North of Boston: The black cottage. In *Robert Frost poems.* Franklin Center, PA: The Franklin Library. (Original work published 1914)

Guralnick, M.J. (Ed.). (2001). *Early childhood inclusion: Focus on change.* Baltimore: Paul H. Brookes Publishing Co.

Hanson, M.J. (1996). Early interactions. In M.J. Hanson (Ed.), *Atypical infant development* (2nd ed., pp. 235–272). Austin, TX: PRO-ED.

Hanson, M.J. (1999, September). *Early Transitions for children and families: Transitions from infant/toddler services to preschool education.*

(ERIC Digest No. E581) Reston, VA: The ERIC Clearinghouse on Disabilities and Gifted Education.

Hanson, M.J. (2003a). National legislation for early intervention: United States of America. In S. Odom, M.J. Hanson, J. Blackman, & S. Kaul (Eds.), *Early intervention practices around the world* (pp. 253–279). Baltimore: Paul H. Brookes Publishing Co.

Hanson, M.J. (2003b). Twenty-five years after early intervention: Follow up of children with Down syndrome and their families. *Infants and Young Children, 16*, 354–365.

Hanson, M.J. (in press). Ensuring effective transitions. In M.J. Guralnick (Ed.), *A developmental systems approach to intervention: National and international perspectives.* Baltimore: Paul H. Brookes Publishing Co.

Hanson, M.J., & Beckman, P.J. (Eds.). (2001). *Me too! series: Introducing me; It's time for preschool; My community, my family; My new friends; On my best behavior; Look what I can do now.* Baltimore: Paul H. Brookes Publishing Co.

Hanson, M.J., & Bruder, M.B. (2001). Early intervention: Promises to keep. *Infants and Young Children, 13*(3), 47–58.

Hanson, M.J., & Hanline, M.F. (1990). Parenting a child with a disability: A longitudinal study of parental stress and adaptation. *Journal of Early Intervention, 14*(3), 234–248.

Hanson, M.J., & Harris, S.R. (1986). *Teaching the young child with motor delays.* Austin, TX: PRO-ED.

Hanson, M.J., Lynch, E.W., & Wayman, K.I. (1990). Honoring the cultural diversity of families when gathering data. *Topics in Early Childhood Special Education, 10*(1), 112–131.

Hill, R. (1949). *Families under stress.* New York: Harper.

Hill, R. (1958). Generic features of families under stress. *Social Casework, 49*, 139–150.

Individuals with Disabilities Education Act (IDEA) of 1990, PL 101-476, 20 U.S.C. §§ 1400 *et seq.*

Individuals with Disabilities Education Act (IDEA) Amendments of 1997, PL 105-17, 20 U.S.C. §§ 1400 *et seq.*

Kübler-Ross, E. (1969). *On death and dying.* New York: Macmillan.

Lazarus, R.S., & Folkman, S. (1984). *Stress, appraisal, and coping.* New York: Springer.

Lynch, E.W., & Hanson, M.J. (2004). *Developing cross-cultural competence: A guide for working with children and their families* (3rd ed.). Baltimore: Paul H. Brookes Publishing Co.

McCubbin, H.I., & Patterson, J.M. (1982). Family adaptation to crises. In H.I. McCubbin, A.E. Cauble, & J.M. Patterson (Eds.), *Family stress, coping and social support* (pp. 26–470). Springfield, IL: Charles C Thomas.

McCubbin, H.I., & Patterson, J.M. (1983a). Family stress and adaptation to crises: A double ABCX model of family behavior. In D. Olson & B. Miler (Eds.), *Family studies review yearbook* (pp. 87–106). Beverly Hills: Sage.

McCubbin, H.I., & Patterson, J.M. (1983b). The family stress process: The double ABCX model of family adjustment and adaptation. *Marriage and Family Review, 6*, 7–37.

McGonigel, M.J., Woodruff, G., & Roszmann-Millican, M. (1994). The transdisciplinary team: A model for family-centered early intervention. In L. Johnson, R. Gallagher, M. LaMontagne, J. Jordan, J. Gallagher, P. Hutinger, & M. Karnes (Eds.), *Meeting early intervention challenges: Issues form birth to three* (pp 95–131). Baltimore: Paul H. Brookes Publishing Co.

Naseef, R.A. (2001). *Special children, challenged parents: The struggles and rewards of raising a child with a disability* (Rev. ed.). Baltimore: Paul H. Brookes Publishing Co.

National Early Childhood Technical Assistance System (NECTAS). (December, 1998). *Part C Updates.* Chapel Hill, NC: Author.

National Early Childhood Technical Assistance System. (2001, October). *Service coordination under IDEA.* Retrieved October 15, 2002, from http://www.nectac.org/topics/scoord/scoord.asp

Noh, S., Dumas, J.E., Wolf, L.C., & Fishman, S.N. (1989). Delineating sources of stress in parents of exceptional children. *Family Relations, 38*, 456–461.

Odom, S.L. (Ed.). (2002). *Widening the circle: Including the child with disabilities in preschool programs.* New York: Teachers College Press.

Orr, R.R., Cameron, S.J., Dobson, L.A., & Day, D.M. (1993). Age-related changes in stress experienced by families with a child who has developmental delays. *Mental Retardation, 1*, 171–176.

Palfrey, J.S., Walker, D.K., Butler, J.A., & Singer, J.D. (1989). Patterns of response in families of chronically disabled children: An assessment in five metropolitan school districts. *American Journal of Orthopsychiatry, 59,* 94–104.

Patterson, J.M. (1988). Families experiencing stress. The Family Adjustment and Adaptation Response Model. *Family Systems Medicine, 6*(2), 202–237.

Patterson, J.M. (1989). A family stress model: The Family Adjustment and Adaptation Response. In C. Ramsey (Ed.), *The science of family medicine* (pp. 95–117). New York: Guilford Press.

Patterson, J.M. (1993). The role of family meanings in adaptation to chronic illness and disability. In A.P. Turnbull, J.M. Patterson, S.K. Behr, D.L. Murphy, J.G. Marquis, & M.J. Blue-Banning (Eds.), *Cognitive coping, families, and disability* (pp. 221–238). Baltimore: Paul H. Brookes Publishing Co.

Patterson, J.M., & Leonard, B.J. (1993). Caregiving and children. In E. Kahana, D.E. Biegel, & M. Wykle (Eds.), *Family caregiving across the lifespan* (pp. 33–158). Newbury Park, CA: Sage.

Rice, M.L., & O'Brien, M. (1990). Transitions: Time for change and accommodation. *Topics in Early Childhood Special Education, 9*(4), 1–14.

Rosenkoetter, S.E., Hains, A., & Fowler, S.A. (1994). *Bridging early services for children with special needs and their families: A practical guide for transition planning.* Baltimore: Paul H. Brookes Publishing Co.

Safford, P.L., & Safford, E.J. (1996). *A history of childhood and disability.* New York: Teachers College Press.

Sandall, S.R., McLean, M.E., & Smith, B.J. (2000). *DEC recommended practices in early intervention/early childhood special education.* Longmont, CO: Sopris West.

Sandall, S.R., & Schwartz, I.S. (2002). *Building blocks for teaching preschoolers with special needs.* Baltimore: Paul H. Brookes Publishing Co.

Santelli, B., Poyadue, F.S., & Young, J.L. (2001). *The parent to parent handbook.* Baltimore: Paul H. Brookes Publishing Co.

Shelton, T., Jeppson, E., & Johnson, B. (1987). *Family-centered care for children with special health care needs.* Washington, DC: Association for the Care of Children's Health.

Singer, G., & Irvin, L.K. (1989). Family caregiving, stress, and support. In G.H.S. Singer & L.K. Irvin (Eds.), *Support for caregiving families: Enabling positive adaptation to disability* (pp. 3–25). Baltimore: Paul H. Brookes Publishing Co.

Sloper, P., & Turner, S. (1993). Risk and resistance factors in the adaptation of parents of children with severe physical disability. *Journal of Child Psychology and Psychiatry, 34,* 167–188.

Solnit, A.J., & Stark, M.H. (1961). Mourning and the birth of a defective child. *Psychoanalytic Study of the Child, 16,* 523–537.

Spiegle, J.A., & van den Pol, R.A. (Eds.). (1993). *Making changes: Family voices on living with disabilities.* Cambridge, MA: Brookline.

Trute, B., & Hauch, C. (1988). Building on family strength: A study of families with positive adjustment to the birth of a developmentally disabled child. *Journal of Marital and Family Therapy, 14,* 185–193.

Turnbull, H.R. (1986). *Free appropriate public education: The law and children with disabilities.* Denver, CO: Love Publishing Co.

Turnbull, A.P., Patterson, J.M., Behr, S.K., Murphy, D.L., Marquis, J.G., & Blue-Banning, M.J. (Eds.) (1993). *Cognitive coping, families, and disability.* Baltimore: Paul H. Brookes Publishing Co.

Turnbull, A.P., & Turnbull, H.R. (1985). *Parents speak out: Then and now.* Columbus, OH: Charles E. Merrill.

Turnbull, A.P., & Turnbull, H.R. (1990). *Families, professionals, and exceptionality: A special partnership* (2nd ed.). Columbus, OH: Charles E. Merrill.

U.S. Department of Education. (2000). *Twenty-second annual report to Congress on the implementation of the Individuals with Disabilities Education Act.* Washington, DC: Author.

Weston, D.R., Ivins, B., Heffron, M.C., & Sweet, N. (1997). Formulating the centrality of relationship in early intervention: An organizational perspective. *Infants and Young Children, 9*(3), 1–12.

Winkler, L.M. (1988). Family stress theory and research on families of children with mental retardation. In J.J. Gallagher & P.M. Vietze (Eds.), *Families of handicapped persons: Research, programs, and policy issues* (pp. 167–

195). Baltimore: Paul H. Brookes Publishing Co.

Winton, P.J., McCollum, J.A., & Catlett, C. (Eds.) (1997). *Reforming personnel preparation in early intervention: Issues, models, and practical strategies.* Baltimore: Paul H. Brookes Publishing Co.

CHAPTER 5

FAMILIES IN POVERTY

Cumulative Risks and Resilience

Poverty demoralizes.
—Ralph Waldo Emerson, 1860 (rev. 1876)

There is something about poverty that
smells like death. Dead dreams dropping off the heart
like leaves in a dry season and rotting around the feet; impulses
smothered too long in the fetid air of undeground caves. The soul lives
in a sickly air.
—Zora Neale Hurston (1996, p. 87)

If a free society cannot help the many
who are poor, it cannot save the few who are rich.
—John F. Kennedy (Inaugural Address, January 20, 1961)

THE FACES OF POVERTY

Poverty wears many faces. The stories that follow suggest the range of U.S. families who struggle through economic hardships, as well as the multiple effects created by economic deprivation on families. Some families are able to struggle valiantly to overcome these difficulties, whereas others succumb to the overwhelming uphill battle. The purpose of this chapter is to explore what it means to be poor, how poverty affects family and child outcomes, and how transactional models of development help family service providers to understand and support family adjustment and adaptation. Begin by considering five different families, all of whom struggle with economic hardship to care for their children with disabilities.

Cecilee

Mary Anne and her daughter, Cecilee, who has cerebral palsy, share dinner with her large family every Sunday when the family meets after church. Mary Anne and her daughter live in a small trailer behind her mother's house; most of Mary Anne's relatives live within 5 miles of them. Mary Anne feels fortunate to have her family close by. Someone is almost always available to care for Cecilee for a short time or give her a ride to her Head Start class or to a medical appointment. Mary Anne is unemployed; she recently had to quit her custodial job at a nearby paper plant because the long hours at night made it impossible to care for Cecilee. Cecilee's grandmother tried to take on her care at night but her arthritic condition prevented her from being able to lift or move to assist Cecilee.

Ge

Ge is a 7-year-old girl who has a visual impairment. Ge's father, Ly Chia, and her mother, Mai Dao, immigrated to the United States from Laos and were settled in a small inland farm community approximately 150 miles from the Pacific Coast in central California. Her family was forced to subsist on welfare after the economic recession that shut down many local factories in their new community. Ly Chia's brother lives nearby. He manages to feed his own family from the produce of his small farm and to help Ly Chia's family, as well.

    Ge is in first grade and is bussed to school with her 9-year-old brother, while her 3-year-old sister remains at home during the day. Ge's brother helps her navigate and get to her classroom where she receives specialized services for her visual impairment.

Lamont

Lamont's family lives in a large, urban area. When Lamont was born at City Hospital, Jonalene, his mother, was told that he had Down syndrome and that he would need pediatric care and an early intervention program. She and her husband, Carl, took him back to the hospital emergency room several times over the next year—once when he fell off the bed and stopped breathing, and once when he had a fever and was coughing and wheezing so much that they were afraid he would die. A public health nurse came to visit the family's small apartment and helped them to get connected to a local agency that provides services to infants with disabilities. Jonalene fully intended to get Lamont registered in the program, but she and her husband split up, and she had to leave the apartment. She was forced to move from shelter to shelter. Just finding a roof over their heads and getting a hot meal each day became her daily existence.

JOSÉ

Arely and her 16-year-old son José immigrated to the United States from El Salvador 10 years ago. They share a small apartment with Arely's sister and her son in a suburban area. Both sisters save whatever money they can to send to relatives in El Salvador who were left homeless by an earthquake. Arely typically works 12 hours per day, and often 6 days per week, cleaning houses. She is extremely worried about her son, who was expelled from high school after threatening another student. She finds solace and support in her church; she goes on Sunday, her one day off of work, and several nights a week to pray.

DAWN AND DAVID

Floyd and Nancy Randall have two children, Dawn and David. Dawn's birth was fraught with difficulties, and she sustained brain damage during delivery. Subsequently, she had numerous hospitalizations and health complications. Floyd works at the local mill and earns minimum wage while Nancy tries to earn a few dollars here and there by helping take care of elderly neighbors or doing some child care. Making ends meet each month is a challenge. This family has borrowed money from Nancy's parents, and they have relied on the assistance of people who attend their church on more than one occasion. They often express exasperation over the fact that their hard work does not seem to get them ahead or even on par with their family's needs.

These families exemplify the many faces of poverty. As discussed briefly in Chapter 1, poverty is found across all regions, races, and family constellations, although higher percentages of families living in poverty are found in certain groups. For instance, poor and impoverished families are more likely to be headed by a single parent (usually a mother), reside in a city, and be undereducated (i.e., to have less than a high school degree). In addition, although a larger *number* of people living in poverty are white, a larger *percentage* of American Indians/Alaska Natives, Latinos, and African Americans are poor (Dalaker, 2001).

Children and Poverty

Poverty rates for children are higher than for any other age group (Dalaker, 2001). Though improvements have been made in the last decade, nearly

12 million children live in poverty; more than four million of them are younger than age 6 (National Center for Children in Poverty, 2003). This number represents 16% of all children (19% of children younger than 6) based on the 2001 federal poverty level of $14,255 for a family of three (National Center for Children in Poverty, 2003). Broken down by race/ethnicity, the poverty rate for children under age 18 is 30% for African American children, 29% for Latino children, and 13% for white children (National Center for Children in Poverty, 2003). For the youngest children—those younger than age 6—the child poverty rates are similar: Specifically, the NCCP study found them to be 35% for African American children, 33% for Latino children, and 15% for white children. Thus, a large proportion of children are likely to live in poverty in the United States.

Furthermore, in 2000, 7% of children in America (9% of those younger than age 6) lived in extreme poverty (i.e., in 2001, earning below $7,127 for a family of three, i.e., half the poverty line or below). It also is noteworthy that 38% of children (42% younger than age 6, or approximately 10 million children) in America live in or near poverty as defined by family income that is 200% of the poverty line, that is, $28,510 and below for a family of three (National Center for Children in Poverty, 2003). The concerns of these families typically mirror those for families considered "poor" and include issues of employment, child care, and health care.

Poverty and Disability

The links between poverty and disability are equally compelling. Findings from a recent Institute for Women's Policy Research analysis of disabilities among families reported that low-income families are nearly 50% more likely to have a child with a disability or a severe disability than are higher income families. Furthermore, they reported that families receiving welfare benefits have an even higher likelihood of having at least one child with a disability: Twenty percent of all families receiving welfare benefits have a child with a disability, and of these 20%, 13% have a child with severe disabilities (Lee, Sills, & Oh, 2002). In addition, this analysis found that single-mother families were more likely to have a child with a disability than were two-parent or single-father families.

Disabilities among single-mothers in low-income families also were higher than were rates for single mothers with higher incomes. Approximately 29% of these low-income single mothers had a disability and 17% had a severe disability (as contrasted with 17% and 5%, respectively, for higher income single mothers). The percentages were even more startling for single mothers receiving welfare or Temporary Assistance for Needy Families (TANF)—38% of these women had a disability and 25% were reported to have a severe disability.

Another review of research related to welfare reform and disabilities cited evidence that estimated that 30%–40% of families receiving welfare had either a mother or a child with some level of disability (Loprest & Acs, 1996; Meyers, Lukemeyer, & Smeeding, 1996). A study conducted by Fujiura and Yamaki in 2000 gathered prevalence data that revealed a growing relationship between poverty and risk for disability. The conditions of poverty that may lead to disability or chronic illness and the provision of resources to impoverished families who have members with disabilities, however, have largely been overlooked in research and policy formation (Rosman & Knitzer, 2001). Recommendations for addressing the needs of these families who receive welfare and who have family members with disabilities have been made regarding expanding access to health care, child care, and vocational training and securing income maintenance through Supplemental Security Income (SSI) (Birenbaum, 2002).

Historical Trends in Poverty Rates

Poverty rates are undeniably linked to time periods (e.g., the Great Depression) and to shifts in family characteristics and societal pressures and opportunities. The increase in mother-only households is often cited as causally linked to increased poverty rates for children. The link may not be so linear or clear cut as is often thought. Although it is likely that mother-only households are characterized by lower income levels, the low earnings of fathers and employment insecurity remain prime contributors to increases (Hernandez, 1997). Certainly, these issues exert a direct effect on family income. In addition, analyses suggest that these issues (e.g., low salaries) may indirectly influence poverty and family trends by necessitating that mothers work outside the home to increase family income and thus, perhaps contribute to separation and divorce (Hernandez, 1997). The issue is not so much family structure as it is the economic and employment experiences and opportunities for both mothers and fathers.

Though poverty rates for families and children have declined over the past decade, they remain high. In a study of poverty between 1998 and 2000 (Dalaker, 2001), the average rates over the 3-year period for various populations were the following: 11.9% for all races; 25.9% for American Indian/Alaska Natives; 23.9% for blacks; 23.1% for Hispanics; 11.3% for Asian/Pacific Islanders; and 9.9% for whites (7.8% for white, non-Hispanic). The overall poverty rate dropped between 1999 and 2000, undoubtedly due to a strong economy. The economic downturn in the early 21st century offered the possibility that more families and children would be returned to impoverished circumstances. The risks posed to the well-being of these families and children are many and comprehensive.

WHAT IT MEANS TO BE POOR

In the discussion thus far, the definition of poverty has centered on income level for a family of three. The official federal poverty line was $14,255 in 2001 for a family of three. Policy makers and social scientists, however, have hotly debated the characteristics used to define poverty or economic deprivation over the years. Income alone hardly paints the whole picture. In fact, these numbers and percentages represent Spartan or conservative markers for children and families living under poor economic resource conditions. A 1988 study by Hagenaars and de Vos (as cited in McLoyd, 1998a) described different methods for defining poverty, which are characterized as *absolute, relative,* and *subjective* poverty. These definitions, respectively, characterize poverty as 1) having the minimum required for basic needs such as food, clothing, and housing; 2) having less than others in terms of what is typical for most members of that society; and 3) feeling one does not have enough to get along.

The absolute poverty marker refers to the official poverty line as determined by the Social Security Administration (SSA), and it is the most commonly used marker for policy and research. An SSA economist developed it in 1965. A number of difficulties are associated with this marker, including 1) the failure to adjust for geographic location in living costs and variation in support programs, such as food stamps and Medicaid; 2) the use of pretax income to determine who is below the threshold of poverty; and 3) the issue that this marker does not reflect the poverty gap, in other words, how far below the threshold the family falls. (For a history of the official poverty measure, see Fisher [1992].)

Other definitions offer a broader view of economic deprivation than that based on a somewhat arbitrary cash marker of family income. In some research studies socioeconomic status (SES) has been used to categorize individuals. This marker includes components such as the father's and mother's occupations and education and certain lifestyle variables.

Both the concepts of poverty income and SES, however, are viewed as ongoing and linked to conditions such as unemployment or low wages (McLoyd, 1998a). As such they may fail to account for events in the family's life that produce economic deprivation. For example, an employed person may experience a sudden loss or drop in income. Although this may not push the individual into poverty, nevertheless the impact of the economic hardship affects the individual's and the family's functioning and dynamics. The issues of the *timing* and *terms* of poverty are not always considered in research and policy studies. Undoubtedly, living in persistent poverty, as opposed to living through bouts of poverty, has a different impact on children and their families. In addition, statistics reveal that race and ethnicity interact with the persistence of poverty. African American and Latino children experience higher rates of poverty and they also are more likely to be poor for longer time periods than are white children (Brooks-Gunn, Duncan, & Maritato, 1997).

Thus, family circumstance and structure, parental education, time, and degree of poverty all may exert a profound effect on the family's economic well-being. These issues, coupled with how individual family members perceive or experience their economic circumstances, make it difficult to tease apart indicators or markers for poverty.

Regardless of the definition of poverty used, most definitions do not begin to capture the many differences in day-to-day living practices that children and families experience when existing under economically deprived conditions. Such challenges run the gamut from lack of basic necessities associated with food, clothing, and housing to irregular work or work schedules, lack of family support, lack of child care, insufficient access to health care, safety issues, exposure to stressful living conditions, and psychological stress, among many others. Similarly, ethnic and cultural factors interact with these issues, as well as the timing of poverty and chronicity of this deprivation. The many factors and dimensions make poverty difficult to define and study. Policy makers and social scientists concur that the effects of poverty are pervasive and potentially devastating, however.

IMPACT OF POVERTY ON CHILD AND FAMILY WELL-BEING

Although many families manage to overcome adverse circumstances, living in poverty unleashes a set of factors and events that pose great risk to the well-being and development of children and their families. A proliferation of research in the 1990s has analyzed the impact of poverty on development (Brooks-Gunn & Duncan, 1997; Brooks-Gunn, Duncan, & Maritato, 1997; Duncan & Brooks-Gunn, 1997; Huston, 1991; Huston, McLoyd, & Garcia Coll, 1994; McLoyd, 1998b) and documented deleterious effects. Highlights from this research are briefly reviewed with respect to what we know about the impact on child development and family functioning.

Poverty and Child Development

Given the crucial importance of early experience to an individual's development, it is alarming that so many children are growing up under circumstances that may place their development at risk. In a recent policy and scientific publication on the science of early childhood development, the authors noted, "One of the most consistent associations in developmental science is between economic hardship and compromised child development" (Shonkoff & Phillips, 2000, p. 275).

Children living in impoverished conditions may be at greater risk of exposure to a variety of risks including inadequate nutrition, environmental toxins, impaired parent–child interaction, trauma and abuse, lower quality child care, and drugs and substance abuse by parents (National Center for Children in Poverty, 2002). These factors further increase the risk of developmental impairment for children living in poverty.

Because nearly one in five young children in the United States lives in poverty, the urgency of this issue is apparent (National Center for Children in Poverty, 2002). Scientific evidence gathered in recent years on early brain development underscores the importance of experience in the early years to the child's emotional, intellectual, and physical development (Shore, 1997). Advances in neuroscience research have documented the course of early brain development and highlighted the sensitive period for optimal brain development in the earliest years (including prenatal development) of the child's life. During these early years, exposure to environmental stimulation has a profound effect on brain growth and development. Likewise, early exposure to risks, such as those factors previously listed, also may impede brain development.

In this light, consider again the risk factors identified by the National Center for Children in Poverty (2002) (see Figure 5.1). Malnutrition in children is associated with delays in physical growth and motor skills development, lower test scores in subsequent years on academic subjects, social withdrawal, and, as a result, lower expectations from parents and teachers. Research studies substantiate the link between degree of poverty and degree of malnutrition (Brown & Pollitt, 1996). Substance abuse during and after pregnancy also has been demonstrated to produce deleterious effects on brain development (Mayes, 1996). Exposure to toxins, too, can damage or stunt brain growth. More than 400,000 children each year have toxic levels of lead in their blood at delivery (The National Health/Education Consortium, 1991), and 55% of African American children living in poverty display toxic levels of lead in their blood (National Center for Children in Poverty, 1997). Furthermore, children who experience trauma or abuse in their early years may have difficulties forming attachments, and they may display more anxiety and depression. The stressors associated with poverty create more trauma for these children (Brooks-Gunn, Klebanov, Liaw, & Duncan, 1995). The quality of care, too, is important to children's well-being, particularly children's emotional and intellectual development. Mothers who suffer from depression are less likely to provide appropriate and needed stimulation and interactions with their infants, resulting in deficits such as lowered activity levels, withdrawal behaviors, and shorter attention spans (Belle, 1990). Positive interactions and exposure to learning environments influence how the brain develops. Poor child care and parent–child interactions likely impede the child's development, whereas high-quality child care experiences have been linked with enhanced child development (Burchinal, Lee, & Ramey,

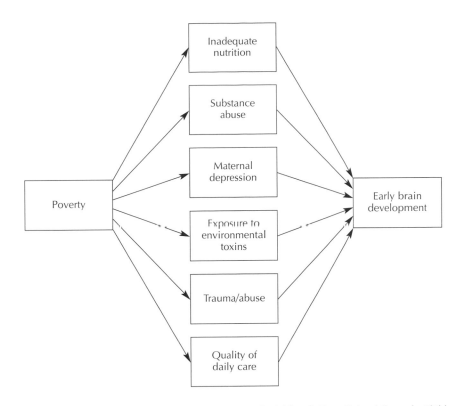

Figure 5.1.   The effect of poverty on brain development in early childhood. (From National Center for Children in Poverty [1997, April]. *Poverty and brain development in early childhood.* Retrieved June 2003, from http:// cpmcnet.columbia.edu/dept/nccp/brain.html; reprinted by permission.)

1989; Cost, Quality & Child Outcomes Study Team, 1995). Children in poverty are disproportionately exposed to risks, and thus their well-being is seriously threatened.

An extensive body of research literature has documented the association between poverty and child outcomes. Family income can dramatically affect outcomes for children and adolescents and these negative effects are more apparent for some outcomes than for others. In addition, these outcomes are linked to the depth and duration of poverty (Brooks-Gunn & Duncan, 1997).

Descriptive studies have linked poverty conditions to teenage pregnancy, low academic achievement, and juvenile delinquency (Brody et al., 1994; McLeod & Shanahan, 1993; Sampson & Laub, 1994). Furthermore, low income has been associated with social-emotional difficulties, including conduct disorders, anxiety, and depression (Bank, Forgatch, Patterson, & Fetrow, 1993; Dodge, Pettit, & Bates, 1994; McLoyd, Jayaratne, Ceballo, & Borquez, 1994).

Brooks-Gunn and Duncan (1997), using data from large-scale, national, cross-sectional databases, provided a comprehensive analysis of the links between family income and child outcomes. The data sets analyzed included the Panel Study of Income Dynamics (PSID), the National Longitudinal Survey of Youth (NLSY), Children of the NLSY, National

Survey of Families and Households (NSFH), the National Health and Nutrition Examination Survey (NHANES), and the Infant Health and Development Program (IHDP). Outcomes were examined in the areas of physical health (low birth weight, growth stunting, lead poisoning), cognitive ability, school achievement, emotional and behavioral outcomes, and teenage out-of-wedlock childbearing.

Brooks-Gunn and Duncan (1997) noted that different indicators of risk or well-being were found at different periods in the child's life (e.g., birth to 2 years, early childhood from ages 3 to 6, late childhood from ages 7 to 10, early adolescence from ages 11 to 15, late adolescence from ages 16 to 19). With respect to physical health, their analyses revealed that poorer children were less likely to be in excellent health. Children born to poor mothers also were more likely to be born at low birth weight, a factor itself associated with potential health, cognitive, and behavioral difficulties in future development. Furthermore, poor children were more likely to manifest growth stunting and experience lead poisoning.

With regard to cognitive abilities, Brooks-Gunn and Duncan (1997) noted that children living in poverty were 1.3 times more likely than children who were not poor to experience developmental delays and learning disabilities. In a related study using the NLSY and IHDP data sets, the poorer children scored lower on standardized tests of IQ, verbal ability, and achievement (Smith, Brooks-Gunn, & Klebanov, 1997). In that study, the effects of poverty were found at each of the ages tested between 2 and 8 years. Furthermore, duration of poverty was found to be a crucial variable. Children who lived in persistently poor families (i.e., families considered poor for more than 4 years) fared worse than those who were never poor, and they scored 6–9 points lower on cognitive assessments. It is also noteworthy that these negative effects appeared to grow stronger as the children got older (as demonstrated on the Peabody Picture Vocabulary Test-Revised [PPVT-R; Dunn & Dunn, 1981] measure for the IHDP sample). Effects of income also were shown as early as age 2 for the IHDP children. In addition, the severity or magnitude of poverty appeared to affect child outcome on cognitive measures. Children in the very poor group (family income below 50% of the poverty level) scored 7–12 points lower than children in the near poor group.

The effect of poverty was noted to have some relationship to school achievement in the older age groups as well (Brooks-Gunn & Duncan, 1997). Poverty was shown to exert a small but negative impact on graduation rates and years of schooling attained. An increase in family income in the early years was associated with more years of schooling completed, however.

Emotional and behavioral child outcomes were also analyzed (Brooks-Gunn & Duncan, 1997). Children who were poor were found to experience emotional and behavioral difficulties more frequently than children who were not poor. Both externalizing behaviors (e.g., aggression, fighting, acting out) and internalizing behaviors (e.g., anxiety, social withdrawal, depression) were studied. Again, results revealed that children growing up in persistent poverty were more likely to experience both externalizing and internalizing behavior problems than were children who had not grown up in persistent poverty (IHDP sample) (Duncan, Brooks-Gunn, & Klebanov, 1994). Children who experienced short-term poverty also demonstrated more behavior problems, but the effects were not as great as for those in persistent poverty. Though studies demonstrated a link between poverty and emotional outcomes, the effects of poverty were not as large in this area as for cognitive outcomes (Brooks-Gunn & Duncan, 1997). Other research studies have noted effects on social-emotional development and diminished adaptive functioning (e.g., relationships with peers, self-esteem, behavior problems, vulnerability to depression) for children living in poverty (McLoyd, 1990, 1997).

The Brooks-Gunn and Duncan (1997) analysis also examined the relationship of income to out-of-wedlock teenage births. Findings revealed that the timing and duration of poverty did not seem to exert an effect, although the rate of teen out-of-wedlock births was nearly three times higher for poor teens than for teens from nonpoor environments.

In research on poverty, it is difficult to ferret out the effects of income poverty from other interacting variables, such as timing of poverty and family structure. With respect to timing, these data (Smith, Brooks-Gunn, & Klebanov, 1997) did not reveal differences on cognitive indices. It must be noted that the time periods were short (within the early years), however, and also that these negative outcomes were apparent by the age of 2.

Brooks-Gunn and Duncan (1997) cited additional data that the timing of family income level affected a child's years of schooling completed. They found that family income levels in the child's early years (younger than age 5) were more strongly linked to number of school years completed than were family income levels when children were between the ages of 5–10 or between the ages of 11–15. They noted further that a $10,000 increase in mean family income between birth and 5 years was associated with an additional full year of school attained for children from low-income families.

The Effect of Family Structure on Income Levels

The impact of family structure as it relates to family income levels and child developmental outcomes has been of interest, as well. Understanding the effect of different family structures and family shifts in response to changing societal programs (e.g., welfare reform) and values is complex. Research suggests that the family structure does make a difference, however, and that growing up in families characterized by disruption does produce negative developmental consequences (McLanahan, 1997).

In the study by Smith and colleagues (1997), family structure did not influence outcomes for either of the two samples across ages when income levels were controlled. In the NLSY sample, however, when income level was *not* considered, the situation of living in a female-headed household and the introduction of another new parent into the family were both associated with lower verbal ability scores for young children. According to a 1994 study by Booth and Dunn, these findings are in accord with others, suggesting that remarriage or first marriage for a never-married mother may bring stresses. Though surveys indicate that the number of single-parent households has declined in recent years, troubling new reports indicate that more children (particularly African American children in cities) are living in households with no parent (e.g., living with relatives, friends, or foster families) ("More Kids Living with No Parent," 2002).

ECONOMIC WELL-BEING AND FAMILY VARIABLES

Economic hardship also has been associated with effects on family variables—parenting behavior, parental and family functioning, marital relationships, and family processes (Brody et al., 1994; McLoyd, 1990). One study, for instance, was conducted on a large sample of families in the rural Midwest in a region that was characterized by economic difficulty. In this research, economic stress was linked to marital and family conflict and conflicts between parents and their adolescent children (Conger, Ge, Elder, Lorenz, & Simons, 1994). Other research has expanded knowledge of the relation between economic hardship and family and child functioning to include more diverse samples. For example, one study examined this phenomenon with an ethnically diverse, low-income sample of children who were African American and Hispanic and who lived in families headed primarily by single mothers (Mistry, Vandewater, Huston, & McLoyd, 2002). Results of this research confirmed that economic stress affected parenting behavior due to adverse effects on parental psychological well-being. Parents reported feeling less effective or capable in child disciplinary situations and were observed to be less affectionate in parent–child interactions. These less-optimal parenting practices were associated with higher ratings of behavior problems for children and lower teacher ratings for positive child social behavior. Thus, a family economic stress model was used to understand the impact of poverty on families and children. Though economic hardship has been strongly associated with family stress, variables such as family ethnicity, work history, geographical location and density (urban versus rural), and community and personal resources may play crucial roles in determining how families actually respond to economic distress (McLoyd, 1990). Bottom line, however, living in poverty does challenge the abilities of families and parents to support and care for themselves and their children (McLoyd, 1990).

Pathways or Mechanisms of Influence

As is evident from the research reviewed, living in poverty can exert powerful negative influences on family functioning and children's developmental outcomes. Of interest are the "pathways" or "mechanisms" whereby income levels influence child outcomes (Brooks-Gunn & Duncan, 1997). These researchers discussed five potential pathways: 1) health and nutrition, 2) home environment, 3) parental interactions with children,

4) parental mental health, and 5) neighborhood conditions. Each is briefly considered and implications for practice are presented at a later point in this chapter.

Poor health can result from living under adverse economic conditions. Health concerns also can serve as a pathway through which other child outcomes are affected. For instance, low birth weight and increased levels of lead in the blood in young children are both associated with deleterious consequences such as lower scores of cognitive ability in later years. Recurrent ear infections and consequent hearing loss have also been associated with lower IQ scores for children regardless of family's income level. Goldstein (1990) suggested that low birth weight, lead, anemia, and recurrent ear infections may have accounted for up to 13%–20% of the difference in IQ scores between 4-years-olds in families considered both "poor" and "nonpoor" who participated in the study. Malnutrition, too, has been associated with depressed scores on measures of cognitive ability in children.

Studies also have revealed links between adverse child outcomes for children living in poverty and measures of home environment. Typically, researchers have utilized the Home Observation of Measurement of the Environment (HOME) Inventory (Caldwell & Bradley, 1984) to study this phenomenon. The HOME scale assesses learning materials in the home, maternal warmth toward the child, and parent experiences with the child. An overview of the research in this area (Brooks-Gunn & Duncan, 1997) suggested that elements of the home environment accounted for a significant portion of the effect of income level on children's outcomes in cognitive ability. Studies have determined that approximately half of the effect of poverty level on children's IQ scores can be explained by its effect on learning experiences in the home (Bradley, 1995).

Moving beyond an examination of home environmental issues such as materials and activities, studies also have linked dimensions of parent–child interactions to child outcomes and poverty. As reviewed by Brooks-Gunn and Duncan (1997), parenting practices affect child achievement and adjustment. Some studies have suggested that in families living in poverty, parents may be more likely to use harsh punishment and display lower quality parent–child interactions. For example, a study on young children's mental health noted that children in poor homes were spanked more than those in nonpoor homes (McLeod & Shanahan, 1993).

Parental mental health is noted as another potential pathway through which poverty affects child outcomes (Brooks-Gunn & Duncan, 1997). Less favorable physical and mental health status is associated with poverty. In turn, parents experiencing conditions associated with poorer mental health, such as depression, are less likely to provide quality learning experiences for their children and to engage in optimal parent–child interactions.

Finally, poverty serves as a mechanism for potentially altering child outcomes in the way that it affects neighborhoods (Brooks-Gunn & Duncan, 1997). Certainly, neighborhood environments characterized by violence, crime, limited resources for enhancing child development (e.g., playgrounds, child care, school facilities), and the like may interfere with families' abilities to support one another and their children. Such factors are likely to be associated with adverse child outcomes. Though family effects may exert a more direct link to child outcomes, the neighborhood effects may indirectly contribute to child outcomes, particularly in the school-age years (Chase-Landale, Gordon, Brooks-Gunn, & Klebanov, 1997). The research suggests that families are the key agents for child outcomes, but neighborhood circumstances may play an increasing role on children's outcomes as they age, when children venture out of the home during school age and beyond (Brooks-Gunn, Duncan, & Aber, 1997a).

EXAMINING RISKS AND SUPPORTS THROUGH TRANSACTIONAL AND ECOLOGICAL MODELS

Scientific inquiry is shifting from "asking *whether* family resources affect child development to asking *why* research shows so consistently that they do" (Shonkoff & Phillips, 2000, p. 267). As such, the impact of poverty on children and families is perhaps best examined and understood through transactional and ecological models that underscore the importance of the child's and family's interactions with the larger world. These models provide a structure through which the complex array of factors and circumstances associated with living under economic hardship can be viewed and the interplay between characteristics of children/families and the environments in which they live can be better understood. The previous discussion of mediators or pathways suggests the importance of this dynamic, transactional process.

Schorr painted a portrait of how a myriad of factors—all influenced by poverty—can place development in jeopardy:

> The child in a poor family who is malnourished and living in an unheated apartment is more susceptible to ear infection; once the ear infection takes hold, inaccessible or inattentive health care may mean it will not be properly treated; hearing loss in the midst of economic stress may go undetected at home, in day care, and by the health system; undetected hearing loss will do long-term damage to a child who needs all the help he can to cope with a world more complicated than the world of most middle-class children. When this child enters school, his chances of being in an overcrowded classroom with an overwhelmed teacher further compromise his chances of successful learning. Thus, risk factors join to shorten the odds of favorable long-term outcomes. (1988, p. 30)

As this scenario so vividly portrays, children and families living in poverty face increased risks for poor developmental outcomes. These risk factors interact with one another to transform the developmental possibilities for individuals. Mediating factors help to illuminate how poverty is related to adverse developmental outcomes and also how protective factors can serve to support the well-being of children and families.

Reconsider for a moment the transactional model described in Chapter 2. This model explains the outcomes in the previous example. It illustrates how environmental factors (e.g., malnutrition, substandard living conditions) can lead to negative developmental consequences for the child (e.g., developmental delay caused by loss of hearing from ear infection). These consequences, in turn, transform the child's development and lead to other outcomes (child's hearing loss, child's inability to benefit from school activities and lessons, other health concerns). These factors produce a transaction: The child's development is negatively affected or transformed such that the child is less likely to be able to interact with or benefit from aspects of the environment. Furthermore, other characteristics of the child's environment (e.g., overcrowded schools, poor or inappropriate teaching methods, inadequate or inappropriate health care, lack of diagnostic and intervention services) can also exacerbate the negative consequences to the child. From this simple example, one can witness that the child whose development is already at risk is placed in an environment that is less likely to benefit, or structure the child's learning. The result is a negative spiral of repercussions. The transactional model, therefore, helps shed light on the mechanisms or pathways through which impoverishing conditions can act to influence child and family functioning and developmental outcomes.

The number and types of risks faced by children and families also influence these risks' total impact on development and functioning. The developmental and health status of the infant and quality of the home environment interact with family economic circumstances (Sameroff, 1983; Sameroff, Seifer, Barocas, Zax, & Greenspan, 1987). These studies have concluded that children born into families who are not poor typically fare better than do those born into impoverishment even when their biologic or health status is more compromised. Those children born at biologic risk (e.g., prematurity, low birth weight) and also born into poverty potentially face a "double hazard" or "double jeopardy" for even poorer developmental outcomes (Escalona, 1982; Parker, Greer, & Zuckerman, 1988).

A common saying is often true: The rich get richer and the poor get poorer. This quip reflects the chronic nature and devastating effects of poverty. Indeed, families often are said to live in a cycle of poverty. This cycle of poverty will likely continue and intensify if children and families are not supported to escape its effects. Given the magnitude and range of negative effects on children and families associated with poverty, research and policy efforts have been directed toward identifying these needed supports.

Several research studies provide clues for supportive interventions that minimize potential deleterious outcomes for children and families living in poverty. For instance, research demonstrated that the developmental outcomes of premature, low birth weight (LBW) children living in poverty were linked to the quality of their caregiving environment (Bradley et al., 1994). Children whose outcomes were more favorable received caregiving that was more responsive, accepting, organized, and stimulating than did children with less optimal developmental profiles. Though the majority of LBW infants in this sample who were born into poverty conditions had poor developmental prognoses, several factors appeared to offset the potential for harm. The dimensions of the caregiving environments that appeared to serve as protective factors included parental responsivity, acceptance of the child's behavior, variety of stimulation, availability of toys and materials, and adequate space for privacy and exploration. Thus, some of the same pathways or mechanisms that conspire to produce negative repercussions also can lead to more positive outcomes.

These pathways or mechanisms occur at all level of families' ecological contexts. Using the terminology proposed by Bronfenbrenner (1979) (reviewed in Chapter 2), these contexts and potential areas of support and intervention are examined. At the *microsystem* level of the child and family within the home environment, characteristics of children and/or parents that may add stress include biologic risk conditions of a child at birth, disability, and chronic illness, to name a few. Parental issues also may contribute positively to the child and family's functioning. These variables include parental mental health and sensitivity, coping strategies, parent–child interaction styles and techniques (e.g., positive disciplinary techniques, provision of learning activities and stimulation, responsivity), appropriate parental expectations, and marital and family functioning. At the *mesosystem* level are the influences of the neighborhood, child care resources, schools, health care facilities, houses of worship, and other community agencies charged with providing direct services to families. These formal and informal institutions are activated based on the family's desire and ability to gain support and resources from them. Government and community agencies (health, educational, social service, employment, housing, and so forth) and other legislative and regulatory networks are considered *exosystem* contexts that influence children and families through the policies and programs that they provide and the priorities that they establish. Finally, at the most global or *macrosystem* level are societal attitudes and values regarding poverty, different ethnic and/or racial groups, families lifestyles and structures, and the impact of these cultural and societal values on the institutions that more directly influence children and families. A review of each of these levels of the ecological context for families reveals a potential intervention point to support individual children and their families living in poverty.

SUPPORT FOR CHILDREN AND FAMILIES LIVING IN POVERTY

What can be done to prevent, ameliorate, and/or counteract the effects of poverty? It is beyond the scope of this text to consider or debate the myriad of government and community programs that have been attempted in an effort to prevent or overcome poverty within this country. Politicians and policy makers will continue to debate appropriate interventions to

mitigate the effects of poverty, including education and employment programs, wage increases, food programs, supplements aimed at nutrition, health care, housing subsidies, child care, and early education programs (Devaney, Ellwood, & Love, 1997). Some families have long historical roots in poverty that extend generation after generation, living in neighborhoods characterized by economic distress and hopelessness, lack of education or opportunities to advance, and lack of access to the systems and services to pull themselves up. Other children and families have been thrust into poverty suddenly by a parent's loss of employment or reduction in earning, the loss of a parent, and/or a change in family structure. For some families, helping members to earn more and receive supplements to earned income (e.g., child support payments/contributions from absent parents) can reduce poverty (Plotnick, 1997). But for many, the complexity of their life circumstances requires radical shifts to change their economic fate.

At times, it is overwhelming to contemplate where to begin to support children and families who face the effects of poverty every hour of every day. What, for instance, can education, health care, and social service personnel do as professionals and as individuals to assist these children and families as they face their economic hardships? Although there are no simple solutions, avenues of hope and intervention are available through activating and supporting families and informal support networks, and through relationship-based professional commitments of the helping services.

Characteristics of interventions that are likely to be supportive for families who live in poverty include helping parents and other family members to feel more efficacious in their abilities to teach and care for their children, develop self-esteem, become more responsive caregivers, respond with warmth and affection to their children, provide stimulating learning opportunities and activities in the home, acquire appropriate developmental and behavioral expectations for their children, and foster harmonious family relationships. These interventions likely will facilitate secure attachments between parents/caregivers and children, build self-esteem for both, and enhance adult–child relationships and interactions. McLoyd (1997) further noted that emotional support for families and policies that help families to overcome concrete problems will often go a long way toward alleviating the stresses associated with poverty and the resulting mental health issues of depression, punitive parenting style, and psychological distress.

A re-examination of the circumstances faced by the five families introduced at the outset of this chapter illustrates some types of support for families living in poverty. Mary Anne, the mother of 4-year-old Cecilee, for example, feels fortunate to live near her family who gives her emotional and physical support in caring for her daughter. Her spiritual faith and the friendship and support of people at her church are important to her, as well. Mary Anne and Cecilee also benefit from the more formal supports found in the Head Start program, the local special education system, and medical specialists with whom they work. Mary Anne is also seeking child care so that she can return to work to earn a living.

Ge's family members, likewise, rely on each other and on the emotional and financial support of close family, their farm community, and the community of Laotians that live nearby to help them through their hard times.

The story of Lamont and his mother, Jonalene, elucidates the importance of health care and early intervention community services. The availability of these services literally saved Lamont's life when he was ill and provided the needed education and health services to address his developmental and health needs. This family also depends on formal supports such as shelter, health care, and food to help them exist until Jonalene can find a job and gain economic independence for her family.

The support of close family and community is evident in the fourth and fifth families, as well. Arely relies on her sister's family and her church, and Floyd and Nancy look to their neighbors and family for loans and work opportunities. Each family also benefits from the resources offered through local schools, social services, and health care facilities.

Service providers cannot possibly give families the monetary support and resources that they need to move beyond life in impoverished conditions. Practitioners can support these families by acknowledging and encouraging families to use their informal resources and sources of support, however, such as kinship, friendship, cultural/linguistic, and faith-based communities.

Acknowledging the competence that families bring to addressing their own needs only facilitates their abilities to care for themselves. When more formal interventions or services are needed, professionals can assist families to obtain information about what is available and how to gain access to the services. Once these resources are identified, professionals can help families navigate the service maze in order to receive the services they need. Providing referrals and assistance in obtaining housing, food stamps, job programs, quality child care, mental health services, and services in the family's primary language can be invaluable to these families. Though poverty presents daily challenges and remains a heavy burden for most of these families, supportive practitioners can help lighten that load.

SUMMARY

Family income level can exert a profound and substantial influence on the development and well-being of children and families. Indeed, the landscape of opportunity for children and families is transformed by economic hardship. Evidence suggests, in fact, that family income may be one of the most powerful influences on children early in their lives (Duncan, Yeung, Brooks-Gunn, & Smith, 1998). The impact of poverty is not universal or evenly distributed demographically, though it does touch all races, ethnicities, ages, and geographical regions. Rather, the effects of poverty are disproportionately experienced by certain groups such as young children; children living in single-parent families; and children who are African American, American Indian/Alaska Native, and Latino. In his book, *The Souls of Black Folk* (1903), author W.E.B. Du Bois underscored the disparity experienced by these families in a land of plenty: "To be a poor man is hard, but to be a poor race in a land of dollars is the very bottom of hardships" (as cited in Tripp, 1970).

The ways in which poverty exacts its toll are becoming better understood. Poverty is linked more clearly with some adverse consequences than with others, particularly with children's cognitive and achievement outcomes. The duration of poverty also is crucial. Living in persistent, long-term poverty likely has more devastating consequences than experiencing poverty for shorter periods of time. The degree or severity of economic hardship also is a factor in that the more adverse the conditions, the more negative the consequences an individual experiences. Timing, too, may play a role, with the experience of poverty in the earliest years having a larger impact than during adolescence or later years. Children experiencing poverty early on and living in extreme poverty for a long period of time are likely to suffer the worst outcomes.

Children who are born at risk or who have disabilities and who also are born into families living in poverty are considered at "double jeopardy." The interaction of biologic factors with the myriad of environmental factors associated with living in impoverished conditions multiplies the risk for adverse outcomes.

Access to health care, social services, quality affordable child care, quality educational programs, and disability services as needed are of critical importance to families living under conditions of economic distress. Typically, the complexities of the risks these children's and families' life situations pose necessitate these services even more. Interventions must also center on fostering conditions that offer families the opportunity to live in neighborhoods that are safe from violence and crime and that are free from racial/ethnic/religious discrimination. These goals are more likely to be achieved by strengthening neighborhood infrastructures and encouraging the participation and input of those that live there (Brooks-Gunn, Duncan, & Aber, 1997a, 1997b).

Prevention and reduction in poverty are critical investments for this nation. According to the National Center for Children in Poverty (2003), a reduction in childhood poverty would mean profound advantages in almost every area of life:

- Children would enter the schools better able to learn.
- Schools would be more successful.
- Children would have better health, placing less stress on health care systems.
- Less strain would be placed on the juvenile justice system.
- Child hunger and malnutrition would be reduced.

Though one of the richest nations in the world, the United States has a higher rate of poverty than most industrialized nations (Rainwater & Smeeding, 1995). The potential for pervasive and devastating consequences for children and families living in persistent poverty is great in our country. This fact alone beckons us all to renew our commitment to designing programs and policies to alleviate conditions that lead to poverty and to support families in sustaining themselves under troubling circumstances.

Inscribed at the base of the Statue of Liberty in New York is the following poem:

> Give me your tired, your poor,
> Your huddled masses yearning to breathe free,
> The wretched refuse of your teeming shore.
> Send these, the homeless, tempest-tost to me:
> I lift my lamp beside the golden door.
> —Emma Lazarus, "The New Colossus," 1883

This poem pays tribute to the United States as the haven of the oppressed and gateway to opportunity. May we continue to work to make it so.

ACTIVITIES TO EXTEND THE DISCUSSION

1. **Put yourself in their place.** Imagine that you live in a family of three and that your family's total annual income is under $14,000. What adaptations would your family have to make? What priorities would you choose? How would you make these choices? What types of support and services would you seek?

2. **Think of the impact.** Think of one of the families with whom you work that you know to be struggling with poverty. How has their economic hardship had an impact on their family? When you discuss the family's issues, be sure to change the family members' names and identifying characteristics to ensure confidentiality.

3. **Draw an "ecological map."** For the family you described in Activity 2, draw an ecological map. What specific elements of their lives are affected by their economic struggles at each level of the ecological framework?

4. **Dare to dream.** Consider again the family that you described in Activity 2. If you could activate any possible services and resources for them, what would those services and supports be?

REFERENCES

Bank, L., Forgatch, M.S., Patterson, G.R., & Fetrow, R.A. (1993). Parenting practices of single mothers: Mediators of negative contextual factors. *Journal of Marriage and Family, 55*, 371–384.

Belle, D. (1990). Poverty and women's mental health. *American Psychologist, 45*(3), 385–389.

Birenbaum, A. (2002). Poverty, welfare reform, and disproportionate rates of disability among children. *Mental Retardation, 40*, 212–218.

Booth, A., & Dunn, J. (1994). *Stepfamilies: Who benefits? Who does not?* Mahwah, NJ: Lawrence Erlbaum Associates.

Bradley, R.H. (1995). Environment and parenting. In M. Bornstein (Ed.), *Handbook of parenting* (pp. 235–261). Mahwah, NJ: Lawrence Erlbaum Associates.

Bradley, R.H., Whiteside, L., Mundfrom, D.J., Casey, P.H., Kelleher, K.J., & Pope, S.K. (1994). Early indications of resilience and their relation to experiences in the home environments of low birthweight, premature children living in poverty. *Child Development, 65*, 346–360.

Brody, G.H., Stoneman, Z., Flor, D., McCrary, C., Hastings, L., & Conyers, O. (1994). Financial resources, parent psychological functioning, parent co-caregiving, and early adolescent competence in rural two-parent African-American families. *Child Development, 65*, 590–605.

Bronfenbrenner, U. (1979). *The ecology of human development: Experiments by nature and design.* Cambridge, MA: Harvard University Press.

Brooks-Gunn, J., & Duncan, G.J. (1997). The effects of poverty on children. *The Future of Children: Children and Poverty, 7*(2), 55–71.

Brooks-Gunn, J., Duncan, G.J., & Aber, J.L. (Eds.). (1997a). *Neighborhood poverty: Vol. I. Context and consequences for children.* New York: Russell Sage Foundation.

Brooks-Gunn, J., Duncan, G.J., & Aber, J.L. (Eds.). (1997b). *Neighborhood poverty: Vol. II. Policy implications in studying neighborhoods.* New York: Russell Sage Foundation.

Brooks-Gunn, J., Duncan, G.J., & Maritato, N. (1997). Poor families, poor outcomes: The well-being of children and youth. In G.J. Duncan & J. Brooks-Gunn (Eds.), *Consequences of growing up poor* (pp. 1–17). New York: Russell Sage Foundation.

Brooks-Gunn, J., Klebanov, P., Liaw, F., & Duncan, G.J. (1995). Toward an understanding of the effects of poverty upon children. In H.E. Fitzgerald, B.M. Lester, & B. Zuckerman (Eds.), *Children of poverty: Research, health, and policy issues.* New York: Garland Publishing.

Brown, L., & Pollitt, E. (1996). Malnutrition, poverty and intellectual development. *Scientific American, 274*(2), 38–43.

Burchinal, M., Lee, M., & Ramey, C. (1989). Type of day care and preschool intellectual development in disadvantaged children. *Child Development, 60*(1), 128–137.

Caldwell, B., & Bradley, R.H. (1984). *Home observation for measurement of the environment.* Little Rock: University of Arkansas, Center for Research on Teaching and Learning.

Chase-Landale, P.L., Gordon, R.A., Brooks-Gunn, J., & Klebanov, P.K. (1997). Neighborhood and family influences on the intellectual and behavioral competence of preschool and early school-age children. In J. Brooks-Gunn, G.J. Duncan, & J.L. Aber (Eds.), *Neighborhood poverty: Vol. I. Context and consequences for children* (pp. 79–118). New York: Russell Sage Foundation.

Conger, R.D., Ge, X., Elder, G.H., Lorenz, F.O., & Simons, R.L. (1994). Economic stress, coercive family process, and developmental problems of adolescents. *Child Development, 65*, 541–561.

Cost, Quality and Child Outcomes Study Team et al. (1995). *Cost, quality, and child outcomes in child care centers.* Denver: University of Colorado at Denver, Department of Economics.

Dalaker, J. (2001). *Poverty in the United States: 2000. Current population reports: Consumer income.* Washington, DC: U.S. Census Bureau, U.S. Department of Commerce.

Devaney, B.L., Ellwood, M.R., & Love, J.M. (1997). *The future of children: Children and poverty, 7*(2), 88–112.

Dodge, K.A., Pettit, G.S., & Bates, J.E. (1994). Socialization mediators of the relation between socioeconomic status and child conduct problems. *Child Development, 65*, 649–665.

Duncan, G.J., & Brooks-Gunn, J. (Eds.). (1997). *Consequences of growing up poor.* New York: Russell Sage Foundation.

Duncan, G.J., Brooks-Gunn, J., & Klebanov, P.K. (1994). Economic deprivation and early childhood development. *Child Development, 65,* 296–318.

Duncan, G.J., Yeung, W.J., Brooks-Gunn, J., & Smith, J. (1998). *American Sociological Review, 63*(3), 406–423.

Dunn, L.M., & Dunn, L.M. (1981). *Peabody Picture Vocabulary Test–Revised.* Circle Pines, MN: American Guidance Service.

Escalona, S.K. (1982). Babies at double hazard: Early development of infants at biologic and social risk. *Pediatrics, 70,* 670–676.

Emerson, R.W. (1860, 1876). Wealth. In *The conduct of life.*

Fisher, G.M. (1992). *The development of the Orshansky thresholds and their subsequent history as the official U.S. poverty measure.* Retrieved June 2003, from www.census.gov/hhes/poverty/povmeas/papers/orshansky.html

Fujiura, G.T., & Yamaki, K. (2000). Trends in demography of childhood poverty and disability. *Exceptional Children, 66*(2), 187–199.

Goldstein, N. (1990). *Explaining socioeconomic difference in children's cognitive test scores.* Working Paper No. H-90-1. Cambridge, MA: Malcolm Wiener Center for Social Policy, John F. Kennedy School of Government, Harvard University.

Hernandez, D.J. (1997). Poverty trends. In G.J. Duncan & J. Brooks-Gunn (Eds.), *Consequences of growing up poor* (pp. 18–34). New York: Russell Sage Foundation.

Hurston, Z.N. (1996, originally published in 1942). *Dust tracks on a road.* New York: HarperPerennial.

Huston, A.C. (1991). *Children in poverty: Child development and public policy.* New York: Cambridge University Press.

Huston, A.C., McLoyd, V.C., & Garcia Coll, C. (1994). Children and poverty: Issues in contemporary research. *Child Development, 65,* 275–282.

Lee, S., Sills, M., & Oh, G.T. (2002). *Disabilities among children and mothers in low-income families.* Research-in-Brief. Washington DC: Institute for Women's Policy Research. Available at: http://www.iwpr.org/pdf/d449.pdf

Loprest, P., & Acs, G. (1996). *Profile of disability among families on AFDC.* Washington, DC: The Urban Institute.

Mayes, L. (1996). *Early experience and the developing brain: The model of prenatal cocaine exposure.* Paper presented at the invitational conference, Brain Development in Young Children: New Frontiers for Research, Policy, and Practice, The University of Chicago, June 12–14.

McLanahan, S.S. (1997). Parent absence or poverty: Which matters more? In G.J. Duncan & J. Brooks-Gunn (Eds.), *Consequences of growing up poor* (pp. 35–48). New York: Russell Sage Foundation.

McLeod, J.D., & Shanahan, M.J. (1993). Poverty, parenting and children's mental health. *American Sociological Review, 58,* 351–366.

McLoyd, V.C. (1990). The impact of economic hardship on black families and children: Psychological distress, parenting, and socioemotional development. *Child Development, 61,* 311–346.

McLoyd, V.C. (1997). The impact of poverty and low socioeconomic status on the socioemotional functioning of African-American children and adolescents: Mediating effects. In R. Taylor & M. Wang (Eds.), *Social and emotional adjustment and family relations in ethnic minorities* (pp. 7–34). Mahwah, NJ: Lawrence Erlbaum Associates.

McLoyd, V.C. (1998a). Children in poverty: Development, public policy, and practice. In I.E. Sigel & K.A. Renninger (Eds.), *Handbook of child psychology: Vol. 4. Child psychology in practice* (5th ed., pp. 135–208). New York: John Wiley & Sons.

McLoyd, V.C. (1998b). Socioeconomic disadvantage and child development. *American Psychologist, 53,* 185–204.

McLoyd, V., Jayaratne, T.E., Ceballo, R., & Borquez, J. (1994). Unemployment and work interruption among African American single mothers: Effects on parenting and adolescent socioemotional functioning. *Child Development, 65,* 562–589.

Meyers, M.K., Lukemeyer, A., & Smeeding, T.M. (1996). *Work, welfare, and the burden of disability: Caring for special needs of children in poor families, Income Security Policy Series, Paper No. 12.* Syracuse, NY: Center for Policy Research, Maxwell School of Citizenship and Public Affairs, Syracuse University.

Mistry, R.S., Vandewater, E.A., Huston, A.C., & McLoyd, V.C. (2002). Economic well-being and children's social adjustment: The role of family process in an ethnically diverse low-income sample. *Child Development, 73,* 935–951.

More kids living with no parent. (2002, July 29). *San Jose Mercury News,* p. A4.

National Center for Children in Poverty (1997, April). *Poverty and brain development in early childhood*. Retrieved June 2003, from http://cpmcnet.columbia.edu/dept/nccp/brain.html

National Center for Children in Poverty (2002). *Early childhood poverty: A statistical profile*. Retrieved March 2002, from http://cpmcnet.columbia.edu/dept/nccp/ecp302.html

National Center for Children in Poverty. (2003, March). *Low-income children in the United States: A brief demographic profile*. Retrieved from http://cpmcnet.columbia.edu/dept/nccp/ecp302.html

The National Health/Education Consortium. (1991, January). Healthy brain development. *The National Health/Education Consortium Report*, 4–5.

Parker, S., Greer, S., & Zuckerman, B. (1988). Double jeopardy: The impact of poverty on early childhood development. *Pediatric Clinics of North America, 35*, 1127–1241.

Plotnick, R.D. (1997). Child poverty can be reduced. *The future of children: Children and poverty, 7*(2), 72–87.

Rainwater, L., & Smeeding, T. (1995, August). *Doing poorly: The real income of American children in a comparative perspective. Luxembourg Income Study Working Paper No. 127*. Syracuse, NY: Maxwell School of Citizenship and Public Affairs, Syracuse University.

Rosman, E.A., & Knitzer, J. (2001). Welfare reform: The special case of young children with disabilities and their families. *Infants and Young Children, 13*(3), 25–35.

Sameroff, A. (1983). Developmental systems: Context and evolution. In P.H. Mussen (Series Ed.) & W. Kessen (Vol. Ed.), *Handbook of child psychology: Vol. 1. History, theory and methods* (pp. 238–294). New York: John Wiley & Sons.

Sameroff, A., Seifer, R., Barocas, R., Zax, M., & Greenspan, S. (1987). Intelligence quotient scores of 4-year-old children: Social-environmental risk factors. *Pediatrics, 79*, 343–350.

Sampson, R.J., & Laub, J.H. (1994). Urban poverty and the family context of delinquency: A new look at structure and process in a classic study. *Child Development, 65*, 523–540.

Schorr, L. (1988). *Within our reach: Breaking the cycle of disadvantage*. New York: Anchor Books/Doubleday.

Shonkoff, J.P., & Phillips, D.A. (Eds.). (2000). *From neurons to neighborhoods: The science of early childhood development*. Washington, DC: National Academy Press.

Shore, R. (1997). *Rethinking the brain: New insights into early development*. New York: Families and Work Institute.

Smith, J.R., Brooks-Gunn, J., & Klebanov, P. (1997). Consequences of living in poverty for young children's cognitive and verbal ability and early school achievement. In G.J. Duncan & J. Brooks-Gunn (Eds.), *Consequences of growing up poor* (pp. 132–189). New York: Russell Sage Foundation.

Tripp, R.T. (1970). *The international thesaurus of quotations*. New York: Thomas Y. Crowell, Publishers.

CHAPTER 6

ADDICTION AND VIOLENCE IN THE HOME

Family Life at Risk

"Life is neither a good nor an evil; it is the scene of good and evil."
—SENECA (AS CITED IN GARDNER & REESE, 1975, p. 107)

Sadly, the home is not always a sanctuary, but a place of fear.
—JO BOYDEN (1993)

Addiction and violence fill headlines and prisons; they break up families and break hearts. They are concerns that touch the entire population—male and female, children and adults, rich and poor, urban and rural. Like many other risk factors, the negative effects of addiction and violence fall disproportionately on groups with limited resources and often on populations of people of color. Their impact on families is profound in economic, social, and medical terms, and their relationship to disability and risks in child development is becoming increasingly clear.

Research, statistics, and recommendations related to addiction and violence abound. The indicators and the outcomes are clear, but as a nation we have not been successful in developing comprehensive prevention and intervention efforts that can break the cycle of negative effects. Addiction and violence put the lives of families and family members at extreme risk. Recall, for example, the family systems framework described in Chapters 2 and 3. Consider the ways in which drug addiction, violence, and abuse affect the system. What might they do to communication within and outside the family? How would they affect the functions that families are expected to perform? In what ways might the family life cycle be altered by violence or addiction?

This chapter discusses addiction, family violence, child abuse, and neglect. It describes their impact on families and highlights promising prevention and intervention practices. The information is detailed, and it is often disheartening. For service providers who are skilled at seeing the brighter side of difficult situations, it may even be difficult to consider. This information is provided, however, because most service providers, no matter where they work, will be exposed to the consequences of addiction and violence in families with whom they work, among their acquaintances, or within their own families. Addiction and its consequences transcend the stereotypes of the popular press. They are a part of the richest and the poorest communities (Arthur & Gerken, 1998). If professionals are to provide support to families who face the challenges of addiction and abuse, service providers must have information and knowledge of the problems and solutions.

Berkow, Beers, and Fletcher defined addiction as "the compulsive activity and overwhelming involvement with a specific activity" (1997, p. 440). Addiction may be physical, psychological, or a combination of both. Drugs or activities that do not cause *physical* dependence may cause *psychological* dependence, the desire to continue to take the drug or engage in the activity because of its pleasurable effects or the reduction in tension and anxiety that occur (Berkow et al., 1997). Physical dependence occurs when the body adapts to the drug and requires the drug to function comfortably. Drugs that cause physical dependence range from illicit drugs such as heroin to common prescription drugs for blood pressure and even laxatives (Berkow et al., 1997).

In this chapter, addiction and substance abuse are used interchangeably to refer to an individual's overwhelming involvement with a drug or other activity—involvement that interferes with daily life, the ability to make sound judgments, and to care adequately for oneself and others. Substance abuse involving alcohol, nicotine, cocaine, marijuana, heroin, and prescription drugs falls into this category, as do gambling and some sexual behavior. Addictive behaviors pose serious risks to families because they become all consuming, more important than anything else in the addict's life.

Addictions to and abuse of drugs, both legal and illegal, also pose significant health threats. For example, needle sharing in intravenous drug use is associated with HIV/AIDS; long-term alcoholism among women may lead to significant birth defects in their babies; nicotine addiction is a major cause of emphysema and lung cancer; and amphetamine abuse results in increased blood pressure and heart rate, which may lead to heart attacks (Berkow et al., 1997). The need to obtain drugs or engage in addictive activity often results in criminal behaviors. In 1997, 19% of state prisoners and 16% of federal inmates reported that they had committed the offense for which they were serving time to obtain money for drugs; and in the 1997 Survey of Inmates in State and Federal Correctional Facilities, 33% of state and 22% of federal inmates reported that they had committed the offense for which they were currently serving time while under the influence of drugs (U.S. Department of Justice, Bureau of Juvenile Statistics, 2000). Crimes against property are not the only offenses associated with drug use and abuse. In 2000, approximately 4% of the homicides in the United States in which the circumstances were known were drug related (U.S. Department of Justice, Bureau of Juvenile Statistics, 2000). According to the data presented in multiple studies of drug use, arrests, and convictions, drug users are more likely to commit crimes than non-users (Spiess & Fallow, 2000).

Finally, when addiction becomes all consuming or substance abuse becomes pervasive, addicts and abusers are unable to put the needs of others above their own. They become unavailable to others psychologically and physically, and parenting or partnering in a relationship becomes secondary. The negative outcomes are clearly articulated by the U.S. Department of Health and Human Services:

> *Alcohol and illicit drug use are associated with child and spousal abuse; sexually transmitted diseases, including HIV infection; teen pregnancy; school failure; motor vehicle crashes; escalation of health care costs; low worker productivity; and homelessness. Alcohol and illicit drug use also can result in substantial disruptions in family, work, and personal life. (2000, p. 9, http://www.healthypeople.gov)*

Working with families who are experiencing a problem with addiction is one of the most challenging tasks for service providers. For even the most family-centered practitioner, it is often difficult to consider the needs of all family members when it is clear that money needed for food, shelter, medical care, and clothing is being used to pay for an addiction. Recognizing that the adult with the addiction needs as much help as the other members of the family is not easy when that adult's behavior is so destructive. The service provider can make a positive difference, however, by sharing his or her knowledge of community resources, supporting family members who are struggling against difficult odds, and being aware of the laws related to reporting situations when children and other family members are endangered.

Violence in communities, neighborhoods, and homes also poses significant threats to families and children. Domestic violence, spousal abuse, and child abuse are especially devastating because the ability to protect children and other loved ones is foundational to all family functions. Chronic exposure to violence, abuse, and the extreme stress that results can lead to a deterioration of basic coping skills (Osofsky & Jackson, 1994)—making effective functioning impossible.

Violence is not an issue that can be viewed in isolation. It permeates society and is both a cause and an outcome of many of society's most intractable problems. As reported by The Violence Study Group sponsored by the organization ZERO TO THREE: National Center for Infants, Toddlers, and Families, "Family violence, community violence and societal violence are all on a similar continuum. They have an impact on each other and frequently affect the same individuals" (1993, p. 38). Nearly a third of the 2.9 million children reported to child protective services in 1998 as suspected victims of child abuse and neglect were confirmed to have been abused or neglected (Children's Defense Fund, 2001). Violence begets violence. One review of studies on child maltreatment and violence against women found that the overlap of violence against children and women in the same families was high (Edleson, 1999). Even when children in abusive families are not themselves abused, many witness violence. Data reported by the Children's Defense Fund (2000, 2001) suggested that between 3.3 million and 10 million children each year in the United

States witness violence against their mothers or in their homes. Not surprisingly, problems with drug and alcohol abuse are linked to family violence and neglect. In families in which parents abuse drugs and alcohol, children are three times more likely to be abused and four times more likely to be neglected than children whose parents do not abuse alcohol or other drugs (Children's Defense Fund, 2000).

What are the results of violence? Physical injury is a risk, of course. Approximately 20% of the 1,000,000 children who are physically abused each year in the United States are permanently injured; 1,200 die (Berkow et al., 1997). Separation from the family is another consequence of violence; children may be removed from their homes and placed in a foster care system that is already overburdened in many states. Children who are physically or sexually abused suffer serious psychological injury as well. They may be fearful, anxious, irritable, aggressive, and unable to form and sustain relationships (Berkow et al., 1997; Mrazek, 1993; Osofsky, 1994). Children who have been neglected may be distrustful, unassertive, and anxious to please adults. They may have limited language skills, and appear to have cognitive impairments (Berkow et al., 1997).

These characteristics in childhood do not predict positive outcomes in adulthood. Adults who experienced abuse or neglect as children or who witnessed violence in childhood may have difficulty forming relationships, and they may allow the patterns of abuse in their childhood to be repeated with their own children (McCloskey & Bailey, 2000). They may also exhibit behaviors in adulthood that may lead to serious, chronic conditions such as obesity, diabetes, depression, and psychological stress (Felitti, 1998).

Perhaps a universal wish for all children and families is that they feel safe and secure, that they are nurtured, and that they have trusting relationships. But this is not just wishful thinking. Safety and security, nurturance, and trusting relationships support the kinds of transactions among parents, infants, and young children that are considered to be optimal in child rearing (Sameroff & Chandler, 1975). In homes in which addiction, violence, and their often lethal combinations occur, risks abound. Marshalling the family's resilience and the protective factors that exist within each individual, family, and community (Mrazek, 1993) is one of the service provider's most difficult, but most important, jobs.

ADDICTION AND SUBSTANCE ABUSE

To assist families struggling with issues of addiction, service providers must have basic information about the way in which addiction is defined, types of addiction, and drugs that are common in addiction. This chapter does not attempt to suggest strategies that early interventionists can use to assist families in overcoming addiction. Rather, it focuses on information to increase awareness and understanding of the psychological, medical, and psychosocial risks that these families face. It is also presented to help interventionists explore and be prepared to call on substance abuse treatment resources within their community. Although the information may seem distant from the daily work of many service providers, it is likely that some day it will become important to understanding and working effectively with a family or, perhaps, a friend.

Definitions

As defined in the introduction to this chapter, an individual is addicted when he or she is compulsively and overwhelmingly involved with a specific activity (Berkow et al. 1997). Orford considered addiction to be a problem of excessive appetite for an activity or substance. In his definition he stated that in addiction, the appetite is "so strong that a person finds it difficult to moderate the activity despite the fact that it is causing harm" (2001, p. 4, electronic version). Although illegal drugs, alcohol, and nicotine typically come to mind when one thinks of addictions, any substance or activity that is excessive and difficult to moderate in spite of negative consequences is considered addictive. Eating, gambling, sexual behaviors, an exercise routine, Internet use, and prescription or over-the-counter drugs may be addictive if the individual is compulsively involved in them and finds it difficult to alter his or her behavior in spite of detrimental effects. Although Orford's model of addiction is controversial, it directly addresses the primary concern of this book—families and their resilience in the presence of risk. More refined definitions of addiction are based on the type of dependence that results.

Types of Addiction

Three types of addiction or dependence can be identified: psychological, physical, and a combination of psychological and physical. Activities such as gambling may become psychologically addicting. The atmosphere of excitement and the euphoria of a winning hand can be pleasurable and mood altering. In this situation, mathematical odds and the consequences of the behavior fade into the background and the obsession with gambling takes over. Certain drugs and substances have similar effects by acting on the brain to create pleasurable sensations, reduce tension and stress, produce a sense of enhanced physical or mental competence, or alter sensory perceptions (Berkow et al., 1997). Marijuana, cocaine, and volatile nitrites such as amyl nitrite (also called "poppers," "Locker Room," and "Rush") create psychological dependence but have not been proved to create physical dependence (Berkow et al., 1997; Merck Manual, 2002d, 2002e, 2002g).

Some drugs, such as heroin, sedatives, alcohol, and nicotine cause physical dependence (Merck Manual, 2002a, 2002c, 2002f). When one of these drugs is used continually, the body adapts to it, developing what is referred to as *tolerance*. Tolerance is defined as the need to continually increase the dosage to achieve the drug's initial effect (Berkow et al., 1997). When the drug use is stopped or blocked, withdrawal symptoms occur. Withdrawal symptoms may include sickness, headaches, paranoia, diarrhea, hallucinations, and tremors. In some instances symptoms may be life-threatening (Berkow et al., 1997).

Drugs such as heroin, sedatives, alcohol, and nicotine are both psychologically and physically addicting. In addition to the pleasurable effects and reduction in tension or stress, the body builds up a tolerance to the substance, requires more and more to achieve the same positive effects, and reacts with withdrawal symptoms when drug use is curtailed. Whether the dependence is psychological, physical, or a combination of the two, the effect on families is similar. Whenever a drug or an activity becomes an individual's highest priority, continues in spite of its negative consequences, and replaces healthy interactions, families are negatively affected.

Drugs of Choice in Addiction and Substance Abuse

The preceding paragraphs describe types of addiction in terms of their psychological and physical effects. To understand families' challenges related to addiction, it is important to know more about the most common types of substance abuse and addiction, the drugs that are used, and their effects. This section discusses four illegal drugs that are commonly abused and associated with visits to hospital emergency rooms. The section concludes with a discussion of two legal drugs, alcohol and nicotine, that profoundly affect family functioning and are positively correlated with disability in infants and young children.

In the year 2000, it was estimated that for every 100,000 people in the United States, 243 drug-related visits to emergency rooms occurred (Ducharme & Ball, 2001). Cocaine, heroin, marijuana, and amphetamines accounted for 35% of all drugs identified as causes for the visits. Data from this report also compare the drugs implicated in emergency room visits across 21 metropolitan areas, allowing for analysis of the differences in drug use in different areas of the country. For example, methamphetamine use that resulted in emergency room visits was almost exclusively confined to the West Coast; whereas, cocaine, heroin/morphine, and marijuana were more prevalent on the East Coast and in the Midwest.

Cocaine

Cocaine is a stimulant that can be taken orally, inhaled in powder form through the nose (snorted), injected into the bloodstream (mainlining), or smoked or injected after being boiled with other substances to convert it into its freebase form known as crack cocaine (Berkow et al., 1997; Merck Manual, 2002e; Office of National Drug Control Policy, 2002d). Freebasing, or inhaling the smoke from this combustible form, provides an intense high comparable to injecting the drug directly into the bloodstream. The high of cocaine is described as a feeling of extreme alertness, power, and euphoria (Berkow et al., 1997; Office of National Drug Control Policy, 2002d) that lasts for 5–20 minutes depending upon the form in which it was taken.

Cocaine users tend to be episodic, recreational users. Crack is most commonly used in low-income, urban communities (Merck Manual, 2002e). Compulsive use is more common among crack users than those who snort cocaine (Merck Manual, 2002e). Although street names for drugs change and sometimes vary from one region of the country to another, "blow" and "nose candy" are sometimes used when describing cocaine; "tornado" may be used to refer to crack (Office of National Drug Control Policy, 2002c).

Survey data suggests that slightly more than 11% of Americans older than age 12 have used cocaine at least once, and 0.5% or 1,213,000 were current users of cocaine in the year 2000 (Office of National Drug Control Policy, 2002c). Admissions for cocaine treatment in publicly funded treatment facilities has declined by 23% since 1993, with the decline attributed to a reduction in users rather than a reduction in the number of individuals seeking treatment (Drug and Alcohol Services Information System, 2002a; Office of National Drug Control Policy, 2002c).

Immediate medical treatment is seldom needed for cocaine because of the short-acting nature of the drug. In the case of an overdose or unanticipated medical emergency, however, other medications may be used to reduce an individual's heart rate, blood pressure, and fever, and medical personnel would carefully monitor the individual's condition (Merck Manual, 2002e). Counseling and psychotherapy are considered to be the best approaches to treating long-term cocaine addiction (Berkow et al., 1997). Support, self-help groups, and cocaine hotlines are also used to help addicts quit; however, the depression that typically results requires careful, professional supervision by psychiatrists, primary care physicians, or social workers as well as depression-treating drugs (Berkow et al., 1997).

Heroin

Heroin is an illegal drug processed from morphine, a naturally occurring opiate that is made from the seed pod of certain varieties of poppies (Office of National Drug Control Policy, 2002e). Legal opiates such as morphine, codeine, and others are used therapeutically in the treatment of severe pain. All are addictive, and an individual may develop tolerance and physical dependence within 2–3 days of taking regular doses of the drug (Merck Manual, 2002f). Though critical to pain management, legalized opiates are prescribed under strict guidelines and medical supervision. Although some individuals are addicted to therapeutically administered opiates, this section deals with heroin, the illegal form.

Heroin in its pure form is a bitter-tasting, white powder (Office of National Drug Control Policy, 2002e). When sold on the street, the color varies from white to dark brown to black depending on the impurities left during processing or the additives. The "rush" associated with heroin is most rapid and intense when the drug is injected intravenously—within 7–8 seconds, a feeling of euphoria may occur.

Heroin addiction used to call to mind an image of addicts injecting heroin directly into their veins in dilapidated buildings under very unsanitary conditions. Heroin use and methods are changing, however. Heroin use among young people of all socioeconomic groups is on the rise. Between 1996 and 1998, the number of users among 12- to 17-year-olds nearly doubled (Drug and Alcohol Services Information System, 2001b). The Youth Risk Behavior Surveillance System survey of 1999 reported that 2.4% of high school students surveyed had used heroin (Office of National Drug Policy, 2002e). Admissions to publicly funded treatment facilities for primary heroin addiction increased between 1993 and 1999 (Drug and Alcohol Services Information System, 2002b).

The increase in use is suspected to be because of the availability of high-quality, smokable heroin and young people's lack of knowledge about the adverse effects of heroin use. Described as "generational forgetting," new users may have seen or known of the negative effects of crack cocaine use but had no knowledge of or experience with long-term heroin users (Drug and Alcohol Services Information System, 2001b; Office of National Drug Control Policy, 2002a). As with other illicit drugs, the street names for heroin vary; however, the following are used in reference to heroin: "Big H," "crop" (for low-quality heroin), "hell dust," "smack," and "thunder" (Office of National Drug Control Policy, 2002e).

Heroin's effects are profound, and physical dependence takes hold soon after regular drug use begins. Initial feelings of euphoria are followed by periods of wakefulness and drowsiness that may last for several hours. Heroin's depressive effect on the central nervous system results in mental cloudiness and confusion, and breathing may slow to the point of respiratory failure (Office of National Drug Control Policy, 2002e). Long-term use has serious medical as well as social and economic consequences. Addicts may develop a wide range of serious health problems, and the consequences of shared needles may include HIV/AIDS and hepatitis.

Treatment for heroin addiction is complicated and is overseen by federal, state, and local regulations to which physicians must adhere. In most instances, referral to a specialized treatment center is the preferred approach (Merck Manual, 2002f). Withdrawal is typically managed by substituting methadone for heroin. A small, daily dose of methadone can significantly limit severe withdrawal symptoms, and weaning from methadone is accomplished by progressively reducing the dosage after the appropriate dose has been established (Merck Manual, 2002f). Therapeutic communities have also been established to treat long-term heroin users. These communities rely on training, redirection, and education to help addicts change the behaviors that led to their drug abuse and to build new lives. Programs of this kind require a long-term commitment, however—often 15 months—and dropout rates are extremely high in the early days and months of such programs (Merck Manual, 2002f).

Marijuana

Marijuana is a mixture of the stems, leaves, seeds, and flowers of the hemp plant (*Cannabis sativa*). Marijuana may be green to brown, shredded or whole, and look like a ground herb. A derivative of marijuana is used therapeutically to counter the nausea of chemotherapy, and "Cannabis Clubs" operate legally and illegally in some states to dispense marijuana to individuals with serious health problems and/or chronic pain. Like the information provided here on heroin usage, however, the following description deals with illegal usage.

Marijuana is usually smoked in cigarette form called a "joint," a cigar called a "blunt," in a pipe, or in a device called a bong—a water pipe in which the smoke passes through water, goes up a tube, and is inhaled. In ground, herb-like form it can be added to foods such as brownies or brewed into a tea. Marijuana, hashish, and other cannabis-derived drugs are psychoactive or mind-altering (Office of National Drug Control Policy, 2002f). The high experienced from smoking or ingesting marijuana is dreamlike in nature, and sensory experiences and perceptions are sometimes heightened (Berkow et al., 1997).

The use of marijuana in the United States is widespread, and it ranks as the most commonly used illicit drug (Merck Manual, 2002d; Office of National Drug Control Policy, 2002f). In the Youth Risk Behavior Surveillance System survey in 1999, nearly 27% of the ninth to twelfth graders surveyed reported that they were current users of marijuana, and nearly half (47.2%) had used marijuana at least once in their lifetime (Office of National Drug Control Policy, 2002f). Street names for marijuana are many. Examples include "grass," "pot," "weed," "Acapulco Gold," "kind bud," "ganja," "Maui Wowie," "locoweed," and "Mary Jane."

The health risks in smoking marijuana may include increased heart rate; anxiety; panic attacks; slower reaction time; and impaired memory, judgment, and learning. Long-term use may also negatively affect the respiratory system (Office of National Drug Control Policy, 2002f). Marijuana has been known to produce a toxic psychosis in which the user does not know who or where he or she is or what time it is; data also suggest that individuals with schizophrenia are much more susceptible to this sort of toxicity (Berkow et al., 1997).

Between 1994 and 2000, the number of visits to emergency rooms for marijuana use–related health conditions increased 141%, from just over 40,000 to nearly 100,000 (Office of National Drug Control Policy, 2002f). Those admitted to publicly funded treatment centers for marijuana use between 1993 and 1999 tended to be young (47% younger than 20 years old) male (77%), white (58%), and referred through the judicial process (57%) (Drug and Alcohol Services Information System, 2002c).

Acute withdrawal symptoms from marijuana use alone do not occur, because marijuana is released from the body over days and weeks. Treatment options to help users quit are similar to options for other drugs—behavioral interventions, self-help groups, counseling, and residential treatment.

Methamphetamines

Methamphetamine, usually called "speed," is a central nervous system stimulant that is usually taken in pill form; it can also be injected, snorted, or smoked (Office of National Drug Control Policy, 2002g). Other terms used to refer to methamphetamine include "meth," "chalk," "crank," "crystal meth," "glass," "ice," and "poor man's cocaine" (Office of National

Drug Control Policy, 2002g). Methamphetamines are highly addictive and can be manufactured easily and cheaply in clandestine "meth labs." Methamphetamines, like other amphetamines, produce a rapid, intense rush followed by increased energy, alertness, and activity; reduced appetite; and a sense of well-being or euphoria that can last 6–8 hours (Berkow et al., 1997). Amphetamines, a type of methamphetamine, were once prescribed as appetite suppressants, but their highly addictive nature and dangerous side effects have caused them to be withdrawn from approval. Long-haul truck drivers have been known to take amphetamines to stay awake, and athletes have used them to enhance performance (Berkow et al., 1997).

Methamphetamine use, originally concentrated in the Western and Southwestern states, has spread to most areas of the nation. In cities with the highest number of arrestees testing positive for methamphetamine (e.g., San Diego, California; Salt Lake City, Utah; Spokane, Washington; Portland, Oregon), more females than males tested positive at the time of arrest (Office of National Drug Control Policy, 2002g). Admissions for treatment of amphetamine abuse have risen in recent years (Drug and Alcohol Services Information System, 2001a).

Since the 1990s, another amphetamine has received considerable attention. MDMA, known on the street as E, X, Ecstasy, or Adam, is one of the drugs associated with "raves" (i.e., all-night dance parties) and after-hours clubs (Berkow et al., 1997). Ecstasy produces stimulant and psychedelic effects, enabling users to dance for longer periods of time and experience mind-altering sensations and perceptions.

The effects of methamphetamine and amphetamine use are significant. Increases in heart rate and blood pressure have resulted in heart attacks and strokes, which are sometimes fatal to even the most physically fit athletes (Berkow et al., 1997). Chronic users may become violent and/or anxious, and they may have insomnia, delusions, paranoia, and auditory hallucinations (Office of National Drug Control Policy, 2002b). Habitual users who use amphetamines several times daily quickly develop a tolerance, requiring ever-increasing doses to produce the same effects. Some individuals increase their dosage to 100 times that of the original; and at this level, virtually 100% of users become psychotic.

Individuals who already have psychiatric disorders are particularly vulnerable to amphetamine-induced psychosis (Berkow et al., 1997). Recovery from even severe and prolonged amphetamine psychosis occurs with treatment, but loss of memory, confusion, and delusional ideation may continue for months (Merck Manual, 2002b). Medical management of withdrawal depends on the individual's symptoms and mental state. Those showing signs of exhaustion and depression may be monitored in inpatient facilities to prevent self-injury or suicide. Those in an acute psychotic episode may be given antipsychotic drugs (Berkow et al., 1997).

Alcohol

Berkow and colleagues defined alcoholism as "a chronic disease characterized by a tendency to drink more than was intended, unsuccessful attempts at stopping drinking, and continued drinking despite adverse social and occupational consequences" (1997, p. 442). An estimated 75% of adults in the United States drink socially (Merck Manual, 2002a). For 10% of this population, however, drinking is not just social; it is a severe problem, routinely abused, and puts them and their families at risk. Alcohol also is abused by larger numbers of teens and adults who binge drink or simply drink episodically or excessively now and then. The ratio of male alcoholics to female is approximately 4 to 1 (Merck Manual, 2002a).

The causes of alcoholism are unknown, however, both biological and social theories related to the addiction continue to be investigated. Arguments for biological contribution are that the biological children of alcoholics are more likely to become alcoholics than the adopted children of alcoholics, suggesting some genetic predisposition toward alcoholism (Berkow et al., 1997). Evidence also indicates that alcoholics' brains are less sensitive to the effects of alcohol and less easily intoxicated than those who do not become alcoholics (Berkow et al., 1997). Personality traits and environmental factors are also associated with alcoholism. Alcoholics tend to be more isolated, lonely, shy, depressed, dependent, hostile, self-destructive, impulsive, and sexually immature than non-alcoholics (Merck Manual, 2002a). In terms of social factors, alcoholics are more likely to come from homes with one parent absent and have disturbed relationships with their parents (Merck Manual, 2002a). These factors often occur within a larger context of poverty, limited education, psychiatric illness, and inadequate treatment options. These disparate facts form an interesting puzzle; however, it is one that is not easily solved. Do these factors lead to alcoholism or are they its result? Regardless of the answer, alcoholics come from all ethnicities, strata of society, and education and income levels.

The health consequences of alcoholism are life threatening, with damage to the liver, the heart, and the brain. Lack of adequate nutrition, which frequently accompanies alcoholism, contributes to peripheral nerve degeneration and brain damage (Merck Manual, 2002a). Tolerance to alcohol occurs in those who drink large quantities over long periods of time with increasing amounts needed to produce the desired effect.

For those who are physically dependent on alcohol, withdrawal symptoms typically occur within 12–48 hours after the last drink. In their mildest form, they may include weakness, sweating, tremors, and limited numbers of seizures (Merck Manual, 2002a). More profound withdrawal symptoms occur when alcohol is withheld after prolonged, excessive use. Medical diagnosis and supervision are critical to effective management of the withdrawal phase in alcoholism. The first step in management is detoxification, which includes withdrawing alcohol and correcting nutritional deficiencies. The next step is changing the individual's behavior so that he or she can remain sober. A variety of interventions are used to help recovering alcoholics change their behavior, such as group therapy, drugs that cause vomiting when alcohol is ingested, and organizations such as Alcoholics Anonymous (AA). AA is believed to have benefited more alcoholics than any other treatment approach (Merck Manual, 2002a).

The consequences of alcohol abuse and alcoholism are profound, including the effects it may have on a developing fetus. It is also the drug that is most familiar to many families—one that does not take sophisticated strategies to interdict, and one that each individual can help to control.

Nicotine

Nicotine is a naturally occurring, colorless liquid that comes from tobacco plants. When smoked, nicotine turns brown. It is one of the most frequently used addictive drugs, and nicotine addiction in the United States occurs most commonly from smoking cigarettes (U.S. Department of Health and Human Services, 2001). Sales of smokeless tobacco products (e.g., chewing tobacco) and cigars are increasing. One absorbs nicotine by inhaling smoke into one's lungs and/or through the skin and the mucous lining of one's nose and mouth (U.S. Department of Health and Human Services, 2001). Nicotine causes a "high" whether smoked in cigarettes or ingested in chewing tobacco (U.S. Department of Health and Human Services, 2001).

Because it is a legal, easily accessible, and heavily marketed drug, nicotine is one of the most commonly used addictive drugs throughout the world. Although ostracism of smokers and bans on smoking in restaurants and bars are changing behavior in some parts of the United States, much of this country and the rest of the world are clouded by cigarette smoke. In the 1999 National Household Survey on Drug Abuse, approximately 57 million Americans reported that they were current smokers, and 7.6 million people reported that they used smokeless tobacco (U.S. Department of Health and Human Services, 2001). Teen smoking is a serious and growing problem that neither legislation nor anti-smoking campaigns have diminished. The number of teenage girls who smoke has increased substantially, surpassing the number of teenage boys who smoke (Berkow et al., 1997). Of teen populations, white teens are most likely to smoke (36.5%) and African American teens least likely (15%); however, rates for both groups have begun to increase again (Children's Defense Fund, 2001) since a slow-down period from 1997 to 2001 (U.S. Department of Health and Human Services, 2001). Men are only slightly more likely to smoke than women, and women are less likely to quit smoking than men (U.S. Department of Health and Human Services, 2001).

The immediate effects of nicotine are not dissimilar to other addictive drugs—a rush, high, or kick caused by the release of adrenaline and glucose. Heart rate, blood pressure, and respiration also increase along with dopamine levels in the areas of the brain that control pleasure and motivation (U.S. Department of Health and Human Services, 2001). In long-term addiction, changes in the brain occur and tolerance develops. Like other drugs in which there is physical addiction, withdrawal symptoms occur when an individual quits smoking. Symptoms may include sleep disturbances, irritability, increased appetite, nicotine craving, and attention or cognitive impairments. The psychological dependence on cigarettes often persists long after the physical dependence and addiction have been managed. The rituals of smoking seem to be particularly pleasurable and difficult to give up (U.S. Department of Health and Human Services, 2001).

Long-term effects of nicotine addiction are well documented. Tobacco use accounts for a third of all cancers in the United States, and 90% of lung cancers are linked to cigarette smoking. Cancers of the mouth, tongue, pharynx, larynx, esophagus, stomach, pancreas, cervix, kidney, ureter, and bladder are also associated with smoking, making smokers twice as likely to die from cancers than nonsmokers (U.S. Department of Health and Human Services, 2001). For heavy smokers, death rates from cancer are 4 times greater than for nonsmokers. Smoking also causes other debilitating lung diseases such as emphysema and chronic asthma. Cancer is not the only disease that is clearly linked to smoking. Since 1940, smoking has been associated with heart disease, stroke, aneurysms, and vascular disease. Estimates suggest that about 20% of deaths from heart disease can be attributed to smoking (U.S. Department of Health and Human Services, 2001).

Smokers are not the only ones whose health is affected by their habit. Secondhand smoke, also called environmental tobacco smoke (ETS), is estimated to cause 3,000 lung cancer deaths annually among nonsmokers; and another 40,000 deaths from heart disease among nonsmokers are attributable to secondhand smoke (U.S. Department of Health and Human Services, 2001). Children are particularly affected; studies have shown that in homes in which an individual smokes, there are more severe cases of asthma, higher rates of sudden infant death syndrome, and fire fatalities from dropped cigarettes (U.S. Department of Health and Human Services, 2001). For interventionists who work with young children with disabilities or children at risk for disabilities, smoking in the home is a serious issue. Although family-centered practice dictates that families, not service providers, establish the rules for how the family operates, interventionists may need to provide information to families about the additional risks secondhand smoke poses to their children.

Nicotine addiction is one of the most intractable addictions. Less than 7% of individuals who attempt to quit smoking without outside help succeed for longer than a week (U.S. Department of Health and Human Services, 2001). Effective treatments are available, however. For individuals who are motivated to quit, a combination of pharmacological (e.g., nicotine patches, inhalers, gum) and behavioral treatments doubles the success rate over efforts to quit without these supports.

Like alcohol addiction, nicotine addiction is common in many homes. It is something many people live—and die—with. It is preventable, it can be treated, and its reduction would account for significant reductions in many other life-threatening diseases as well as a reduction in premature births and low birth weight infants among mothers who smoke.

THE CAUSES AND CONSEQUENCES
OF SUBSTANCE ABUSE AND ADDICTION

Few, if any, individuals wake up one morning and decide to become addicted to legal or illegal drugs. Most of those who are addicted would prefer not to be. None of the consequences of addiction are positive. So why is addiction so prevalent? Why don't people "just say no"?

Causes

Addiction is the result of multiple, complex, and interacting variables. As discussed previously, personality, social, economic, and physiological variables contribute to each individual's reactions to drugs. These variables may predispose a person to addiction or serve as protective factors that reduce the likelihood of addiction. Although it is not possible to predict the outcomes for an individual, a number of societal variables are associated with risky behaviors that often lead to addiction. For adults, lack of opportunity, unemployment, poverty, limited access to treatment, violence at home and in the neighborhood, and association with substance abusers contribute to drug abuse and addiction.

Ethnic differences emerge when examining drug use and its patterns. As reported by the Office of National Drug Control Policy (2002h) based on data from 2000 National Household Survey of Drug Abuse, the rates of those who reported that they had used an illicit drug at least once in their lives differ across ethnic groups. The highest rate was among American Indian/Alaska Natives (53.9%), followed by people of multiple races (49.2%), white non-Hispanics (41.5%), African Americans (35.5%), Latinos (29.9%), and Asians (18.9%). The Monitoring the Future study sponsored and reported by the Office of National Drug Control Policy (2002h) examined drug use among high school students. Their findings showed the lowest rates of use for most drug types among African American students. More Latino eighth graders used drugs than white, non-Latino or African American eighth graders. Although Latino twelfth graders' rate of drug usage fell between that of white, non-Latinos and African Americans, it is likely that this change is not a reduction in use but an artifact of the high percentage of Latino students who drop out of school before twelfth grade. These disparities suggest that drug abuse and its consequences are entangled in a number of social, political, and economic issues.

Remarkably, many individuals face extremely difficult circumstances and escape addiction. For young people the risk and protective factors are clear. According to the National Institute on Drug Abuse (2002), the following increase the risk of drug abuse among youth: 1) chaotic home environments, especially those in which parents have mental illness or are substance abusers; 2) lack of parent–child attachment and nurturing; 3) shy or aggressive classroom behavior that is inappropriate; 4) school failure; 5) poor social coping skills; 6) friendships and affiliations with peers who display deviant behavior; and 7) perception that drug use is acceptable. As might be anticipated, risks that often lead to drug abuse also lead to other forms of antisocial behavior such as delinquency, youth violence, school incompletion, risky sexual behaviors, and teen pregnancy. Conversely, a number of protective factors help prevent drug abuse and other antisocial behavior. These factors, as identified by the National Institute on Drug Abuse and others, include 1) family bonds that are strong and positive; 2) parental monitoring of their children's behavior and activities and that of their children's peers; 3) clear, consistently enforced rules of conduct within the family; 4) parental involvement in their children's lives; 5) school success and strong bonds with community institutions such as school, church, mosque, or synagogue; and 6) acceptance of conventional norms about drug use. The role of the service provider is clear in these situations. Everything that service providers do to help family's marshal protective factors contributes to more positive outcomes for the entire family.

Consequences

The consequences of drug abuse and addiction in the United States can be measured economically, but their cost in human potential is even more profound. Every day spent snorting cocaine is an evening in which relationships with children and partners are secondary to the desire for the drug. Every dollar spent to support an addiction is money that cannot be spent for food, housing, or medical care. In all types of homes across the United States, every behavior related to the addiction prohibits or interferes with behaviors that support strong families. In any home, an addiction may interfere with a woman's healthy pregnancy and delivery, and substance abuse is correlated with low birth weight, preterm delivery, and fetal alcohol syndrome (FAS)—all significant risk factors for disability (Office of Applied Studies, Substance Abuse and Mental Health Services Administration, 2002).

The use of illicit drugs such as cocaine, crack, and heroin during pregnancy received considerable research and media attention in the late 1980s and early 1990s; however, parental cigarette smoking and alcohol abuse present risks of equal magnitude to the developing fetus. Antismoking campaigns and the information that is available on the hazards of smoking has not reached or changed the behavior of all women (Office of Applied Studies, Substance Abuse and Mental Health Services Administration, 2002). The percentage of women who smoke or live with someone who smokes has decreased minimally in 20 years, and the number of women who smoke heavily has increased. Cigarette smoking during pregnancy results in low birth weight; as the mother's smoking increases, the infant's birth weight typically decreases (Wunsch, Conlon, & Scheidt, 2002). Premature rupture of the membranes and pre-term labor along with uterine infections are also common problems among smokers. Birth defects involving the heart, brain, and face are more common among the infants of smokers as is sudden infant death syndrome (Berkow et al., 1997).

Drinking alcohol during pregnancy is the leading known cause of birth defects and mental retardation. Although "How much is too much?" remains an unanswered question, it is evident that alcohol usage is having a serious impact: For every 1,000 births, from 0.5 to 3 children are diagnosed with some degree of FAS (Berkow et al., 1997; Streissguth, 1997). FAS is a birth defect that primarily affects the brain. Even if a woman who drinks does not bear a child with FAS, miscarriage and fetal alcohol effects (FAE) or possible fetal alcohol effects (PFAE) such as severe behavioral disturbances and attention deficit disorders in the developing child may result from alcohol use during pregnancy (Berkow et al., 1997; Streissguth, 1997). According to Streissguth, these behavioral difficulties may continue throughout life:

> Extremely high rates of mental illness as well as high rates of disrupted school experiences, trouble with the law, and alcohol and other drug problems are alarming. . . . Many individuals with FAS/FAE need ongoing help across the life span—anything from a protective environment to a trusted friend, spouse, or advocate to help them stay grounded and focused. (1997, p. 6)

Use and abuse of illegal drugs are also associated with poor neonatal outcomes ranging from premature delivery to significant disabilities. Women who are drug dependent often live in environments and under circumstances that are not conducive to healthy pregnancy and delivery. They often receive little to no prenatal care, have medical complications such as infections, and are poorly nourished (Baer, 1995). They also may be subject to violence and battering, which harms them and the developing fetus.

The consequences of drug abuse and addiction on families are often devastating—violence, loss of resources, frequent interactions with the police and justice systems, and limited options for treatment and recovery. Loss of a sense of home as a safe haven and loss of trust in loved ones are perhaps as undermining to an individual's well-being as the loss of material possessions. The consequences of drug addiction and abuse threaten every aspect of family life and make the successful performance of family functions close to impossible.

Treating Drug Abuse and Addiction

Large-scale evaluations of drug prevention and treatment programs have concluded that treatment is effective overall (Office of National Drug Control Policy, 1996). Like so many evaluations of educational and social programs, which programs work for which individuals under what conditions has not been determined. Among the models that have been shown to be effective are therapeutic communities (i.e., residential treatment in which personal support, education, and psychological support are combined), pharmacological treatment, outpatient treatment without medication or pharmacological management, and inpatient treatment (Office of

National Drug Control Policy, 1996). Prevention strategies with young people have included providing prevention education, developing alternative drug-free activities, identifying substance abuse problems early and referring for treatment, building community-based interventions, and working with schools and other institutions to create an environment that reduces risk factors and enhances protective factors (Office of National Drug Control Policy, 2002a).

Finally, for any prevention strategy or treatment to work, it has to be available to those who need it when they need it. Making options available, accessible, and culturally competent continues to be a challenge to systems and to professionals in those systems who work with and care about families.

VIOLENCE

Violence is part of nearly every newscast and is featured on evening television 7 days a week in the United States. It is common in movies, computer games, comics, and cartoons; in every genre, guns figure prominently. Research on children's exposure to violence on television, in movies, and through video games consistently demonstrates that exposure to violence results in increases in violent behavior. Children with higher levels of exposure to violence are more apt to solve conflicts through violence, lack sensitivity to the victimization of others, be desensitized to violence and violent acts, and view the world as a frightening place (Miller, 2001). Several studies suggest that this exposure to violence persists in young adulthood. In Anderson's (as cited in Larkin, 2000) study of more than 200 college students in the United States, those who reported playing violent video games in the past were more aggressive in their behavior and had lower grades in college. In another study conducted by Anderson and cited in Larkin, college students who had played a violent video game 15 minutes prior to the experimental condition "punished" their opponents with a longer blast of a loud noise than did those who did not play the violent video game. Six major professional societies—the American Academy of Pediatrics, American Medical Association, American Academy of Family Physicians, American Academy of Child and Adolescent Psychiatry, American Psychiatric Association, and the American Psychological Association—concur that there is a direct, causal link between some children's exposure to media violence and their aggressive behavior (Anderson & Bushman, 2002).

It should, therefore, not be surprising that when children younger than 15 in the United States are compared with children in the same age group in 25 other industrialized countries combined, U.S. children are "9 times more likely to die in a firearms accident, 11 times more likely to commit suicide with a gun, 12 times more likely to die from gunfire, and 16 times more likely to be murdered with a gun" (Children's Defense Fund, 2001, p. xxii).

Violence in schools, communities, and throughout the nation has punctuated lives throughout the nation for several decades. Children shooting children, high school students killing classmates and teachers, parents killing their children, and random shootings in restaurants or other public places have become all too familiar. These incidents, combined with the mind-numbing terrorist attacks on September 11, 2001, have brought new images and new fears into American homes and headlines. Each of these is worthy of our individual and collective best efforts to understand and prevent future occurrences, but community violence is outside the scope of this book. The following sections of this chapter focus on violence at home—usually violence against women and children. Although violence at home is frequently nested in society's larger problems, this section focuses on what happens to those who are battered and abused and how that affects families and their ability to function.

Violence at Home

Violence between domestic partners or former partners accounts for much of the abuse in America's homes. In domestic violence, both men and women are perpetrators, but women are far more likely to be victims than men. Violence against women is typically not characterized by isolated incidents, but rather, by an ongoing pattern of behavior over months, years, and decades (Watts & Zimmerman, 2002). Data from the National Violence Against Women Survey co-sponsored by the National Institute of Justice and the Centers for Disease Control and Prevention provide a picture of spousal and intimate partner violence in the home. A nationally representative sample of 8,000 women and 8,000 men participated in telephone interviews. Findings from the late 1990s related to spousal or intimate partner violence include the following (Tjaden & Thoennes, 1998):

- Rape and/or physical assaults by an intimate partner were committed against approximately 1.5 million women and 800,000 men.

- Husbands, former husbands, cohabiting partners, boyfriends, or dates carried out 76% of the reported violent incidents against women.

- Women were significantly more likely to be abused by a partner than were men.

In this study, as is typical of other research, physical assault was defined broadly to include a range from hair pulling, biting, hitting, slapping, and kicking to beating; choking; trying to drown; threatening; or hurting with a knife, gun, or other weapon. Women were 2–3 times more likely than men to report that they had been grabbed, shoved, kicked, or had something thrown at them. For the more violent assaults of being beaten up, choked, or threatened or assaulted with a gun, women were 7–14 times more likely than men to report such experiences (Tjaden & Thoennes, 1998). Men are almost always the perpetrators of violence against both men and women. Men committed 93% of the reported acts of violence against women, and 86% of violent acts against men were committed by men (Tjaden & Thoennes, 1998). Throughout the world, rape is typically committed by intimate partners, males in the family, acquaintances, or men in positions of authority (Watts & Zimmerman, 2002). Because the violent act of men battering women is so much more prevalent than female violence against male partners, the focus in this chapter is on issues faced by women and mothers who are abused.

According to one study, 172 women are physically and/or sexually abused every hour in the United States (National Center for Victims of Crime, 2002). As jarring as this number is, violence is almost always underreported because of short-term reconciliation, fear of retribution, or embarrassment on the part of the victim (Watts & Zimmerman, 2002). Physical and sexual violence are not the only forms of abuse that occur in many of these destructive relationships. Verbal and psychological abuse often are co-occurring and can serve to change women's perceptions of their own worth, their relationships, and their rights and place in the larger world (Johnson & Ferraro, 2000). These altered perceptions contribute to women's inability to leave an abusive relationship. Contrary to what is sometimes suggested in the popular press and reports of research, however, many women do leave these relationships (Johnson & Ferraro, 2000). It may take several attempts, temporary safe housing, legal advocacy, personal counseling, and supports provided by service agencies, but women do leave. This is one of the reasons that professional family support is so important.

Johnson and Ferraro (2000) detailed four types of partner violence in an elaboration of Johnson's earlier work. They describe "common couple violence," which is typical of a more generalized pattern of control. This sort of violence occurs in specific arguments in which one or both partners lash out at the other. It typically does not accelerate over time, is generally confined to a low level of violence, and is likely to be mutual. "Intimate terrorism" describes a pattern of behavior that is based on the desire to control the partner. It is usually just one strategy of control used in the relationship, but it is often characterized by violence, psychological abuse, escalation over time, and serious injury. Intimate violence is usually practiced by only one partner. The pattern of abusive behavior in which a partner fights back has been labeled "violent resistance." This type of violence is most often attributed to women and sometimes results in death or serious injury of the perpetrator of the original violence. Little research has been conducted on it. It is this sort of violence that is often used in a self-defense plea in homicide cases. Some relationships are defined by mutual combat between partners who are both violent and controlling. Johnson and Ferraro defined this as "mutual violent control" (2000, p. 3 electronic version).

Violence between partners is one of the most complex forms of violence. Resolving it is seldom, if ever, a simple task; and many professionals, from police officers to psychiatrists, spend years training and practicing strategies for intervention. When a service provider is confronted with domestic violence, it is essential to know the reporting laws of the state, the reporting policies of his or her agency, and the community resources that are available to help the family. Inserting oneself into the situation as either an advisor or an adjudicator is not recommended. The knowledge, expertise, and experience required to assist partners at war are typically quite different from those required of service providers whose work focuses on supporting the optimal functioning of young children who are at risk or have disabilities and their families.

Who batters women? What is known about men who treat their partners with aggression and abuse? Jacobson and Gottman's (1998) research studied couples involved in violent relationships. Through interviews, observations, psychometric evaluations, and observations during arguments in the laboratory, at least two types of men who resort to violence seemed to emerge. One type could be called *sociopathic.* They seem to be completely physiologically detached from their vicious verbal attacks on their partners, and their pasts were marked by violence and antisocial behavior exhibited by themselves and others. The other type of violent man is physiologically attuned to what is occurring during heated, vicious arguments but can be described as dependent and needy. Jacobson and Gotmann's data suggested that abusive men have personalities and pre-established patterns of behavior such as the need to control, irritability, and use of violence to solve problems, which are likely to lead to abusive relationships with women. Given the longstanding nature of these person ality traits and types, in many instances, abuse is no surprise.

Rates of assault against women differ by race/ethnicity. The Violence Against Women Survey (Tjaden & Thoennes, 1998) found that American Indian/Alaska Native women are significantly more likely to report that they were victims of rape or assault than white non-Hispanic, African American, and Asian/Pacific Islander women. Conversely, Asian/Pacific Islander women are significantly less likely to report rape and/or assault. Latino women are less likely than non-Latino women to report that they have been raped, but the percent of physical assaults not including rape were similar between the groups. Although not discussed in the report, the percentage of women of mixed race reporting rape and assault is higher than for any group other than American Indian/Alaska Natives. The reasons for these differences cannot be accounted for by the information gathered in the study. They may be artifacts of small sample size for American Indian/Alaska Natives and Asian/Pacific Islanders. They may be the result of different cultural variables, immigration, and comfort in reporting. They may also speak to deeper cultural and sociocultural issues and the nation's ability or inability to address inequities across groups. Race/ethnicity may be a factor that makes some women more vulnerable to abuse than others, however. An important next step is determining why these differences occur and finding ways to reduce abuse in all relationships.

Outcomes of Domestic Violence

The effects of domestic violence are many and affect all members of the family, including children.

Effects on Abused Women

The most obvious outcomes of violence are the negative physical and psychological effects on women including injury, pain, hospitalization and recuperation, embarrassment, fear, and depression. Abuse limits women's options for education, work, and even opportunities to leave the house. It also limits women's ability to create alone (or with a partner) a safe haven for their children. It is not uncommon for some abusers to prevent their wives or partners from obtaining or maintaining a job or career. An abuser's controlling tactics are often insidious, including depriving the partner of transportation, beating a woman before a job interview, turning off the alarm clock to intentionally make a partner late for an appointment, harassing a partner when she is at work, and failing to be available for childcare as promised (Johnson & Ferraro, 2000).

In a qualitative study conducted by Levendosky (2000), women in abusive relationships discussed the effects of domestic violence on their parenting. The majority reported that their parenting suffered because of the violence. Women described lack of energy, physical illness and injury, and generalized anger as results of abuse that interfered with parenting. Even in the face of these challenges, a number of women mobilized their resources to protect and provide for their children in spite of abuse. They used their circumstances to support positive parenting. For example, some reported being more empathic toward their children and their needs because of their own experiences. Others put considerable effort into helping their children develop self-esteem so that the children would be less likely to be victims of abuse (Levendosky, 2000).

Effects on Children

Children who witness violence are also affected by it. Depression, anxiety, poor problem solving, psychosomatic complaints, and low self-esteem are common (Szyndrowski, 1999). These patterns of behavior often persist, as evidenced by data indicating that women in college who recall violence between their parents are less socially competent, are more depressed, and have lower self-esteem (Henning, Leitenberg, Coffey, Bennett, & Jankowski, 1997). Individually or in combination, these characteristics often interfere with school success. Of even greater concern are the long-term outcomes for children who witness abuse. These children are at risk for becoming direct victims of the violence and for posttraumatic stress disorder (PTSD), which may cause developmental delays and difficulty concentrating and becoming involved in intimate relationships (Accardo & Whitman, 2002). Children who witness domestic violence learn that violence is a part of intimate relationships, and no countervailing force teaches other ways of communicating and solving problems (Groves, 1996). Victimization places children at risk for delinquency, criminal acts, and violent criminal behavior (National Institute of Mental Health, 2000). Although direct links to the causes of witnessing violence are difficult to determine because of associated variables, it would not be surprising to find that witnessing violence also places children at similar risk. Direct effects of violence on children who are abused are discussed in a later section of this chapter.

The transmission of violence is frequently discussed in the professional literature in social work, psychology, criminology, and sociology. Transmission is believed to have both environmental and genetic components. In other words, children who witness or experience violence and those who live in homes where violence is condoned are in environments in which models of behavior put the child at risk for later violence as a victim or a perpetrator. It is also thought that there may be genetic predispositions to personality and behavioral types that are characteristic of abusers. Children exposed to violence at home and in the community have a higher risk of becoming either a victim or perpetrator of violence as adults (Anderson & Cramer-Benjamin, 1999, Stith et al., 2000). Likewise, men whose childhoods were spent in homes in which there was domestic violence have been reported to be more likely to be violent as husbands and partners than those who have not grown up with violence (Johnson & Ferraro, 2000).

Homelessness Related to Violence

Homelessness is a serious and, to this point, intractable problem in the United States. In one study at least half of homeless women were forced onto the streets and into shelters because of extreme violence against them in their homes (Zorza, 1991). In another interview study of homeless women and women living in low-income housing, a third reported that they had experienced severe physical violence from their current or most-recent partner (Browne & Bassuk, 1997).

Other "Costs"

Because battering is a crime, the effects on police departments, courts, jails, and rehabilitation programs are also significant. Every dollar spent on the crime of battering subtracts from the resources available for prevention and treatment. At another level, the modeling of violence in the home has a range of incalculable personal costs.

Preventing Domestic Violence

Domestic violence is a result of many interconnected factors and issues. It requires attention and coordinated approaches that involve prevention and intervention at the individual, community, societal, and political levels. As the statistics demonstrate, domestic violence has no quick fix. In fact, one of the hallmarks of the progress in this area is getting society to accept the fact that battering is not "the woman's problem." Domestic violence must become unacceptable in homes and communities. Children should learn at an early age that violence in the home is unacceptable.

Families need opportunities to learn childrearing techniques that do not include physical punishment and to learn communication and problem-solving skills that do not rely on physical force or verbal abuse. As society's tolerance of abuse decreases, it will be critical to support programs for batterers and ensure that they are available and accessible. Otherwise, violence will become an even more private and intractable problem. One does not have to condone a problem to condone its treatment; this must become equally true for supporting treatment for perpetrators of domestic violence. Programs must be delivered to meet the diverse characteristics—racial, cultural, educational, economic, life experience—of those they serve.

In addition to treatment for batterers, partners and their children must have alternatives that keep them safe and help them regain their sense of control and personal efficacy. Temporary shelters, job training, protection, child care, education, psychological counseling, legal advocacy, and social support are essential to help women leave violent relationships. Because of the relationship between substance abuse and domestic violence, programs that prevent and treat drug addiction and alcoholism are key to reducing domestic violence. Making guns unavailable would eliminate or at least reduce access to weapons that are often a part of intimate partner and child violence.

These programs and services are neither cheap nor easy to develop in coordinated and collaborative ways that maximize resources and effectiveness. They are, however, essential if the nation is serious about the problem—and serious about the importance of families and their ability to function effectively. Service providers who are trained to work in family-centered ways have a great deal to contribute to improving their own community's response to family violence. Knowledge of community resources, the ability to work as team members, and advocacy skills are as important to reducing family violence as they are to providing effective intervention with individual families and children.

CHILD ABUSE AND NEGLECT

Unfortunately, the scope of the problem of child abuse and neglect is great. Child maltreatment is a significant and growing problem in the United States. A child's risk of being harmed in 1993 was 1.5 times greater than in 1986 (Sedlak & Broadhurst, 1996). Between these same years, physical abuse increased by almost 100%; sexual abuse increased by over 100%; and emotional abuse, physical and emotional neglect increased by 250% (Sedlak & Broadhurst, 1996). In 2000, 3 million referrals for suspected child abuse and neglect were made, with an average of one report every 10 seconds (Childhelp USA, 2002). The 3 million referrals involved the health, safety, and welfare of 5,000,000 children. Two thirds received further assessment and investigation, and of those, it was determined that one quarter (28%) of the referred children were being maltreated or at significant risk for maltreatment (The Administration for Children and

Families, Children's Bureau, 2003). Twelve hundred children died as a result of abuse and/or neglect. Forty-four percent of those who died were younger than 12 months of age; 85% were younger than age 6.

Child maltreatment includes neglect, medical neglect, physical abuse, sexual abuse, and psychological maltreatment. In the National Incidence of Child Abuse and Neglect Studies commissioned by Congress, standardized definitions were used in the determination of child abuse and/or neglect. Standards were developed using certain criteria. The Harm Standard is met when children have already suffered harm from abuse or neglect. The Endangerment Standard is met when children have already experienced abuse or neglect that puts them at risk for harm (Sedlak & Broadhurst, 1996). In the 2001 statistics, the largest percentage of maltreated children was physically or medically neglected (59%), 19% were physically abused, 10% were sexually abused, and 7% suffered psychological maltreatment. The percentage of boys and girls who were physically abused was very similar (48% were boys and 52% were girls); however, the rate of sexual abuse is greater for girls (The Administration for Children and Families Children's Bureau, 2003). Conversely, boys are more likely to suffer serious physical injury from abuse and significantly more likely to be emotionally neglected than girls (Sedlak & Broadhurst, 1996).

Overwhelmingly, children who experience abuse and neglect are poor (Child Welfare League, 1999; Sedlak & Broadhurst, 1996). Risks were significantly greater for every type of maltreatment for children in families earning less than $15,000 per year in 1993 than for children from families earning $30,000 or more (Sedlak & Broadhurst, 1996). The relationship of poverty to other social factors related to child abuse such as transient residence, more limited and poorer education, higher rates of substance abuse, and parental mental illness may help to explain the risks for abuse and neglect that poor children face. The relationship to substance abuse is particularly striking, with almost half of the substantiated cases of child abuse and neglect related to a parent's abuse of alcohol or drugs (Child Welfare League, 1998).

Data from Administration for Children and Families, Children's Bureau (2003) indicated that 50% of children who were abused and/or neglected in the year 2001 were white and 25% were African American. Percentages among Latinos (15%), American Indian/Alaska Native (2%), and Asian/Pacific Islanders (1%) were lower (Administration for Children and Families, Children's Bureau, 2003). Data from the three National Incidence Studies of Child Abuse and Neglect have found no significant differences by race (Sedlak & Broadhurst, 1996). Their findings do, however, suggest that families from different races receive differential treatment within various service systems, resulting in what appear to be different rates of abuse among families of color (Sedlak & Broadhurst, 1996).

Young children are most vulnerable to abuse and neglect, and child maltreatment is the leading cause of death for children age 4 and younger (Childhelp USA, 2002). Family size and structure are related to abuse and neglect. Data from the third National Incidence Study indicate that children of single parents are more likely to be physically abused and/or neglected than children living in two-parent families (Sedlak & Broadhurst, 1996). Children in large families (four or more dependent children) were found to be at considerably greater risk for educational and physical neglect than "only" children and children in two- to three-child families. Unexpectedly, only children had higher rates of educational and physical neglect than their counterparts in two- to three-child families (Sedlak & Broadhurst, 1996). Although the data do not explain why this is the case, Sedlak and Broadhurst hypothesize that it may be that too many expectations are focused on only children. Also, first children tend to have parents who are younger and less experienced.

Data from the third National Incidence Study provides information, albeit incomplete, on the characteristics of those who abuse and/or neglect children (Sedlak & Broadhurst, 1996). According to data from that study, children are most likely to be maltreated by their birth parents. Birth parents were responsible for 72% of physical abuse incidents and 81% of the cases of emotional abuse against children. The statistics differ in cases of sexual abuse. Half of the children who were sexually abused were molested by someone other than a parent or someone in a parenting role. One fourth were sexually abused by a birth parent. An alarming finding was that sexual abuse perpetrated by a birth parent was more likely than such abuse by a non-birth parent to result in a serious injury or impairment. Data from the same study indicated that of people who physically neglect their children, women are more likely to do so than men, a finding consistent with the fact that women are typically the primary caregivers. Male abusers, in general, were more likely to abuse children than were women, in part because of men's higher rates of sexual abuse. When all types of abuse committed by birth parents were considered, differences in gender were nearly nonexistent. Birth mothers are more likely than birth fathers to physically abuse their children (Sedlak & Broadhurst, 1996).

These facts and findings are difficult to comprehend in a country that describes its children as its most precious resource. Realizing that in 1996, 478 children younger than 12 months of age died from abuse or neglect compared with 55 police officers killed in the line of duty puts the scope of the problem in stark perspective (Child Welfare League, 1999).

Child Abuse and Neglect and Disability

A national study funded by the National Center on Child Abuse determined that 14.1% of the children who had been maltreated had one or more disabilities (American Academy of Pediatrics, 2001). Children with disabilities are at greater risk for child abuse and neglect than children without disabilities. Children with disabilities were 1.8 times more likely to be neglected, 1.6 times more likely to be physically abused, and 2.2 times more likely to be sexually abused than children without disabilities (American Academy of Pediatrics, 2001). Like estimates of domestic violence, the numbers of children with disabilities who are abused are likely to be under-reported. This is especially likely because child protective services workers who are typically on the front line of child maltreatment cases are not trained to recognize disabilities. Unless a disability is very apparent, these children are likely to be recorded in the general population rather than in the population of children with disabilities. Numbers may also be higher because of the inability of some children and youth with disabilities to provide any corroborating information of their experiences.

The causes of child maltreatment for children with disabilities do not differ dramatically from the causes for children without disabilities; however, children with disabilities typically place higher demands on caregivers physically, emotionally, and financially (American Academy of Pediatrics, 2001). These extra demands and additional stressors may be overwhelming to some parents, whose frustration and inability to cope are turned on the child (Sobsey, 1994).

Sexual abuse of children with disabilities may stem from factors associated with the disability itself. Some disabilities necessitate more physical care and support, making the boundaries of appropriateness blurred. Children with disabilities may have a number of caregivers and personal assistants who have intimate contact with them, for example, providing increased opportunities for sexual molestation. On the positive side, when multiple caregivers are involved, it may be more likely that one will discover and report the abuse (American Academy of Pediatrics, 2001). Children and youth with disabilities may not have knowledge of appropriate and inappropriate sexual behavior. It may not be included in their educational curriculum or taught by parents or other caregivers. This makes it even more difficult for children to know about appropriate boundaries and to tell someone when they are being sexually abused. Societal attitudes may also contribute to increased risk of abuse. Beliefs that individuals with disabilities are "less than" others, asexual, or do not feel pain or that all caregivers are good and saintly people may interfere with recognition and reporting of abuse (Administration for Children and Families, 2001a).

Family attitudes may also affect the likelihood of abuse or neglect. Those who view the child as unacceptably different, as an embarrassment, or as a punishment for their own behavior may be more likely to engage in abuse and neglect or ignore abuse perpetrated by others (Burrell, Thompson, & Sexton, 1994; Rycus & Hughes, 1998). As with all other forms of domestic violence and abuse, parents with other serious problems such as alcoholism and drug abuse are more likely to abuse their child with a disability than parents who do not have such problems.

Outcomes of Child Abuse and Neglect

Like the outcomes of domestic violence, the immediate outcomes of the physical and sexual abuse of children are physical injury, pain, disability, and death. Negative psychological and cognitive outcomes of experiencing victimization and witnessing abuse have been well documented. They include fear, sadness, bleakness, aggression, learning problems, and depression (Osofsky, 1996; 2000). Children who are abused tend to think less of themselves, feel guilty, and feel that they have no control over their own lives—beliefs that can have long-term, negative consequences.

Effects in Adulthood

Abused children do not leave their childhoods behind when they grow up. Abuse suffered as a child follows the child into adulthood. Both retrospective and prospective studies of mental health outcomes attest to the risks inherent in childhood abuse and neglect. The relationship is not one to one. Being abused or neglected as a child does not mean that adult outcomes will be negative; however, it does increase the likelihood of mental health problems in adulthood (MacMillan, Fleming, Streiner, & Lin, 2001). In a 20-year prospective study, adult men who were physically or sexually abused or severely neglected as children were found to have diagnoses of antisocial personality disorder and more symptoms of the depressive disorder referred to as *dysthymia* as adults than matched controls (Horwitz, Widom, McLaughlin, & White, 2001). Dysthymic disorders are characterized by a depression that begins in early life and alters one's personality. Individuals with this type of depression are usually gloomy, pessimistic, unable to enjoy life, self-deprecating, lethargic, introverted, and hypercritical (Berkow et al., 1997). Adult women who experienced abuse and/or neglect as children were more likely to be dysthymic, have antisocial personality disorders, and report more problems with alcohol abuse and dependence than their matched controls (Horwitz et al., 2001).

Women exposed to physical and verbal abuse as victims or as observers of their mother's battering were more likely to engage in risky sexual behaviors such as early intercourse and promiscuity (i.e., having 30 or more sexual partners during one's lifetime). As the number of categories of childhood abuse increases during a girl's life (e.g., experiencing abuse or neglect, witnessing violence against one's mother), so does the likelihood that, when she becomes a woman, she will engage in risky sexual behaviors (Hillis, Anda, Felitti, & Marchbanks, 2001). The relationship between childhood abuse and neglect and adult outcomes is complex, but abuse and neglect are certainly contributors to greater risk and less-than-optimal outcomes.

Effects on Society

The economic costs are perhaps the least of the concerns that surround child abuse and neglect, but it would be naive to ignore the financial burden that child abuse and neglect place on communities. Abuse and neglect tax our hospitals, clinics, courts, jails, and community services. Every hour a child spends in treatment for being injured, terrified, or disabled as a result of abuse is an hour that child will not spend playing, learning, and developing a positive sense of self. These costs are immeasurable and have, as pointed out previously, serious long-term consequences that exacerbate the problem. At a deeper level, hurting children affects who we are as a society. If the youngest and most vulnerable cannot be protected from interpersonal violence, our society can claim little in the way of compassion and social justice. A society in which the problem is growing rather than abating is one that has considerable work remaining to be done.

Preventing Child Abuse and Neglect

Child abuse and neglect results from a multiplicity of personal, social, cultural, political, and societal problems. Prevention cannot be achieved without addressing each individually and as part of a larger set of issues. Prevention of child abuse and neglect, like other areas of prevention, can be conducted at three levels: primary, secondary, and tertiary. Primary prevention calls attention to the problem by informing the public and decision makers of its scope and the needs that exist. Secondary prevention focuses on children and families that are known to be at risk for child maltreatment, such as children of substance-abusing parents, families reported for domestic violence, extremely low-income families, and families of children with disabilities. Programs directed to these families may include parent education, substance abuse treatment programs, respite care for families of children with disabilities, and information and referral services for low-income families. Tertiary prevention focuses on families in which neglect and abuse have already occurred and on the children who have been victimized. Mental health workers may provide intensive counseling to family members and children may be removed to safer environments (Administration for Children and Families, 2001b).

In addition to this three-pronged approach to prevention, issues that are deeply embedded in society such as racial discrimination, gender inequity, economic disparity, and the condoning (if not glorification) of violence must be examined. Each contributes to the conditions that allow child abuse to occur; and each individual and each community must reflect on and make the necessary changes to improve our chances of protecting children.

SUMMARY

Drug abuse, addiction, family violence, child abuse, and child neglect are significant problems in the United States. Their costs and human consequences are devastating, and their prevention continues to be elusive. Substance abuse and violence affect every component of the family system. The family structure often changes as members come and go physically and psychologically. Healthy communication and acceptable boundaries among subsystems are thwarted, and the family's ability to carry out its functions is severely challenged. Even the family life cycle is affected because of changing roles, extended illnesses or incarcerations, and the transience of caregivers. The legal, political, and policy decisions related to substance abuse, domestic violence, and child maltreatment also affect families. Whether the political climate favors punishment or treatment significantly affects abusers and victims alike. It is difficult to reconcile the scope of the problems of substance abuse and family violence in a nation that prides itself on being caring and compassionate. As nations search for terrorists within and outside their national boundaries, it is important to pause and reflect. What are we doing to prevent terrorism within our own homes and families?

ACTIVITIES TO EXTEND THE DISCUSSION

1. **Form a small group to discuss the effects of substance abuse on families.** Using the family systems framework, detail the ways in which family characteristics, functions, and life cycle might be affected by a parent who is an alcoholic. After you have considered and recorded the possibilities, do the same for a situation in which a teen in the family is an alcoholic.

2. **Learn more about your own community's approach to domestic violence.** Contact a community agency that works with victims or perpetrators of domestic violence and interview an administrator or staff member about the scope of the problem in the community and the programs and services that their agency provides.

3. **Search the Internet for information about child abuse and neglect.** How is it defined? What national studies or interventions are being conducted? What are states doing to prevent child abuse and neglect? Are there any local resources on the Internet about the community's efforts to prevent child abuse and neglect?

REFERENCES

Accardo, P.J., & Whitman, B.Y. (Eds.). (with Behr, S.K., Farrell, A., Magenis, E., Morrow-Gorton, J.). (2002). *Dictionary of developmental disabilities terminology* (2nd ed.). Baltimore: Paul H. Brookes Publishing Co.

Administration for Children and Families. (2001a). *In focus: The risk and prevention of maltreatment of children with disabilities.* Retrieved June 26, 2002, from http://www.calib.com/nccanch/pubs/prevenres/focus.cfmactions/risk.cfm

Administration for Children and Families. (2001b). *National clearinghouse on child abuse and neglect information: Prevention fundamentals.* Retrieved July 9, 2002, from http://www.calib.com/nccanch/pubs/prevenres/fundamentals.cfm

Administration for Children and Families, Children's Bureau. (2003, May.) National clearinghouse on child abuse and neglect information: Child maltreatment 2001: Summary of key findings. Retrieved July 30, 2003, from http://www.calib.com/nccanch/pubs/factsheets/canstats.cfm

American Academy of Pediatrics. (2001). Assessment of maltreatment of children with disabilities [Electronic version]. *Pediatrics, 108*, 508–513.

Anderson, C.A., & Bushman, B.J. (2002). *Science, 295*(5564) [Electronic version]. Retrieved May 23, 2003, from EBSCO Host Research Databases.

Anderson, S.A., & Cramer-Benjamin, D.B. (1999). The impact of couple violence on parenting and children: An overview and clinical implications [Electronic version]. *American Journal of Family Therapy, 27*, 1–20.

Arthur, C.R., & Gerken, K.C. (1998). Prenatal exposure and public policy: Implications for pregnant and parenting women and their families. *Infants and Young Children, 10*(4), 23–35.

Baer, B.M. (1995). Drugs and the effects on health and development of the fetus, neonate, infant, and child. In K.D. Lewis (Ed.), *Infants and children with prenatal alcohol and drug exposure: A guide to identification and treatment* (pp. 21–56). Northbranch, MN: Sunrise River Press.

Berkow, R., Beers, M.H., & Fletcher, A.J. (Eds.). (1997). *The Merck manual of medical information: Home edition.* Whitehouse Station, NJ: Merck Research Laboratories.

Boyden, J. (1993). *Families: Celebration and hope in a world of change.* London: Gaia Books.

Browne, A., & Bassuk, S.S. (1997). Intimate violence in the lives of homeless and poor housed women: Prevalence and patterns in an ethnically diverse sample. *American Journal of Orthopsychiatry, 67*, 262–278.

Burrell, B., Thompson, B., & Sexton, D. (1994). Predicting child abuse potential across family types. *Child Abuse and Neglect, 18*, 1039–1049.

Child Welfare League. (1998). *Alcohol and other drugs survey of state child welfare agencies.* Washington, DC: Author.

Child Welfare League. (1999). *Child abuse and neglect: A look at the states, CWLA's 1999 stat book.* Washington, DC: Author.

Childhelp USA. (2002, June). *National child abuse statistics.* Retrieved July 5, 2002, from http://www.childhelpusa.org/child/statistics.htmx

Children's Defense Fund. (2000). *Yearbook 2000: The state of America's children.* Washington, DC: Author.

Children's Defense Fund. (2001). *Yearbook 2001: The state of America's children.* Washington, DC: Author.

Drug and Alcohol Services Information System. (2001a, July). *The DASIS report: Amphetamine treatment admission increase: 1993–1999.* Retrieved June 27, 2002, from http://www.samhsa.gov/oas/facts.cfm

Drug and Alcohol Services Information System. (2001b, July). *The DASIS report: Heroin—changes in how it is used.* Retrieved June 27, 2002, from http://www.samhsa.gov/oas/facts.cfm

Drug and Alcohol Services Information System. (2002a, January). *The DASIS report: Cocaine treatment admissions decrease: 1993–1999.* Retrieved June 27, 2002, from http://www.samhsa.gov/oas/facts.cfm

Drug and Alcohol Services Information System. (2002b, January). *The DASIS report: Heroin treatment admissions increase: 1993–1999.* Retrieved June 27, 2002, from http://www.samhsa.gov/oas/facts.cfmx

Drug and Alcohol Services Information System. (2002c, January). *The DASIS report: Marijuana treatment admissions increase: 1993–1999.* Retrieved July 1, 2002, from http://www.samhsa.gov/oas/facts.cfm

Ducharme, L., & Ball, J. (2001, July). *Major drugs of abuse in ED visits, 2000.* Retrieved June 26, 2002, from http://www.DrugAbuseStatistics.SAMHSA.gov

Edleson, J.L. (1999). The overlap between child maltreatment and woman battering. *Violence Against Women, 5*, 134–154.

Felitti, V. (1998). Relationship of childhood abuse and household dysfunction to many of the leading causes of deaths in adults: The adverse childhood experiences (ACE) study. *American Journal of Preventive Medicine, 14*, 245–258.

Gardner, J.W., & Reese, F.G. (Eds.). (1975). *Quotations of wit and wisdom* (p. 107). New York: W.W. Norton.

Groves, B.M. (1996). Children without refuge: Young witnesses to domestic violence. *Zero to Three, 16*(5), 29–34.

Henning, K., Leitenberg, H., Coffey, P., Bennett, T., & Jankowski, M.K. (1997). Long-term psychological adjustment to witnessing interparental physical conflict during childhood. *Child Abuse and Neglect, 21,* 501–515.

Hillis, S.D., Anda, R.F., Felitti, V.J., & Marchbanks, P.A. (2001). Adverse childhood experiences and sexual risk behaviors in women: A retrospective cohort study. *Family Planning Perspectives, 33*(3), 206–211.

Horwitz, A.V., Widom, C.S., McLaughlin, J., & White, H.R. (2001). The impact of childhood abuse and neglect on adult mental health: A prospective study. *Journal of Health and Social Behavior, 4*(2), 184–201.

Jacobson, N., & Gottman, J. (1998). *When men batter women: New insights into ending abusive relationships.* New York: Simon & Schuster.

Johnson, M., & Ferraro, K.J. (2000). Research on domestic violence in the 1990s: Making distinctions [Electronic version]. *Journal of Marriage and Family, 62,* 948–964.

Larkin, M. (2000). Violent video games increase aggression, *Lancet, 355*(9214). Retrieved May 23, 2003, from EBSCO Host Research Databases.

Levendosky, A.A. (2000). Mothers' perceptions of the impact of woman abuse on their parenting [Electronic version]. *Violence Against Women, 6,* 247–275.

MacMillan, H.L., Fleming, J.E., Streiner, D.L., & Lin, E. (2001). Childhood abuse and lifetime psychology in a community sample [Electronic version]. *The American Journal of Psychiatry, 158,* 1878–1883.

McCloskey, L.A., & Bailey, J.A. (2000). The intergenerational transmission of risk for child sexual abuse [Electronic version]. *Journal of Interpersonal Violence, 15,* 1019–1036.

Merck Manual. (2002a). *Alcoholism* [Electronic version]. Retrieved June 27, 2002, from htp://www.merck.com/pubs/mmanual/section15/chapter195/195b.htm

Merck Manual. (2002b). *Amphetamine dependence* [Electronic version]. Retrieved June 27, 2002, from htp://www.merck.com/pubs/mmanual/section15/chapter195/195b.htm

Merck Manual. (2002c). *Anxiolytic and hypnotic drug dependence* [Electronic version]. Retrieved June 27, 2002, from htp://www.merck.com/pubs/mmanual/section15/chapter195/195d.htm

Merck Manual. (2002d). *Cannabis (marijuana) dependence* [Electronic version]. Retrieved June 27, 2002, from http://www.merck.com/pubs/mmanual/section15/chapter195/195e.htm

Merck Manual. (2002e). *Cocaine dependence* [Electronic version]. Retrieved June 27, 2002, from http://www.merck.com/pubs/mmanual/section15/chapter195/195f.htm

Merck Manual. (2002f). *Opioid dependence* [Electronic version]. Retrieved June 27, 2002, from htp://www.merck.com/pubs/mmanual/section15/chapter195/195c.htm

Merck Manual. (2002g). *Volatile nitrites* [Electronic version]. Retrieved June 27, 2002, from http://www.merck.com/pubs/mmanual/section15/chapter195/195k.htm

Miller, K.E. (2001). *American Family Physician, 64*(5) [Electronic version]. Retrieved May 23, 2003, from EBSCO Host Research Databases.

Mrazek, P.J. (1993). Maltreatment and infant development. In C.H. Zeanah, Jr. (Ed.), *Handbook of infant mental health* (pp. 159–170). New York: Guilford Press.

National Center for Victims of Crime. (2002). *2001 crime clock.* Retrieved July 5, 2002, from http://www.ncvc.org/vroom/crimeclock/

National Institute on Drug Abuse. (2002, February). *Risk and protective factors in drug abuse prevention* [Electronic version]. NIDA Notes, 16(6). Retrieved July 3, 2002, from http://www.drugabuse.gov/NIDA_Notes/NNVol16No6/Risk.html

National Institute of Mental Health. (2000). *Child and adolescent violence research at the NIMH.* Retrieved June 24, 2002, from http://www.nimh.nih.gov/publicat/violenceresfact.cfm

Office of Applied Studies, Substance Abuse and Mental Health Services Administration. (2002, May). *Substance use among pregnant women during 1999 and 2000: The NHSDA report.* Retrieved June 27, 2002, from http://www.samhsa.gov/oas/2k2/preg/preg.pdf

Office of National Drug Control Policy. (1996). *Treatment protocol effectiveness study.*

Retrieved July 1, 2002, from http://www.whitehousedrugpolicy.gov//treat/shanprot.html

Office of National Drug Control Policy. (2002a). *CSAP's prevention strategies.* Retrieved July 1, 2002 from http://www.whitehousedrugpolicy.gov/prevent/high%5Frisk/e%5Fsum3. htm

Office of National Drug Control Policy. (2002b). *Drug facts: Club drugs.* Retrieved June 27, 2002 from http://www.whitehousedrugpolicy.gov/drugfact/club/club_b.html

Office of National Drug Control Policy. (2002c). *Drug facts: Cocaine.* Retrieved June 27, 2002 from http://www.whitehousedrugpolicy.gov/drugfact/cocaine/cocaine_b.ht ml

Office of National Drug Control Policy. (2002d). *Drug facts: Crack.* Retrieved June 27, 2002 from http://www.whitehousedrugpolicy.gov/drugfact/crack/crack_b.html

Office of National Drug Control Policy. (2002e). *Drug facts: Heroin.* Retrieved June 27, 2002 from http://www.whitehousedrugpolicy.gov/drugfact/heroin/heroin_b.html

Office of National Drug Control Policy. (2002f). *Drug facts: Marijuana.* Retrieved July 1, 2002 from http://www.whitehousedrugpolicy.gov/drugfact/marijuana/marijuana_b.html

Office of National Drug Control Policy. (2002g). *Drug facts: Methamphetamines.* Retrieved June 27, 2002 from http://www.whitehousedrugpolicy.gov/drugfact/methamphetamines/meth_b.html

Office of National Drug Control Policy. (2002h). *Drug facts: Minorities and drugs.* Retrieved June 27, 2002 from http://www.whitehousedrugpolicy.gov/drugfact/minorities/minorities_b.html

Orford, J. (2001). Addiction as excessive appetite [Electronic version]. *Addiction, 96,* 15–32.

Osofsky, J.D. (1994). Introduction. *Zero to Three, 14*(3), 3–6.

Osofsky, J.D. (1996). Introduction. *Zero to Three, 16*(5), 5–8.

Osofsky, J.D. (2000). Treating traumatized children: The costs of delay. *Zero to Three, 20*(5), 20–24.

Osofsky, J.D., & Jackson, B.R. (1994). Parenting in violent environments. *Zero to Three, 14*(3), 8–12.

Rycus, J.S., & Hughes, R.C. (1998). *Field guide to child welfare: Vol. III. Child development and child welfare.* Washington, DC: Child Welfare League of America.

Sameroff, A.J., & Chandler, M.J. (1975). Reproductive risk and the continuum of caretaking casualty. In F.D. Horowitz, M. Hetherington, S. Scarr-Salapatek, & G. Siegel (Eds.), *Review of child development research* (Vol. 4, pp. 187–244). Chicago: University of Chicago Press.

Sedlak, A.J., & Broadhurst, D.D. (1996, September). *Executive summary of the third National Incidence Study of Child Abuse and Neglect.* Washington, DC: National Clearinghouse on Child Abuse and Neglect Information.

Sobsey, D. (1994). *Violence and abuse in the lives of people with disabilities: The end of silent acceptance?* Baltimore: Paul H. Brookes Publishing Co.

Spiess, M., & Fallow, D. (2000). *Drug-related crime fact sheet.* Rockville, MD: ONDCP Drug Policy Information Clearinghouse. Retrieved June 26, 2002, from http://www.whitehousedrugpolicy.gov

Stith, S.M., Rosen, K.H., Middleton, K.A., Busch, A.L., Lundenberg, K., & Carlton, R.P. (2000). The intergenerational transmission of spouse abuse: A meta-analysis [Electronic version]. *Journal of Marriage and Family, 62,* 640–655.

Streissguth, A. (1997). *Fetal alcohol syndrome: A guide for families and communities.* Baltimore: Paul H. Brookes Publishing Co.

Szyndrowski, D. (1999). The impact of domestic violence on adolescent aggression in the schools [Electronic version]. *Preventing School Failure, 44,* 9–12.

Tjaden, P., & Thoennes, N. (1998, November). *Prevalence, incidence, and consequences of violence against women: Findings from the National Violence Against Women Survey* [Electronic version], National Institute of Justice and Centers for Disease Control and Prevention: Research in Brief. Retrieved July 5, 2002, from http://www.ncjrs.org/pdffiles/172837.pdf

U.S. Department of Health and Human Services. (2000, November). *Healthy people 2010.* Retrieved June 24, 2002, from http://www.health.gov/healthypeople/document/html/uih/uih_4.htm #tobaccouse

U.S. Department of Health and Human Services. (2001). *Nicotine addiction* (National

Institute on Drug Abuse Research Report Series, NIH Publication Number 01-4342). Retrieved July 3, 2002, from http://www.drugabuse.gov/researchreports/nicotine/nicotine.html

U.S. Department of Justice, Bureau of Juvenile Statistics. (2000, January). *Drug use and crime.* Retrieved June 25, 2002, from http://www.ojp.usdoj.gov/dcf/duc.htm

The Violence Study Group, ZERO TO THREE/National Center for Clinical Infant Programs. (1993). Call for violence prevention and intervention on behalf of very young children. *Zero to Three, 14*(3), 38–41.

Watts, C., & Zimmerman, C. (2002). Violence against women: Global scope and magnitude [Electronic version]. *The Lancet, 359,* 1232–1237.

Wunsch, M.J., Conlon, C.J., & Scheidt, P.C. (2002). Substance abuse: A preventable threat to development. In M.L. Batshaw (Ed.), *Children with disabilities* (5th ed., pp. 107–122). Baltimore: Paul H. Brookes Publishing Co.

Zorza, J. (1991). Woman battering: A major cause of homelessness. *Clearinghouse Review, 25,* 421.

SECTION III

FAMILY SUPPORT AND SERVICES

CHAPTER 7

FORMING FAMILY–PROFESSIONAL ALLIANCES

Research and Practice

The greatest gift I've ever had was
the birth of my son...because of him,
I educated myself...I started my lifelong love affair
with libraries...I've learned an awful lot because of him.
—MAYA ANGELOU (AS QUOTED BY VENICE JOHNSON, 1995)

"As parents of [a child with disabilities] we feel that
advocating in school for our child is not just a privilege, but
a responsibility that we are obligated to fulfill in order to
ensure the best possible education for our daughter."
—SALLY AND RON JAWOROWSKI (1978, p. 29)

This is a book of encouragement; it is about the resilience of families and about the ways in which families and professionals can work together to improve their lives and the lives of children. Although family–professional partnerships are important for all who work with children and families, they are foundational to working with families of children with disabilities. The importance of these alliances has been recognized in the literature for many years, but partnerships of all kinds are easier to describe than to create and maintain. Tension between families and professionals is not unusual; in fact, some tension is a healthy result of the different roles that family members and professionals play in the lives of children who have—or who are at risk for—disabilities. Parents and family members know their child better than anyone else. They understand the needs of their family system and the beliefs and behaviors that they value and by which they live. On the one hand, family members are typically the child's best advocate because they are trying to meet the child's needs rather than balance the child's needs against larger social, political, and economic needs that professionals confront within their organizations, communities, and states. Professionals, on the other hand, bring advanced knowledge and skill training, extensive experience, and a range of tools and techniques that have been honed over time. They know more children and families than a family by itself will probably meet in a lifetime. Although family service professionals are often strong advocates for the children and families that they serve, most work within a bigger picture of priorities and needs than those of a family or child alone. Sometimes, admittedly, for family service professionals the bigger picture takes precedence.

This chapter discusses family–professional tensions and alliances in the context of a family-centered approach to intervention from the perspectives of research and practice. It defines the goals and principles of family-centered service, attempts to dispel the myth that professionals have little to contribute in this approach, and discusses family–professional roles and relationships. It concludes with suggestions for putting effective partnerships into practice.

A SHORT HISTORY OF CHANGE IN FAMILY–PROFESSIONAL RELATIONSHIPS

Family-centered services have become the gold standard of early intervention systems, programs, and services since the mid-1980s. In a review of early education programs and outcomes, Bronfenbrenner (1975) concluded that active parent involvement was a major contributor to the success of these programs. In his book *The Future of Children* (1975), Nicholas Hobbs, eminent child psychologist, asserted that the true role of intervention programs was to marshal socializing agents within the family, neighborhood, and community as a way of strengthening families and their functioning. That assertion was more fully described in a later book by Hobbs and colleagues, *Strengthening Families* (1984). The notion of using informal supports rather than formal supports was viewed as a more natural, normalized way of assisting families. The emphasis on the importance of families and of determining family needs from the family's point of view emerged as central to child health care (Baird, 1997).

Fields such as child health care adopted this new model, and research and ideology in areas such as early intervention began to shift. Building on their research with families, philosophy, and evolving notions of best practice, Dunst (1985) and others (Bailey et al., 1986; Dunst, Trivette, & Deal, 1988) challenged the traditional view of child-directed services as the optimal model for early intervention. Turnbull, Summers, and Brotherson's (1984) contributions to the application of family systems theory to families of children with disabilities or children at risk for disabilities moved the field forward in both philosophy and practice. (See Chapters 2 and 3 for details of the family systems framework.) The Education of the Handicapped Act Amendments of 1986 (PL 99-457) (retitled as the Individuals with Disabilities Education Act [IDEA] Amendments of 1997 [PL 105-17]) gave planning grants to states to develop early intervention services for families with children from birth to 3 who have, or who are at risk for, disabilities. It also mandated free and appropriate public education for preschoolers with disabilities. The new legislation created a vehicle for putting new ideology into practice through the individualized family service plans (IFSPs) for children birth through age 3. The IFSP gives families a central role in determining services and the ways in which they are delivered (Hauser-Cram, Upshur, Krauss, & Shonkoff, 1988). It also underscores the need for systems, programs, and individual service providers to re-think their approach to serving children and families. This bill was set to be reauthorized as the Improving Education Results for Children with Disabilities Act (HR 1350) in 2003.

This re-thinking changed the locus of services from children to *children in the context of their families*. Determining family priorities and needed

supports became as important as child-centered activities, approaches, and interventions. Family-centered approaches incorporate family support in service delivery, and family support emphasizes family strengths (Dunst, Trivette, Starnes, Hamby, & Gordon, 1993; Singer & Powers, 1993). Professional contributions to family support typically enhance families' well-being and competence, and model and teach relationship skills. Professionals must reflect ethical behavior in all interactions, employ strategies for training specific skills and behaviors, and demonstrate knowledge and ability to teach strategies that enhance supports. Optimally, they must display a commitment to collaborative partnerships and place value on the power of self-help groups (Singer & Powers, 1993). These skills are foundational to family-centered practices, and wisdom from the family support movement provided evidence that families were quite capable of identifying their own needs.

This view has been reinforced by research in subsequent years in which families of children with disabilities were asked about their own needs and preferences related to information gathering and services. In a qualitative study that examined parents' and professionals' expectations of family outcomes in early intervention and the preferences of each group for gathering information about family strengths and needs, Summers and colleagues (1990) found that family members looked to early intervention professionals to provide emotional support and friendship. Contrary to professional training curricula that emphasize professional distance and boundaries, these findings underscore the value of personal, informal relationships between professionals and family members when parents are first learning that their son or daughter has a disability. The study also found that early interventionists and early intervention programs were expected to provide information, assist in linking families with other families in similar situations, and help parents and other family members develop skills that would facilitate later relationships with service systems. Professionals were also expected to help parents develop the skills necessary to work more effectively with their son or daughter with disabilities. This last point is critical, for it has been so frequently omitted as programs have attempted to become family-centered. Although the role of professionals in family-centered practice has changed, its importance and value have not.

In a similar qualitative study, parents' primary expectation for early intervention was accurate information, positive reactions, and uncensored information about what is available so that parents can decide (Able-Boone, Sandall, & Frederick, 1990). Family members expressed their desire to have the knowledge that would empower them to make informed decisions. This study, too, supported families' desire for professionals who are knowledgeable and who bring their knowledge and skills to the partnership.

In addition to participating in research conducted by professionals, parents and other family members have developed models and approaches to services that underscore the many tenets of family-centered practice (Santelli, Poyadue, & Young, 2001). Parents throughout the country have

developed Parent to Parent networks. In Parent to Parent networks, a trained, supportive parent of a child with a disability or risk condition provides information and emotional support as needed to a matched parent who requests assistance (Singer et al., 1999). The veteran parent is often available around the clock for questions, conversations, and emotional support (Santelli, Turnbull, Sergeant, Lerner, & Marquis, 1996). The veteran and referral parents are often matched by children's disability or risk condition, the children's ages, or the even geographic proximity of the families. Parent to Parent programs have been cited as particularly valuable in providing information and emotional support for families of children with disabilities (e.g., Meyer, 1993; Santelli, Turnbull, Lerner, & Marquis, 1993; Santelli et al., 1996; Turnbull & Turnbull, 2001). The opportunity to talk with someone who has "been there" is often an invaluable resource for families who are encountering new feelings, new demands, and new systems. Parent to Parent programs do not include professionals and do not represent models of family–professional collaboration; they underscore the importance of personal contact and knowledge of daily life with a child with disabilities or serious risks—something that most professionals have not experienced.

Cognitive Coping

Cognitive coping, according to Turnbull and Turnbull, entails "thinking about a particular situation in ways that enhance a sense of well-being" (1993, p. 1). The ability to re-frame a situation that is negative or is perceived to be negative in a more positive light is another way to define cognitive coping. Parent-professionals—recognized researchers who are also parents of children with disabilities—have driven research on cognitive coping in the area of developmental disabilities. Contrary to much of the writing in the field of developmental disabilities and societal views, many families feel enriched by their son or daughter with a disability (Turnbull et al., 1993). Expressing these feelings of being enriched by living with, learning from, and loving a child with a disability is an example of cognitive coping. The research on cognitive coping underscores the family-centered principles of empowerment and respect for family perspectives.

A Realignment of Priorities and Ways of Working Together

The change from child-centered to family-focused or family-centered services was akin to a shift in planetary alignment—all elements within the model now relate differently to one another. This new family-focused approach required that professionals and parents alike develop new ways to work together. As stated by Vacca and Feinberg,

> *The new paradigm requires that early interventionists learn to adapt to the culture and aspirations of the families with whom they work. A unidirectional strategy in which parents are expected to become acculturated to the world of the early interventionist is replaced by a bidirectional system in which both the clinician and family learn from and adapt to each other. (2000, p. 41)*

Though a family-centered approach remains the gold standard, it has been challenging to implement and plagued by considerable misunderstanding of what family-centered really means.

WHAT DOES FAMILY-CENTERED REALLY MEAN?

Several tenets characterize family-centered practice: It 1) recognizes parents or primary caregivers as experts on their child; 2) acknowledges the family as the ultimate decision maker for their child and themselves; 3) views the family as the constant in the child's life and the service providers and systems as transitory; 4) respects and works to support family priorities, their goals for service, and the extent to which they choose to be involved; 5) values trusting, collaborative relationships between parents and professionals; and 6) works to ensure culturally competent services (e.g., Baird, 1997; Dunst et al., 1988; Hanson, 1996; Hanson & Lynch, 1995; Lynch & Hanson, 2004). Although many professionals and program administrators asserted that they had already been doing this, generally that was not the case. Consider the story of Marta, which describes service delivery in an approach that is not family-centered.

Marta

Marta is 28 months old. Her parents are very concerned because she seems to be regressing instead of progressing in the areas of socialization and communication. Until recently, Marta had seemed to be developing typically:

She had said her first words at 12 months in both English and Spanish and had developed a vocabulary that allowed her to name her favorite objects and put two words together. Although she was never as cuddly as her older sister had been, she enjoyed being held and was socially engaging.

The family physician and a university clinic staff member assess Marta and tell her parents that they think that her increasing problems in social and communication areas place her on the spectrum of pervasive developmental disorder or autism. They suggest an early intervention program. Marta's mother contacts the program to express her concern and interest. Although the person who answers the telephone is friendly and sounds supportive, she makes it clear that they only accept referrals from other professionals. Marta's mother must ask the family physician or someone at the clinic to make the referral and send any reports that have been written so that program personnel can determine the appropriateness of the referral before they meet Marta or her parents.

Marta's mother agrees, requests the referral, and has the reports sent to the program. Program staff decide that it is an appropriate referral but want to conduct their own assessment. In their assessment, various staff members administer various tests, play with Marta, and observe Marta's behavior. The only questions they ask Marta's parents have to do with birth history and developmental milestones. The staff ask them no questions about their observations as parents, their immediate concerns, what they have been told up to this point, or what they need as a family to make this challenging time easier for them.

The program staff determine that Marta is eligible for services and develop goals, objectives, and outcomes that they present in a very nice rough draft to Marta's parents at the IFSP meeting. Marta's mother and father were hoping that she could continue to attend the community toddler/preschool program that her sister attends, but program staff state that they just cannot spread themselves that thin. They need to see Marta at their center 3 days a week. They also emphasize the importance of weekly home visits—something difficult for her parents to arrange because of their work schedules. The meeting ends with the staff's suggestions and rough draft accepted as is, and Marta begins to attend the program. During the subsequent home visits, a staff member demonstrates how to work with Marta. The staff member then leaves activities for Marta and her parents to do together and data collection forms for Marta's parents to complete before the next home visit.

Let us examine this vignette in relation to the principles of family-centered services. In this example, staff members did not recognize parents or primary caregivers as experts on their child. They demonstrated this by requiring a professional referral and professional reports before talking with the family about their concerns. In the assessment, program staff relied on the administration of various tests, observations, and play activities without soliciting or listening to the parents' concerns and asking about their observations. IFSPs and individualized education programs (IEPs) are to be jointly developed by parents and staff members. In this

IFSP, no opportunity was given for the family's expertise to be incorporated. Finally, the home visits were used only for instruction on the goals and objectives developed by the program. They were not related to any concerns expressed by the parents or integrated into the family's normal routines.

The professionals in this vignette did not acknowledge the family as the ultimate decision maker for their child and family. If families are the decision makers, their referral and concerns should be adequate for program staff to begin assessment for eligibility. Referral from another professional would not be required. Parental requests at the IFSP would have been heeded rather than ignored, and the need for, time, or place for home visits would have been discussed and negotiated.

When families are viewed as the constant in the child's life and the service providers and systems viewed as transitory, every effort is made to incorporate intervention into the daily life and routines of the family. Interventions that create additional burdens are less likely to be continued and less likely to be effective over the long term. Viewing families and family members as the constant also leads to efforts to empower parents for a lifetime of negotiations and decision making related to their son or daughter.

In this vignette, Marta's parents' priorities, goals, and level of involvement were neither respected nor supported. Her parents were never really asked about their priorities and goals. The program staff developed the IFSP outcomes without consultation. The community toddler/preschool program that Marta's parents preferred was ruled out without investigation; and the home visits were conducted at the staff's—not the parents'—convenience.

When programs value trusting, collaborative relationships between parents and professionals, the family-centered principles are not ignored. An ongoing attempt is made to examine practice, consider alternatives, and seek family input to determine ways to improve. Although these staff members may be competent in the technical skills of their professional disciplines, they have not shown that they value family–professional relationships.

To be family-centered is to acknowledge, respect, and tailor programs and services to meet the cultural and sociocultural needs of families (i.e., to be culturally competent). In the case of Marta and her family, culture or preferred language was not considered. The service providers made the assumption that there was nothing salient about the family's cultural beliefs, values, or language that would affect intervention. When culture is not broached, it is never addressed; and services cannot be considered to be culturally competent.

In this example the program and professionals associated with it were not malevolent people. They did not deliberately bypass a family-centered approach. They may have been technically competent in their professional disciplines. They were simply operating on a set of principles that are no longer acceptable in intervention, whether it takes place in health care, early intervention for children with disabilities, child care, or Head Start.

Myths and Misunderstandings in Family-Centered Practice

Although family-centered practice is the goal, all too often, programs and professionals have embraced the words without understanding the content. The subsequent paragraphs illustrate some of the myths, misunderstandings, and mistakes that occur when service providers, programs, and policy makers do not fully understand family-centered practice.

Myth: The Role of Professionals Is Diminishing

Standards of practice in all fields change over time. They are influenced by research, philosophy, politics, economics, and policy decisions. It is not uncommon for the pendulum of practice to swing wildly from one approach to another in an attempt to align with the current trend. This often occurs before all of the data are in and is often based on a cursory reading and understanding of the underlying principles and goals of the trend. This certainly was and continues to be the case with family-centered practice. In a rush to become family-centered, professionals and their skills were initially devalued and their roles disregarded. The children who had been the reason behind the families and professionals getting together in the first place were barely registering on the radar screen. Child-focused interventions were minimized in favor of a family focus. Professionals often misinterpreted critical research (e.g., Able-Boone, Sandall, & Frederick, 1990; Summers et al., 1990) on family preferences and needs and asked new or recently referred parents what they wanted or needed without providing information to assist in decision making. In the absence of accurate information, it is impossible to make an informed decision.

Put yourself in the following situation. Imagine learning that you have a significant health problem. You find the specialists in this field, ask about their experiences with various treatment regimens, and request their recommendations for your particular situation. In this scenario you would expect the specialists to listen to you, but you would also expect the professionals to share information freely and provide recommendations based on their knowledge of the possibilities as well as your own unique circumstances. You would also assume that professionals involved in the treatment would use their skills in treatment. Few people would stay with a professional who assured them that they could treat themselves effectively but never taught them how.

The same can be said of working with families. By the time families seek professionals for assistance and support because of concerns about their children, they want more than a friendly face. They want knowledge and the ability to put that knowledge into the family's context—their values, beliefs, strengths, and needs. Any interpretation of family-centered practice that excludes professional knowledge, experience, and expertise is faulty as is any interpretation that leaves the child out of the picture. An article by Dunst provided a revised vision and version of family-centered practice. In it he stated,

> It now seems to me that any model that is going to be useful needs to explicitly incorporate parent–child and child features into it if the debate about family-centered/family support models versus any other kind of model is to be abated. (2000, p. 101)

Professionals are vital to effective intervention. Their training, knowledge, skills, and experience complement the family's knowledge of their own child, understanding or family preferences and priorities, and their commitment to care over a lifetime. Without equal respect for what each person brings to the relationship there can be no partnership; this is one of the guiding principles of family-centered practice.

Myth: Only Family Concerns Are Important

An extension of the devaluation of professionals is the myth that service providers should address only those issues that the family identifies as important. Thus, if the family is only concerned that the child's behavior is a serious problem, the professional should not mention her concerns that the child may have a significant hearing loss. This perspective, in fact, runs counter to family-centered practice. If families are to be the ultimate decision makers, they must be provided with the necessary information to make informed decisions (Able-Boone et al., 1990). If families and professionals are to develop real partnerships, professionals cannot withhold information that they consider to be important. They may consider the family's concerns first and work on one issue at a time, making the family's concerns the priority, but they should also voice their own concerns and request the family's permission to proceed. Most important, information given to families should be given in ways that support their self-confidence and ability to parent, and facilitate their learning without threatening their knowledge and ability (Bruder, 2000).

Myth: Formal Supports Are Bad

Another misunderstanding is that formal supports such as counseling, classes, or workshops on behavior support or agency-organized inclusive playgroups are inherently bad and should be avoided. Some people prefer formal supports. One of the guiding principles of family-centered practice is the individualization of services to meet the preferences of diverse families. The definition of early intervention proposed by Dunst, Trivette, and Jodry (1997) included formal supports as part of the mix of supports that families may need.

Consider, again, the example from an earlier paragraph in which you learn that you have a significant health problem. In addition to seeking out the experts in the field, you may talk to friends and family members, attend a support group of individuals who have had the same problem, read articles about the problem in everything from medical journals to popular magazines to Internet sites, and investigate alternative treatments. Each person performing this exercise might do it differently; for example, he or she might do one or all of these, and the value that the individual places on each would probably vary. All are strategies for learning about the problem and facing it emotionally.

This range of responses is no different for families with a child with disabilities, behavioral challenges, or health concerns. Considerable attention has been paid in recent years to informal support, the marshaling of resources that are part of a family's daily life, such as other family members, friends, neighbors, colleagues at work, and faith communities. These personal networks have been shown to be important resources for families and research has suggested that informal support through personal networks showed the strongest relationship to child and family outcomes (Dunst, 1999). Supports may be direct as well, however. They may include opportunities for families to participate in learning about resources, their child's disability, and strategies for working more effectively with the child, professionals, and agencies. Although informal supports are important and often make us feel good, they are seldom sufficient to address all of the issues surrounding a child with a disability or serious behavioral problems.

Myth: Only Professionals Must Change

A third myth is that for family-centered practice to be effective, only professionals have to change. Rather, for family-centered practice to be achieved, professionals, families, agencies, and policy makers may have to change. Family-centered practice is not easy to develop or maintain (Bruder, 2000). At a time when an increasing number of families have more complex problems and children have more complicated needs, early interventionists are trying to provide comprehensive, coordinated, family-centered services (Krahn, Thom, Hale, & Williams, 1995). Professionals have had to engage in additional training, obtain new certifications in some instances, and spend increasing amounts of time collaborating with adults at other agencies when they entered the field to work with children. Sometimes all of the effort that professionals have put into retraining themselves has been negated by policy decisions at the state or agency level. The belief that well-trained professionals could single-handedly make family-centered practice a reality is a myth.

Hence, other changes must occur for family-centered practice to be effective. Family members must have the resources and desire to participate in new ways. Participation may vary widely across families and within families over time, but each family must decide on what they want for their child and how they want to be involved in all aspects of intervention. In family-centered practices, services vary. Service providers do not assume that a service that is helpful for one family is equally helpful for another. Customizing services requires that families put forth additional effort to make selections that they consider best for their child and family and that professionals work to ensure that customized services are integrated. Just as implementing a specific teaching strategy or behavior change technique takes learning and time, so do making decisions about priorities, formulating long- and short-term objectives, and monitoring outcomes.

Agencies and policy makers must also change if family-centered support is to become the norm. The current emphasis that some intervention programs place on offering a menu of services as opposed to integrated programs in early intervention has some serious, negative consequences. As McCollum articulated so well when discussing the fee-for-service approach to early intervention,

> *The consequences have been a return to fragmented services at the level of the child and family and less opportunity for collaboration among professionals working with each child and family. It has become much more difficult for service providers of all disciplines to be "family-centered," to embed their interventions within the contexts of families' daily lives, and to integrate their interventions with those of other professionals in recognition of the integrated nature of early development. (2000, pp. 85–86)*

Until the entire system can be designed to facilitate family-centered services, the burden will continue to fall on those closest to the issues—families and direct-service professionals.

Avoiding Myths and Misunderstandings

Each of these myths, misunderstandings, and mistakes can be overcome. At its simplest level, family-centered practice is providing supports and services that the family desires and values in order to enhance child and family outcomes within a respectful partnership between families and professionals. If practice is guided by this definition, myths and misunderstandings are likely to decrease.

FAMILY AND PROFESSIONAL ROLES AND RELATIONSHIPS

This section focuses on power, becoming empowered as a parent, and the variables that families and professionals identify as important to effective collaboration.

Power and Becoming Empowered

In most situations in which families and professionals interact, power is a factor, and professionals hold considerable power over information, possibilities, and outcomes of the interaction. Their power comes from real and attributed knowledge, the power of "the system," and long-held assumptions that the system cannot be critically questioned. This has certainly been true in systems of care and education for children with disabilities and their families. Interventions in the not-so-distant past tended to focus on direct, hands-on, professional intervention with children. Parents were considered secondary in the treatment or intervention and were generally expected to follow directions dictated by professionals. Parents were provided with parent education opportunities typically designed and taught by professionals. Very often these opportunities focused on what professionals wanted parents to do rather than on what parents wanted to learn. As discussed in earlier sections of this chapter, this approach would not be considered to be family-centered.

One of the guiding principles of a family-centered approach is empowerment (Dunst et al., 1988). Proactive Empowerment through Partnerships (PEP), described by Dunst (1985), included three tenets that emphasized 1) family strengths rather than deficits in early intervention practice; 2) family control over services rather than dependency-producing, disempowering practices; and 3) collaborative rather than professional-centered practice. These principles not only spawned considerable research but also became guiding principles in family-centered practice. Empowerment in its most basic form is providing the tools that individuals need to gain access to services and make decisions about them. Empowerment enhances capability. To be empowered is to have the information and sense of personal competence necessary to advocate for oneself or someone else. Thus, for family–professional partnerships to flourish, balancing the power between families and professionals is critical to success. Being passionate about an issue does not necessarily empower individuals to do something about it. Empowerment often requires some coaching. Many families may need information and support to become empowered when it comes to issues involving their children. Part of the role of the professional in family-centered services is to help family members become empowered—to ensure that families and professionals recognize that each comes to the relationship with different but equally valued knowledge and skills.

Although providing the tools and support to assist family members to become empowered is a cornerstone of family-centered services, it is a concept that does not resonate equally with families across cultures. In a pilot study comparing African American and Latino mothers in Southern California with white, non-Latino parents of children with disabilities in Australia, issues of disempowerment and empowerment were clearest to the African American mothers (Hall, Lynch, Macvean, & Valverde, 2000). Many had had experience with the Civil Rights movement and were very aware of the parallels between the need to feel empowered as black women as well as mothers of children with disabilities. The Latino mothers interviewed had not had similar experiences, and empowerment and disempowerment were not terms that were familiar to them. Even when these terms were translated conceptually rather than literally, Latino mothers were less able to describe situations related to their child in which they felt a sense of competence and control rather than a sense that they had no control.

Because of the importance of issues of empowerment within a family-centered framework, cross-cultural work on empowerment needs to be pursued. Approaches to empowerment that conflict with cultural and sociocultural beliefs and approaches to interaction are, by definition, disempowering.

Variables that Support or Interfere with Collaborative Partnerships

Professional and Family Variables

In a large, national study of families and professionals, the variables that families and professionals bring to interactions were examined to determine variables that support and those that hinder collaboration. Five categories and one subcategory of variables important to collaboration for both families and professionals emerged (Dinnebeil, Hale, & Rule, 1996). The categories included

- Dispositions/personal and family characteristics
- Philosophical beliefs and attitudes
- Ways of working together
- Knowledge base
- Outside influences

The subcategory of putting beliefs into practice was an amalgamation of philosophical beliefs and values and ways of working together. Dispositions and characteristics were important to both family members and professionals. Being optimistic, friendly, open-minded, and caring were considered to be important traits. When the sociocultural and lifestyle match between professionals and families was missing, it was more difficult to collaborate. Philosophical beliefs and values contributed to or interfered with collaboration. Family-centered practices such as trusting, being nonjudgmental, respecting, and accepting differences contributed to effective collaboration as did positive beliefs about disabilities. Some families thought that the professional's (in this study, the professionals were service coordinators) willingness to be involved as a friend was helpful; however, not all service coordinators felt that friendship enhanced the collaboration. Ways of working together that supported collaboration included open communication, honesty, tact, establishing a positive atmosphere, and using expertise to share information and model ways of working more effectively with the child. Although the importance of the professional's knowledge base was mentioned fewer times than dispositions and philosophical beliefs, it was nonetheless considered important by family members. Knowledge of disability, strategies, and resource information contributed to collaboration, as did cultural knowledge and the ability to communicate in the family's language. Outside influences such as scheduling constraints, size of caseloads, limited options for service, and so forth were also identified as barriers or facilitators, when the constraints had been overcome, of collaboration. These influences were considered to be very important to effective collaboration, but they were not considered to be under the control of families or professionals. Additional influences such as bad weather, distance from services, lack of resources, lack of transportation, and lack of opportunity for staff to be trained in collaboration were also identified. It is interesting to note that issues such as scheduling and availability of services were considered to be outside the control of professionals and parents alike. Given a model that supports empowerment, it would seem that professionals would begin by working to change the system to more satisfactorily accommodate family needs. The subcategory, putting beliefs into practice, showed that professionals "practiced what they preached." They scheduled appointments that were convenient for families, kept appointments, respected families as decision makers, and supported approaches to service that allowed families to live more normal lives.

A case study approach was used to determine the characteristics of professionals that lead to effective collaboration; five themes related to interpersonal interactions as well as two themes related to knowledge of children emerged (McWilliam, Tocci, & Harbin, 1998):

- Having a family orientation
- Being positive and viewing the family in a favorable light
- Sensitivity to the family
- Responsiveness or willingness to do what needs to be done
- Treating parents as friends
- Child and community skills, which included knowledge about disabilities and methods for interacting with and teaching children and integrating their work into the larger community

Although many would seek the majority of these characteristics in their search for a competent and understanding professional, the one area in which these descriptors and professional preferences may depart is in the area of friendship. Throughout a professional's career, many parents become friends; but a professional is neither trained nor encouraged in training to develop friendships with the families they serve. McWilliam and his colleagues acknowledged this difference in expectations and suggested that many professionals would "be more comfortable with the *friendly professional* stance than with a *professional friend*" (p. 215).

In a study of parents' and professionals' perspectives on services needed and services provided, professionals were enthusiastic about their family-centered practices but families reported that they were receiving less than a quarter of the services that they needed (Filer & Mahoney, 1996). Worth noting is that families rated child-level activities provided by early intervention programs as more important than family-level activities. Professionals reported substantially greater needs for service in four out of five categories that parents reported. Professionals felt that families needed 1) more information about their children and how to interpret test results, 2) additional support in preparing for the child's future and advocating for their son or daughter, 3) ways of coping with their child and getting support, and 4) assistance in finding resources or services. The findings of this study are particularly interesting because of families' emphasis on more direct assistance to the child. This certainly does not suggest that family support services are not critical to families. What it does indicate is that a truly family-centered model determines what families believe is most important and builds services on that basis. For these families, the most important support would have been more services for their children such as child care, therapies, and medical treatments.

Issues that cause conflict in early intervention programs were identified in informal conversations with other family members (Vohs, 1998). In these conversations parents spoke about the lost promise of IFSPs—that in many programs IFSPs have been reduced to paperwork. Programs were perceived as not using information from outside sources such as the family physician, or that they did not willingly provide needed services. A number of parents said that they had lost trust in the early intervention system because they felt that professionals had not been open and honest with them about their child's need for service and therapies. Although these areas of conflict might also have surfaced in a family-centered model, their resolution would be more likely if families and professionals were involved in collaborative partnerships based on some of the characteristics described previously.

Program Variables

The study by Dinnebeil, Hale, and Rule (1999) that examined family and professional variables influencing collaboration also investigated program variables that support or interfere with collaboration. More collaborative programs had a philosophy and climate that supported collaboration, operated within a community context, used a team-based approach, implemented policies and procedures conducive to collaboration, and delivered services in ways that demonstrated that collaboration was valued. A subcategory was qualified personnel. Respondents frequently addressed the importance of having well-trained personnel with good communication skills. These findings suggest that program-level decisions, procedures, and processes influence the collaborative process and set the tone for developing partnerships.

Synthesis

These studies provide an extensive list of professional, program, and family characteristics that support family–professional collaboration. They also describe characteristics and behaviors that are not conducive to cooperation, collaboration, and partnership. It is clear that the ability to establish and participate in trusting relationships, communicate effectively, and respect families' roles and responsibilities as the ultimate decision makers for their child and family is critical. It is equally clear that possessing knowledge and skills related to children with disabilities, working within the context of the family and community, being positive and open-minded, and following through on promises contribute to effective collaboration with families. Professionals who are perceived to be dishonest with families, do not share information fully, do not respect family roles and responsibilities, display negative attitudes toward families or their job, and are not well trained for their jobs are not able to form collaborative partnerships. Though based on research, these findings are almost intuitive. In any relationship, respect, positive attitudes, and honesty are critical elements. In programs and services for families, they are essential.

Program variables also help or hinder collaboration. Even the most highly trained and experienced service provider can appear non-collaborative when working within agency policies and procedures that do not support collaboration. Putting all interactions "on the clock" in fee-for-service systems, working only during traditional hours, following required assessment protocols that minimize family input, or refusing needed services in order to under-spend the budget in an effort to look good to superiors can make the most family-centered professional look bad. A family-centered professional would also use his or her skills and creativity to help change the system to make it more responsive to families and children rather than simply view the complaints as unsolvable problems, however.

In most articles, chapters, and books (including this one) about family–professional collaboration, the emphasis is on the characteristics of professionals and systems and how they can change to enhance family–professional collaboration. This is appropriate in that it is the job of the professional to be the collaborator, to meet families "where they are," and to support family goals and priorities—often not easy tasks. Parents and families sometimes have characteristics that interfere with collaboration and partnering. Dinnebeil and colleagues' (1996) research identified certain lifestyles, personality traits, attitudes, and a lack of communication skills as family characteristics that make collaboration extremely difficult. In a study of more than 350 families, Mahoney and Filer (1996) found that families with the most positive characteristics such as enough time and resources, positive family functioning (cohesion, control, expressiveness), and the interpersonal skills to negotiate the system received the most services. These findings, if they can be generalized, are not surprising; but they are troubling. They suggest that families with the greatest needs may be the least well served. Families that do not function well, those that lack the skills to negotiate the system, and those that do not have the time to be involved may be in double jeopardy. They have more problems at the outset and are receiving less help in resolving them. Considering the numbers and range of families that this might include—teen parents; families whose primary language is not English; those who are living in poverty; families with mental health problems; and families who have problems with substance abuse, addiction, and violence—the findings suggest that family–professional collaboration is far from reality in many situations. Some data is promising, however. Unger, Jones, Park, and Tressell (2001) studied the involvement of low-income, single caregivers in an urban environment. Most of the 104 caregivers who participated were African American, lived alone, and were the biological mothers of the children being studied who were attending an early intervention program. In this study, caregivers who were stressed, had difficulties with family functioning, and were less knowledgeable about child development were more likely to become involved with the program. Their involvement was predicated on a welcoming climate and teachers' efforts to reach out to them.

No family will like every professional equally, nor will professionals resonate with each family in the same way. As humans we respond to different characteristics in different ways. As individuals we are inexplicably drawn to some people and not to others. It is the professional's responsibility to provide the same level of information, support, and energy to all families, however. For those who have worked with challenging families, the concern is usually that as professionals they have done everything they can do, but the family "continues to miss home visits," "doesn't follow through," "is so involved in their own issues that they have no time for the child," "doesn't have the skills/ability to parent effectively," "is unrealistic," or "wants everyone else to do the impossible but doesn't want to do anything themselves." All of these may be true, but it is the role of the professional to continue to meet the family "where they are" and to work to support the family and the child. When should a professional give up? The answer is never, where the child is concerned. When a professional feels that she or he may be endangered by continued interaction with the family, however, it is time for a change. Concerns about safety for the child, another family member, or oneself should be immediately reported to supervisors and any other authority or agency determined by state law and program policies.

In addition to families with limited resources, difficult circumstances, and inadequate interpersonal skills, there are families whose resources to challenge the system seem unlimited. They are often knowledgeable, articulate, and well defended (personally and with advocates and attorneys). They typically get what they ask for. For many of these families, the concerns are centered on the needs of the child and the families' willingness to go to any length to obtain what is necessary to improve functioning, opportunity, and daily life. For others, challenging systems has become a way of life. Being litigious in every interaction is one way of gaining power in a situation that one is powerless to change, such as having a child with a disability. As difficult as it is to work effectively with these families, it is essential to try and try again. If the energy that they spent fighting for their son's or daughter's needs could be used to effectively change the shortcomings of service delivery systems, they could be our most important allies.

BUILDING FAMILY–PROFESSIONAL ALLIANCES

Considerable work remains in evaluating parent/caregiver involvement and family support in programs for young children who are at risk or who have special needs (Bailey, 2001). Until more comprehensive evaluation has been undertaken, professionals must rely on what is known about models and practices that support family-centered practices. Several of the studies discussed in this chapter suggest that family–professional collaboration requires more than a positive attitude or philosophy about the role of families in service delivery. Collaboration requires that these attitudes and philosophies be put into practice. This section describes promising and proven models and strategies for putting collaboration into practice.

Every interaction between a family member and a professional supports or interferes with collaboration. Whether the interaction is on the phone, through a form that has been mailed, or face-to-face, it influences the likelihood of collaboration. Therefore, interactions, procedures, and policies must be examined to determine the extent to which they facilitate collaboration or act as barriers. The systems-level issues are in some ways the easiest because they often do not require a change in personal behavior or a retooling of interpersonal skills.

Making Policies and Procedures More Family-Centered

Almost all organizations have policies and procedures that are not customer friendly. Whether it is the registration process at a university, duplicate questions on job application forms, or the policies and procedures in an agency serving children and families, improvement can always occur. One method of examining policies and procedures within programs and agencies is to commission a task force of parents to examine the policies and procedures to determine how they affect collaborative partnerships. The charge to the task force should be clear with timelines attached and should indicate that the program is committed to making its approach to services more family-centered. It should also indicate that every concern identified will be considered and task force members will assist in sorting and prioritizing the concerns that they identify.

Staffing the task force with a professional who can act as an administrative assistant may be helpful, but it is important not to overload the group with professionals and administrators at the beginning. Those who have been involved in such groups know the temptation of administrators and program professionals to defend policies and procedures whenever they come under scrutiny. Although resolving issues jointly is a critical part of collaborating and developing alliances, identifying policies and procedures that inhibit collaboration may be something that should begin with families working together, apart from professionals, so that families will not have to work through their concerns *and* professional defensiveness.

In the second phase of the process, several professionals including a program administrator would join the task force. Family members should be in the majority, however. At this point, the initial charge should be re-stated and elaborated. The task of this expanded group is to sort and prioritize the concerns. Sorting may be done along a variety of dimensions.

One approach is to sort by categories such as "can make changes internally," "requires external approval," and "cannot be changed because of regulation or law." The last category should have few, if any, items. Policies and procedures are often designed to enact law, but there are many ways to conform to law more creatively. Another approach to sorting is by the strength of families' concern. These categories might include "serious deterrent to collaboration, needs immediate attention," "needs to be changed but is not an immediate priority," and "room for improvement." Another approach to sorting and prioritizing concerns is to put issues into the component of the program that they involve. For example, problems might occur at intake, initial assessment, program planning (IFSP or IEP), intervention, progress monitoring, and transition. Although this categorization can be helpful, issues may overlap and it may place greater emphasis on child-level rather than family-level services. These approaches are simply illustrations. The group may have other ways of organizing and prioritizing concerns. The important piece is that the group develops priorities, action plans, and timelines.

In the third phase, those responsible for the action plan report periodically to the task force on their progress. Although it may ultimately be the administrator's responsibility to make changes, family members on the task force and others should be part of the process. For example, if the intake paperwork is determined to be unfriendly to families, task force members and other families should be involved in the revisions, assist in field tests of new forms, and give approval for the new and improved version.

Processes like the one described take time and energy. To be effective, the process must be authentic and result in change. Any process that is, or is perceived to be, a sham only makes matters worse. And nothing leads to the perception of deception more than filling a task force with the program's most supportive parents. Always include a parent that the team would rather not include, and listen carefully to what she or he says. Regardless of the times and energy involved, processes like this result in improved policies, procedures, and collaborative relationships. As family members gain ownership over program policies and procedures, the possibilities for partnerships and alliances increase.

Encouraging Family-Centered Interactions

Changing the system is sometimes easier than changing individuals within it. Family-centered practice relies on the knowledge, interpersonal style, and commitment of the professionals who see families every day. Policies and procedures that are models of family-centered practice do not make up for the actions and interactions of a single individual who believes that families really do not know what is best for their children. Therefore, it is critical for new professionals to be well trained in family-centered principles and for veteran professionals to have opportunities to reevaluate their practices.

Providing Preservice Training

Perhaps the greatest shortcoming in training programs for professionals entering family/child service fields is the lack of interaction with parents of children with disabilities. Although students typically take courses on working with families, are able to faultlessly recite the literature on family-centered practice, and have typically heard presentations by parents and other family members in their classes, few have been trained by parents or alongside parents in their classes. When such training opportunities do occur, they produce some remarkable benefits for students and parents alike (McBride, Sharp, Hains, & Whitehead, 1995). The author of this chapter has had several recent experiences that confirm the value of this model—having a parent as a facilitator in a class on working with families and having students who were also parents of children with disabilities in classes taught. In each situation, the parent perspective increased dialogue and reflection and enhanced professional understanding. One of the most important and needed changes in preservice training is creating structures that enable faculty to align their instruction with the family-centered, interdisciplinary demands of early intervention (Stayton & Bruder, 1999).

Providing Ongoing Professional Development

Since the early 1990s, intervention programs throughout the country have put considerable emphasis on training staff members to be more family-centered and collaborative. Because of these efforts, changes have been made. In any profession, however, ongoing opportunities to learn, reflect on practice, develop new skills, and hone old ones are necessary. Knowledge about collaboration is not new, and it is unlikely that anyone currently in early intervention or an allied field has not been exposed to it. Each professional's skills in developing family–professional collaboration varies, however. Much of what is required is based on interpersonal skills, and the characteristics and behaviors that support collaborative partnerships are well documented in the research reported earlier in the chapter. Based on what is known, the following are important to effective collaborative partnerships: friendliness, optimism, patience, sincerity, open-mindedness, caring, trust, respect, commitment to the relationship, effective communication, responsivity, willingness to share and disclose information, honesty, tact, a positive climate, flexibility, and knowledge (Dinnebeil, Hale, & Rule, 1996). Others also include empathy and an attitude of humility (Jones, Garlow, Turnbull, & Barber, 1996). The question is, can these skills and behaviors be taught? The answer is yes; these are behaviors that can be taught and learned, but what is equally important is that the underlying attitudes and beliefs exist within professionals who work with families. If that is not the case, the Japanese proverb will be affirmed: "Sooner or later you will act out what you really believe."

These characteristics and behaviors can be put into practice in every component of service delivery. They are part of getting acquainted with families and their children (intake), learning about the child as well as the family's values, strengths, and needs (assessment), jointly deciding on and planning services (IFSP/IEP), jointly reviewing progress and evaluating outcomes (monitoring progress), and assisting the family as they make plans for the future (transition). At every step in the early intervention process, professionals have the opportunity to collaborate, form partnerships, and develop alliances with families.

SUMMARY

Family–professional collaboration is one of the goals of programs that serve families and their children who have disabilities or who are at risk. Collaboration requires mutual respect, trust, and the ability to agree on and pursue mutual goals. Family-centered services, a hallmark of quality services for children and their families, provide a first step toward family–professional collaboration. Its principles include 1) a recognition of parents or primary caregivers as experts on their child; 2) acknowledgment of the family as the ultimate decision maker for their child and themselves; 3) a view of the family as the constant in the child's life and the service providers and systems as transitory; 4) respect for and work toward supporting family priorities, goals for service, and their choice in involvement; 5) valuing trusting, collaborative relationships between parents and professionals; and 6) work toward ensuring culturally competent services.

Family-centered services are also linked to empowerment— supporting families to increase the control that they have over their own lives. The literature is replete with characteristics and behaviors that support and hinder family–professional collaboration, and research suggests that the characteristics and behaviors are the same that we would look for in any good relationship. The literature also supports the fact that some of the families who may be most in need of a professional partner are least likely to have the skills to be a good partner, however. This suggests the need for professionals to continue to grow and develop and to reach out to families so that we may grow and develop together.

ACTIVITIES TO EXTEND THE DISCUSSION

1. Think about a relationship that you value, and list the characteristics of that relationship that make it successful. Which of those characteristics would be important in family–professional partnerships?

2. Select the word *collaboration* or *partnership* and brainstorm characteristics that are important for that type of relationship to succeed. For example, the c in *collaboration* might remind someone of the characteristic of *communication*.

3. Think about an agency, organization, or professional office with which you are familiar and discuss one way in which it could be more effective in developing collaborative relationships with its clientele. It may be your work setting, the university, or a physician's or dentist's office where you have received services. Reflect on its services and the extent to which there is an attempt to form partnerships with its clientele.

REFERENCES

Able-Boone, H., Sandall, S.R., & Frederick, L.L. (1990). An informed, family-centered approach to public law 99-457: Parental views. *Topics in Early Childhood Special Education, 10*(1), 100–111.

Bailey, D.B. (2001). Evaluating parent involvement and family support in early intervention and preschool programs. *Journal of Early Intervention, 24*, 1–14.

Bailey, D.B., Simeonsson, R.J., Winton, P.J., Huntington, G.S., Comfort, M., Isbell, P., O'Donnell, K.J., & Helm, J.M. (1986). Family focused early intervention: A functional model for planning, implementing, and evaluating individualized services in early intervention. *Journal of the Division for Early Childhood, 10*(2), 156–171.

Baird, S. (1997). Seeking a comfortable fit between family-centered philosophy and infant–parent interaction in early intervention: Time for a paradigm shift? *Topics in Early Childhood Special Education, 17*, 139–164.

Bronfenbrenner, U. (1975). Is early intervention effective? In B.Z. Friedlander, G.M. Sterritt, & G.E. Kirk (Eds.), *Exceptional infant: Vol. 3. Assessment and intervention* (pp. 449–475). New York: Brunner/Mazel.

Bruder, M.B. (2000). Family-centered early intervention: Clarifying our values for the new millennium. *Topics in Early Childhood Special Education, 20*, 105–115.

Dinnebeil, L.A., Hale, L.M., & Rule, S. (1996). A qualitative analysis of parents' and service coordinators' descriptions of variables that influence collaborative relationships. *Topics in Early Childhood Special Education, 16*, 322–347.

Dinnebeil, L.A., Hale, L.M., & Rule, S. (1999). Early intervention program practices that support collaboration. *Topics in Early Childhood Special Education, 19*, 225–235.

Dunst, C.J. (1985). Rethinking early intervention. *Analysis and Intervention in Developmental Disabilities, 5*, 165–201.

Dunst, C.J. (1999). Placing parent education in conceptual and empirical context. *Topics in Early Childhood Special Education, 19*, 141–147.

Dunst, C.J. (2000). Revisiting "rethinking early intervention." *Topics in Early Childhood Special Education, 20*, 95–104.

Dunst, C.J., Trivette, C., & Deal, A. (1988). *Enabling and empowering families: Principles and guidelines for practice.* Cambridge, MA: Brookline Books.

Dunst, C.J., Trivette, C.M., & Jodry, W. (1997). Influences of social support on children with disabilities and their families. In M.J. Guralnick (Ed.), *The effectiveness of early intervention* (pp. 499–522). Baltimore: Paul H. Brookes Publishing Co.

Dunst, C.J., Trivette, C.M., Starnes, A.L., Hamby, D.W., & Gordon, N.J. (1993). *Building and evaluating family support initiatives: A national study of programs for persons with developmental disabilities.* Baltimore: Paul H. Brookes Publishing Co.

Education of the Handicapped Act Amendments of 1986, PL 99-457, 20 U.S.C. §§ 1400 *et seq.*

Filer, J.D., & Mahoney, G.J. (1996). Collaboration between families and early intervention service providers. *Infants and Young Children, 9*(2), 22–30.

Hall, L.J., Lynch, E.W., Macvean, M.L., & Valverde, A. (2000, December). *Parent empowerment through early intervention and collaborative research.* Competitively selected poster session at the Division of Early Childhood's 15th Annual International Early Childhood Conference on Children with Special Needs, Albuquerque, NM.

Hanson, M.J. (1996). Early intervention: Models and practices. In M.J. Hanson (Ed.), *Typical and atypical development* (2nd ed., pp. 451–476). Austin, TX: PRO-ED.

Hanson, M.J., & Lynch, E.W. (1995). *Early intervention: Implementing child and family services for infants and toddlers who are at risk or disabled* (2nd ed.). Austin, TX: PRO-ED.

Hauser-Cram, P., Upshur, C.C., Krauss, M.W., & Shonkoff, J.P. (1988). Implications of Public Law 99-457 for early intervention services for infants and toddlers with disabilities. *Social Policy Report, 3*(3), 1–16.

Hobbs, N. (1975). *The future of children.* San Francisco: Jossey-Bass.

Hobbs, N., Dokecki, P., Hoover-Dempsey, K., Moroney, R., Shayne, M., & Weeks, K. (1984). *Strengthening families.* San Francisco: Jossey-Bass.

Individuals with Disabilities Education Act Amendments of 1997, PL 105-17, 20 U.S.C. §§ 1400 *et seq.*

Jaworowski, S., & Jaworowski, R. (1978). A baby goes to school. In S.L. Brown & M.S. Moersch (Eds.), *Parents on the team.* Ann Arbor: The University of Michigan Press.

Johnson, V. (Ed.). (1995). *Voices of the dream: African American women speak.* San Francisco: Chronicle Books.

Jones, T.M., Garlow, J.A., Turnbull, H.R., & Barber, P.A. (1996). Family empowerment in a family support program. In G.H.S. Singer, L.E. Powers, & A.L. Olson (Eds.), *Redefining family support: Innovations in public–private partnerships* (pp. 87–112). Baltimore: Paul H. Brookes Publishing Co.

Krahn, F.L., Thom, V.A., Hale, B.J., & Williams, K. (1995). Running on empty: A look at burnout in early intervention professionals. *Infants and Young Children, 7*(4), 1–11.

Lynch, E.W., & Hanson, M.J. (Eds.). (2004). *Developing cross-cultural competence: A guide for working with children and families* (3rd ed.). Baltimore: Paul H. Brookes Publishing Co.

Mahoney, G., & Filer, J. (1996). How responsive is early intervention to the priorities and needs of families? *Topics in Early Childhood Special Education, 16,* 437–457.

McAnaney, K.D. (1992). *I wish . . . dreams and realities of parenting a special need child.* Sacramento, CA: United Cerebral Palsy Association of California.

McBride, S.L., Sharp, L., Hains, A.H., & Whitehead, A. (1995). Parents as co-instructors in preservice training: A pathway to family-centered practice. *Journal of Early Intervention, 19,* 343–389.

McCollum, J.A. (2000). Taking the past along: Reflecting on our identity as a discipline. *Topics in Early Childhood Special Education, 20,* 79–86.

McWilliam, R.A., Tocci, L., & Harbin, G. (1998). Family-centered services: Service providers' discourse and behavior. *Topics in Early Childhood Special Education, 18,* 206–221.

Meyer, D.J. (1993). Lessons learned—cognitive coping strategies of overlooked family members. In A.P. Turnbull, J.M. Patterson, S.K. Behr, D.L. Murphy, J.G. Marquis, & M.J. Blue-Banning (Eds.), *Cognitive coping, families, and disability* (pp. 81–93). Baltimore: Paul H. Brookes Publishing Co.

Santelli, B., Poyadue, F.S., & Young, J.L. (2001). *The parent to parent handbook: Connecting families of children with special needs.* Baltimore: Paul H. Brookes Publishing Co.

Santelli, B., Turnbull, A.P., Lerner, E., & Marquis, J. (1993). Parent to parent programs—a unique form of mutual support for families of persons with disabilities. In G.H.S. Singer & L.E. Powers (Eds.), *Families, disability, and empowerment: Active coping skills and strategies for family interventions* (pp. 27–57). Baltimore: Paul H. Brookes Publishing Co.

Santelli, B., Turnbull, A., Sergeant, J., Lerner, E.P., & Marquis, J.G. (1996). Parent to parent programs: Parent preferences for support. *Infants and Young Children, 9*(1), 53–62.

Singer, G.H.S., & Powers, L.E. (1993). Contributing to resilience in families. In G.H.S. Singer & L.E. Powers (Eds.), *Families, disability, and empowerment: Active coping strategies for family interventions* (pp. 1–25). Baltimore: Paul H. Brookes Publishing Co.

Singer, G.H.S., Marquis, J., Powers, L.K., Blanchard, L., Divenere, N., Santelli, B., Ainbinder, J.G., & Sharp, M. (1999). A multi-site evaluation of Parent to Parent programs for parents of children with disabilities. *Journal of Early Intervention, 22,* 217–229.

Stayton, V., & Bruder, M.B. (1999). Early intervention personnel preparation for the new millennium: Early childhood special education. *Infants and Young Children, 12*(1), 59–69.

Summers, J.A., Dell'Oliver, C., Turnbull, A.P., Benson, H.A., Santelli, E., Campbell, M., & Siegel-Causey, E. (1990). Examining the individualized family service plan process: What are family and practitioner preferences? *Topics in Early Childhood Special Education, 10*(1), 78–99.

Turnbull, A.P., Patterson, J.M., Behr, S.K., Murphy, D.L., Marquis, J.G., & Blue-Banning, M.J. (Eds.). (1993). *Cognitive coping, families, and disability.* Baltimore: Paul H. Brookes Publishing Co.

Turnbull, A.P., Summers, J.A., & Brotherson, M.J. (1984). *Working with families with disabled members: A family systems approach.* Lawrence: University of Kansas, Kansas Affiliated Facility.

Turnbull, A.P., & Turnbull, H.R. (1993). Participatory research on cognitive coping: From concepts to research planning. In A.P. Turnbull, J.M. Patterson, S.K. Behr, D.L. Murphy, J.G. Marquis, & M.J. Blue-Banning (Eds.), *Cognitive coping, families, and disability* (pp. 1–14). Baltimore: Paul H. Brookes Publishing Co.

Turnbull, A.P., & Turnbull, R. (2001). *Families, professionals, and exceptionality* (4th ed.). New York: Prentice Hall.

Unger, D.G., Jones, W.C., Park, E., & Tressell, P.A. (2001). Promoting involvement between low-income single caregivers and urban early intervention programs. *Topics in Early Childhood Special Education, 21,* 197–212.

Vacca, J., & Feinberg, E. (2000). Why can't families be more like us?: Henry Higgins

confronts Eliza Doolittle in the world of
early intervention. *Infants and Young Children, 13*(1), 40–48.

Vohs, J.R. (1998). Parent perspectives on conflict in early intervention. *Infants and Young
Children, 11*(1), vi–x.

CHAPTER 8

COMMUNICATING AND COLLABORATING WITH FAMILIES

Cornerstones of Family-Centered Practices

Seek first to understand, then to be understood.
—S.R. Covey (1989, p. 235)

Clapping with one hand only will not produce a noise.
—Malay Proverb

Communication is an essential aspect of human existence. *Effective* communication is fundamental to building relationships with others and to advancing understanding among individuals. You are invited to pause for a moment to reflect on the role of communication in daily interactions. Imagine your daily routines and count the many interactions that occur with other human beings. Think back through yesterday or today. In reviewing the day, certain interactions will come to the fore— usually those that were particularly gratifying or those that left feelings of anger or distress. Maybe you became agitated when your co-worker did not come to a meeting on time and expected you to take on the majority of the task at hand. Maybe the grocery clerk was surly. Conversely, maybe a neighbor noticed that your dog had gotten loose and brought it back to you. Maybe someone merely told you that you looked nice. Each one of these daily, routine interactions and how you chose to respond had an impact on your feelings and behavior. Cumulatively, they added up and left you with a feeling of having had a "good" day or a "bad" day. So many human interactions occur throughout the day that their impact may escape notice. But each interaction is a transaction and each can influence the way that an individual will behave or feel.

Families of children with disabilities, chronic health disorders, social service needs, and other special needs are thrust into interactions with even more individuals than those encountered in most daily family routines. Many of these interactions may be emotionally draining. The children's conditions and families' needs place these families in contact with a variety of support and service personnel, often from varying disciplines or agencies. The appointment calendars for these families often rival those of the busiest executives in large corporations. The communications they have and the relationships they develop with service providers often will dictate the effectiveness of the services. Services will influence the families, and the process or way in which services are provided, in most cases, is as important as the actual services provided.

The roles and styles of service delivery are particularly compelling for those individuals who work in the helping professions. Professional approaches can determine if the service providers are "part of the problem or part of the solution" for families. To achieve the family-centered service approaches advocated in this text, each individual must make a commitment and concerted effort to develop effective working partnerships with families and engage in supportive interactions. Although most professionals have the best intentions in their work with families, some strategies or processes are more promising than others in building true partnerships or alliances.

This chapter builds on the discussion of effective roles and relationships advanced in the previous chapter and describes strategies and applied practices that can lead to more satisfying and effective communication and relationships between professionals and families. All facets of service delivery necessitate effective working relationships or partnerships between professionals and family members built on effective communication and collaboration. From the first contact that a parent has with a health care provider or an agency to the actual implementation and evaluation of services and subsequent transition to the next service environment, effective communications and relationships will be the key to positive outcomes. At every step along the service continuum, family–professional partnerships and effective communication will enhance the journey for both parents and professionals.

APPLYING PRINCIPLES OF FAMILY-CENTERED SERVICE DELIVERY

Dunst, Trivette, and Deal (1994) offered a framework for describing principles of family support. Based on a literature review and their own research, they identified six principles used to describe policies, practices, and personnel beliefs and behaviors that are conducive to family-centered service. These principles form the basis for structuring effective communication and collaboration.

- Principle 1: Service delivery approaches should *enhance a sense of community*. Such efforts support the interdependence and reciprocal exchanges among members of the community. This sense of community can serve to increase the range of supports and resources that are available within that community environment. This approach also increases the likelihood that the services and supports within the community will be better matched to the family's values, cultural background, and preferences.

- Principle 2: Efforts should focus on *mobilizing resources and supports* to build and activate informal social support networks in ways that are responsive to the individual needs of families. This principle acknowledges that families bring a wealth of resources and personal support networks and the services should focus on enhancing these natural supports rather than creating a system of dependency on more formalized services.

- Principle 3: *Shared responsibility and collaboration* characterize family support services. Roles and relationships that are *mutually* agreed on by the family members and professionals define collaborative partnerships. These relationships differ from the traditional roles of case manager and client that often have dominated in the field.

- Principle 4: Supportive services are concerned with *protecting family integrity*. On the one hand, the unique cultural and personal characteristics of the family must be preserved and respected and on the other hand, resources must be provided that serve to enhance healthy family relationships and family functioning.

- Principle 5: Supportive services are aimed at *strengthening family functioning* by building on family strengths and promoting practices that allow families to develop and demonstrate their own competencies and capabilities. This focus is in sharp contrast to the approach of prescribing services, correcting weaknesses, or attempting to "fix" child and family concerns.

- Principle 6: *Proactive human service practices* serve to prevent risk conditions and promote healthy and positive family functioning. Again, the central feature is emphasizing family strengths and supporting families to develop their capabilities.

Personal Actions that Promote Family-Centered Practices

What behaviors or personal actions can service providers take to enhance the likelihood that their services will be more family friendly and family centered? This section outlines nine family-friendly strategies that every family service provider should put into practice in every interaction with families.

Respect Family Values, Beliefs, and Practices

Each family has a unique set of routines and rituals that characterize their style of living. The family's culture, their history, their ancestry, the family's spiritual beliefs, their socioeconomic status, the opportunities they have, and their place of residence influence family practices. In the course of service delivery, service providers will encounter families whose values, practices, and styles differ, sometimes even radically, from their own. Only when providers respect different families' perspectives can they effectively enter into a working relationship.

Trust that the Family Knows Best

Service providers must *trust that the family knows best* about what is needed for their child and their family. Clearly, in the case of families in which neglectful or abusive practices occur, the practitioner must intervene on behalf of the safety of the child. In most cases, however, families are doing their best. Professionals are in their lives for what may seem only a moment while the family must adjust and adapt to the many facets and circumstances encountered by all of the family members and across all the events of their lives.

Be Sensitive to Diverse Backgrounds

Be sensitive to and supportive of the needs of families from diverse cultural, linguistic, and socioeconomic backgrounds. Review your daily routine again as you did at the outset of this chapter. Only this time, pretend that you are transported to another country where you are less familiar with the customs, the services, and the regulations. In addition to this unfamiliarity, you do not speak the language fluently. Or pretend that you are homeless and do not have ready access to even the most basic survival needs such as food and warm or clean clothing. These are the situations in which many families find themselves as they try to procure services for their children and families. The jargon and policies associated with individualized education programs (IEPs) and individualized family service plans (IFSPs) and medical services, for instance, are foreign to most individuals and they may be even more perplexing to someone who is a recent immigrant to this country and speaks a language other than English. In some cases and for some families, the service options may even violate cultural preferences or practices. Furthermore, families struggling to survive day to day may have more critical or urgent priorities than providing special services for their children.

Acknowledge Family Members as Decision Makers

Regardless of the situation and of professionals' judgments about what families need, family members are the ultimate decision makers regarding their priorities and life choices. Practitioners can support family members in this process by ensuring that they have equitable access to resources and information, are full and equal partners and participants in service decisions, and are provided the supports that they need to make informed choices. The acknowledgment of families as decision makers also means that one must respect the choices and decisions that they make.

Treat the Family Members as People First

Practitioners from the helping professions are trained to focus on a particular dimension of the individual or family. It may be the child's motor, speech, or cognitive development or the social support services needed by the family. Regardless, the child and family members are people first, not cases, not disabilities, and not problems waiting to be "fixed."

Recognize that You Are a Guest in the Family's Home and Life

Family members are involved with one another for the long haul. Professionals participate for only a short time in their lives. It is a privilege not to be taken lightly. Whether the service is needed for a long or a short time, service providers often come into a family's home on a regular basis and are sometimes privy to an individual's intimate feelings and routines. This invitation into families' lives carries heavy responsibility for maintaining confidentiality and a respectful presence.

Maintain Appropriate Boundaries

Most people would agree that a warm and positive relationship is to be valued; however, professional boundaries may be crossed. These breaches of conduct may interfere with the family's ability to develop a natural support system or make their own decisions. Reflective practice and consultation with other team members and supervisors can be useful in preventing blurred boundaries and difficult situations. A family, for example, may request or come to rely on the professional to find needed services such as housing, food stamps, or health care, and they may expect the helping professional to be on call to drive them to appointments. Although these services may be crucial for the family, the professional will not always be available or able to obtain services. Rather than fostering a long-term dependency, when the professional gives families strategies and supports that they can use to obtain the services they need, it is likely that the family will use these skills at other times and in other places. If skills are generalizable, family members are more likely to feel competent about their own abilities to effect change and advocate on behalf of the family.

Be Flexible

Given that families are characterized by a broad array of sizes, groupings, and dynamics and have a myriad of needs and goals, flexibility is a hallmark of the helping professions. As previously discussed, families are highly dynamic systems with their needs and perspectives constantly shifting. Hence, services and service delivery structures must be able to adapt and adjust to these changing demands. For instance, during a crisis one family may prefer to have intensive supports whereas another may prefer to be left alone to cope with the issue as a family. Likewise, for some individuals, conducting frequent visits and talks supplemented by providing written materials may be the optimal method for learning strategies and information about the child's needs. Other family members may prefer less frequent or less structured approaches or they may best acquire new strategies through listening to other parents or professionals tell stories or through observing others.

Enjoy the Children and Families

Service providers are indeed fortunate that they are welcomed into the lives of a variety of families. At the least it is a wondrous education and, at the most, an opportunity for personal growth in understanding, knowledge, and skills. For many family members, particularly when practitioners are involved in interventions in a child's early years, the service provider will hold a special place of respect and honor in their hearts for years to come. Often the professional will be in the position of offering special support or lending a helping hand at a particularly emotional or difficult transition in the family's life. The opportunity to engage at this level and in this type of relationship can bring joy and fulfillment to our lives as well as to the lives of families.

ESTABLISHING RELATIONSHIPS

The relationship between the service provider and the family forms the foundation for intervention (Dunst, Trivette, & Deal, 1994; McGonigel,

1991). It has been argued that this relationship is fundamental to the outcome of intervention regardless of the professional discipline: "The success of all interventions will rest on the quality of the provider–family relationships, even when the relationship itself is not the focus of the intervention" (Kalmanson & Seligman, 1992, p. 48).

No one can provide a recipe or cookie-cutter approach to establishing relationships with others. In fact, one of the exciting challenges that service providers face is the need to individualize services and relate to children and families "in the moment." Hence, the needs of one child and family are different from those of all others, and those needs will differ on different occasions and at different points in time. Likewise, each family is a dynamic system constantly changing with every new prospect and demand.

Each family will present different styles and preferences for type of interaction and communication style. The family's characteristics and life cycle also will influence the type of relationship and style of interaction that develops.

Definition and Characteristics of Partnerships

Dunst and Paget suggested an operational definition of *parent–professional partnership*. They defined this partnership as an association between families and professionals who "function collaboratively using agreed on roles in pursuit of a joint interest or common goal" (1991, p. 29).

Characteristics of partnerships include beliefs, attitudes, communicative style, and behavioral actions (Dunst, Trivette, & Johanson, 1994). Beliefs are defined as the attributions about how one should behave toward others and attitudes are the emotional feeling states about people, situations, or relationships. Communicative style refers to the methods and modes of exchanging or sharing information among partners, in other words, how information is given and received. Behavioral actions refer to the translation of attitudes and beliefs into action.

Dunst, Trivette, and Johanson (1994) described optimal parent–professional partnerships as those that embrace effective helping through empowerment and enablement of families to accomplish their own goals and demonstrate competence. Beliefs that contribute to this approach are mutual respect, trust, honesty, nonjudgmental and accepting perspectives, and the presumption of capabilities. Attitudes that are confident, warm and caring, and understanding and empathetic and that reflect a sense of humor foster this approach. With respect to communicative styles, those that reflect openness, active listening, disclosure, and information sharing are most likely to contribute to these partnerships. Finally, the behavior enactment of these beliefs and attitudes is manifest through services that are flexible, open, reciprocal, and respectful and those that are characterized by problem solving, humor, shared responsibility, and mutual support.

Stages or Phases of Partnerships

The dynamic qualities and the evolving nature of family–professional relationships have been noted in the clinical literature (Walker & Singer,

1993). The working relationship is not a fixed phenomenon that is established prior to the onset of services but rather a changing and developing progression characterized by ups and downs as in any relationship. The process of establishing family–professional relationships has been described as occurring in stages or phases (Beckman, Newcomb, Frank, & Brown, 1996; Walker & Singer, 1993; Wasik, Bryant, & Lyons, 1990).

Phase 1: Getting Acquainted

The initial phase is typically when the foundations of trust and rapport are established. During this phase of getting acquainted, families and professionals exchange information. With some families this phase will occur quickly; for others it will develop over a prolonged period of time depending on the comfort of the family, characteristics of the service provider, match between the provider and family, issues of immediate concern to the family, and other external events.

Phase 2: Exploration

The second phase, the exploration phase, typically continues the discussion of resources and services. The need to listen carefully to families is particularly crucial. Initial goals for intervention are explored and developed. The development of trust between the service provider and families is often a major focus at this stage.

Phase 3: Collaboration

During the collaboration phase, agreed-on intervention goals and procedures are implemented and continually monitored to meet child and family needs. As with all phases, the service provider must be attentive to the differences among family members in terms of their priorities and concerns and their preferences for types, frequency, or intensity of services.

Phase 4: Closure

The final phase, closure, is often overlooked. The end of the working relationship may occur for a variety of reasons—the child "graduates" to the next level of service or a new environment, the family relocates, the child or family no longer needs services, and so forth. During this stage, the service provider and family end their working relationship. This can be difficult for both parties and may engender a sense of loss in anyone in the relationship. This phase should include a review or reflection on the experiences the parties in the relationship have undergone together. Future goals and needs should be addressed as well. Often, the professional is in an ideal position to help the child and family make the transition to a new service or place by transferring to the family the information and skills they need to best benefit from the demands of their new environment.

Creating Partnerships

Many issues can prevent effective family–professional partnerships. Salisbury (1992) described common barriers to such partnerships, including attitudes, perceptions, and values of service providers about the families with whom they work. Providers may not acknowledge the skills and knowledge that families bring to the working relationship, and/or a mismatch may occur between the goals and expectations of the professionals and the family members.

Communication issues also can form major barriers to effective partnership and include concerns related to use of language, languages spoken, literacy levels, and affective components of communication. Lack of service provider knowledge or time and logistical issues such as lack of child care or transportation, too, function as barriers to the establishment of effective working partnerships between families and professionals.

On the other side of the coin, service providers can create more effective partnerships through a variety of strategies. Strategies include identifying the families' concerns, priorities, and resources through holding discussions with them on their own terms and in their language of preference. Other suggestions center on asking family members about their preferred level and method of involvement, time schedules and constraints, preferred type of communication regarding their child's program, and the times and places in which they would like services to occur

(Rosin, 1996). The potential for effective partnerships will be enhanced if families are provided a menu or range of service options so that they can choose those that best fit the needs, comfort levels, and preferences of the family.

Family service professionals and program resources must be committed to the *process* of developing partnerships because true partnerships develop over time and take time to establish. Partnerships must be based on flexible and creative models in order to meet the needs of individual children and families who come from such diverse backgrounds and perspectives.

EFFECTIVE COMMUNICATION

Effective communication is absolutely essential to establishing and maintaining relationships and partnerships with families. Treating others with dignity, respect, and honesty is the foundation of effective communication. From this foundation, trustful relationships can evolve.

Communication is fundamental to the social interactions that characterize human beings. Effective communication is likewise fundamental to productive and satisfying relationships between family members and professionals. Often, during periods of stress, these relationships are particularly challenged and even seemingly minor occurrences can exacerbate painful responses or alleviate distress and concern. Although all people have experienced stressful events and frustrating or negative communications, they usually are of somewhat short duration and most individuals have a chance to refuel at some point following the event. Families of children with disabilities or chronic health conditions or other special needs, however, may experience these challenges every day. Hardly a day passes without an interaction with some professional—a teacher, a health care provider, a therapist, a bookkeeper for an insurance agency, and so forth. In some of these interactions, effective communications occur and each individual is able to convey and receive information in a respectful and satisfying manner. In other interactions, the communication breaks down. Regardless, central to family-centered practice is the idea that every one of these interactions is a transaction and every one of them has an impact on that family.

Let us examine the influence of communicative events and reflect on the choices each practitioner brings to interactions. These choices involve both how the practitioner will respond to the communicative bids of others and also how he or she will choose to communicate to others. Think back to a particularly stressful event in your own life that occurred in the last month. Maybe your car broke down as you were rushing down the freeway on your way to a meeting. Maybe your child fell down at school and suffered a concussion. Maybe your supervisor called you into the office and told you that the company was downsizing and that your job would be curtailed or cut altogether. Maybe a family member who lives in another state became seriously ill and you had to plan a trip to care for her. Try to picture the events that transpired as you tried to understand the stressful situation, adjust to the demands, and procure the services or supports that you needed. How did different styles and attempts at communication influence the outcomes and the subsequent interactions?

Using as an example one of these hypothetical events, one can examine the types of experiences and communicative episodes that the individuals involved may have encountered. Pretend that your elderly mother who lives 1,000 miles away had to have surgery suddenly and you had to travel to be at the hospital with her and also take care of her when she was released to her home. After putting your affairs in order in your own life (e.g., your home, your children, your pets, your job), which was no small matter, you try to book a flight. Maybe you were put on hold for what seemed like an eternity. When you did talk to a ticket agent, you were told that the only flight that was available over the next 2 days left at 7 A.M. the next morning. You booked the flight, and your trip was a nightmare fraught with delays, overbooking, nearly missed connections, and no food service. You arrived to find your mother agitated and frightened. You met with the surgeon who only had about 5 minutes to talk. He told you that he had explained everything to your mother already and that you could check with her and the nurse. You do not know how long the surgery will be, what are the risks, when your mother could expect to come home if all goes well, or what her care needs will be when she is released. Now think about how each interaction and communication involved in such a scenario would have either met your needs or added to your stress level. Consider, for instance, how different your feelings might be if communications were altered at various points. For instance, how much more helpful it would be if, in contrast to the perfunctory overview of your mother's prognosis and surgery, your surgeon and his nurse had outlined the procedures, discussed the options, and referred you to home care services for when your mother returns home.

We all want to be treated with dignity and sensitivity in all of our interactions. When we are embroiled in an emotional situation in which we are stressed, worried, or fearful, these interactions take on even more importance. Simple courtesies and effective, positive communications can exert a major influence in our interactions!

What Service Providers Can Do to Improve Communication with Families

Effective communication requires careful attention and consideration for each partner. Service providers can hone their listening skills and endeavor to communicate information clearly and respectfully to optimize the likelihood of achieving effective working relationships or partnerships with families. The discussion that follows provides more important strategies to enhance these skills. The following are some examples of listening skills.

Listen Actively

Active listening is foundational to the ability to understand others. Good communication cannot occur without the ability to understand the other person's point of view or perspective. Edelman, Greenland, and Mills (1992a) described the key elements to active listening: 1) be attentive, 2) be impartial, 3) reflect back, 4) listen for feelings, and 5) summarize. Attention involves not only paying attention but also conveying attention through body language. Impartial listening requires that the listener just listen and does not give opinions or even agree or disagree. Reflecting back refers to paraphrasing or using similar words to capture what the speaker was attempting to say. This technique not only establishes clearer communications but also it helps to establish rapport and shows the listener's desire to listen. Listening or acknowledging feelings is the fourth technique. Many interactions between family members and service providers will be about issues of tremendous concern to the families. Family members have feelings about these topics and these feelings should be acknowledged. For example, a professional may reflect, "It sounds like you are feeling frustrated with his progress." Finally, active listening involves summarizing. The listener should try to capture the speaker's intent and summarize the key points. This establishes whether the message has been both clearly communicated and received. It also serves to convey understanding. For instance, the professional may state, "Let me make sure that I understood. Dan is not responding when you do those exercises. You would like to adapt the procedure by using a new toy and . . . . " These elements or components appear simple, but most people, particularly in the role of "professional," have a tendency to jump in too soon and provide an opinion or "prescription" for the family.

Communicate Clearly and Respectfully

Other strategies or "do's and don'ts" for clear and respectful communication were offered by Edelman and colleagues (1992a, pp. 34–36):

- *Avoid making assumptions.* The service provider should not draw conclusions prior to meeting and discussing issues with the family. Informed opinions can only come from a period of data gathering.

- *Avoid jargon and explain technical terms.* Professional fields are fraught with technical jargon understood only by those people educated in the field. Terms such as NICU (neonatal intensive care unit), IEP (individualized education program), IFSP (individualized family service plan), OT (occupational therapy), PT (physical therapy) typically make no sense to the layperson and should be avoided or explained to families.

- *Share complete, honest, and unbiased information.* Families can only make informed decisions if they have all of the information they need. For some, information may need to be provided in several modalities (e.g., written, oral) or in a different modality or form from the one being presented. Some families may prefer written materials and others may be more comfortable with oral descriptions or simple graphics. The family members' preferred style of learning, language(s) spoken, and literacy level may influence the way that information is provided and received. In addition, a period of time may be needed for the family members to process the information and analyze their situation. Family members also must be given the opportunity to ask questions and express their concerns.

- *Offer opinions and specify that these are suggestions and they are not the only options.* Being family-centered does not mean not offering professional opinion or expertise. Family members come to professionals to obtain a professional opinion. Clinical advice, however, is one of many factors that the family must consider when making decisions. Professionals must respect their right to agree with the clinical opinion or follow another course of action.

- *Respond to questions directly and specify when the answer is not known.* If service providers do not know the answers to a query, they must be honest and tell the family that they do not know and that they will research the topic and get back to them.

- *Avoid patronizing language and tone.* Using proper greeting titles, such as "Mr.," "Mrs.," or "Ms.," avoids demeaning or overly casual approaches until the service provider knows the parent's preference. "Talking down" to parents is inappropriate in all circumstances.

- *Recognize individuals' differing abilities to understand.* Given the range of experiences and backgrounds of family members, different means of conveying information must be utilized. Some people will prefer written information whereas others will prefer verbal accounts. Literacy levels will vary also—some family members are strong readers and some do not read or they have limited reading abilities. Cultural backgrounds, too, will differ and influence the family members' levels of understanding, knowledge, and concerns. Ample time also must be allowed for family members to process information and discuss issues of concern.

- *Clarify mutual expectations.* A shared vision of the roles and responsibilities of the family members and the professionals is essential to avoid misunderstandings. It may be useful to ask family members to relate what they heard and what they consider the expectations and roles to be. If each partner restates his or her expectations, mutual goals can be developed and achieved.

- *Identify next steps.* Specifically identifying the "who, what, when, where, and how" of the steps or procedures will prevent miscommunications. Often it is useful to write down next steps or diagram procedures.

- *Realign the power.* Traditionally, professionals have "called the shots" with respect to decisions about service delivery and service models. Partnerships will be enhanced when families are treated as equal partners and their suggestions and priorities are considered the driving force behind services.

- *Respect different cultural perspectives.* The power and influence of cultural issues must be understood as families express their preferences and concerns related to their child's services (Hanson, 2004). Learning about the family's culture and background and asking the family their preferences will help establish more culturally responsive services.

- *Respect constraints in families' time and resources.* Children's special needs and services are only two of the myriad factors with which the family must grapple each day. Although the services provided by professionals may appear crucial to them, the family members have to organize their time and resources to meet the needs of *all* family members. Again, asking families to describe the services they need and their preferences for service delivery will be useful.

- *Note and respond to nonverbal cues.* With many people and in many cultures, what is *not* said is more important than what is said. Body language is often worth many words. Service providers are well advised to be aware of their own body language and the family's cultural interpretation of that language, as well as the family's nonverbal cues. For instance, a family member may nod his or her head up and down in response. The professional may interpret this signal as meaning that the family member is agreeing, when in fact the individual may be merely indicating that the information was heard. Another example relates to the use of eye contact. In some cultures, looking one directly in the eye is considered respectful, whereas in other cultures a direct gaze is considered disrespectful. One's gender, status, age, and other factors also may be taken into account in judging the appropriateness of body contact (e.g., shaking hands, pat on the back), eye contact, order of speaking, and proper greeting.

- *Create opportunities for open communication.* Communicating with families in environments or spaces that are private, comfortable, and warm and inviting will do much to facilitate the interaction. These space considerations can help to overcome the natural distance and power issues between families and professionals.

Communication is an extremely complex process. It involves many components: the person or people chosen to address or engage, the things said or not said, the timing of expression, the place in which intent is expressed, and the ways in which the information is expressed. The "who, what when, where, and how" of communication *all* will play important roles in the ability to communicate effectively with family members.

What to Do When Communication Is Particularly Challenging

If communicating clearly and effectively was easy there would not be shelves of self-help and psychology books devoted to this topic. Communication is crucial to all human interactions and it can be a difficult process in many cases. In the helping professions, most professionals will encounter situations that are particularly challenging such as the need to deliver bad news or distressing information. At some time most people will be embroiled in a conflict. These circumstances, communicative attempts will require even more care and scrutiny.

Be Honest and Expect Conflict

No one wants to hear about distressing medical or health problems, limitations to one's abilities or options, or loss of services or supports. Yet at some time most professionals will be called on to deliver such information to families. A number of researchers and clinicians have examined family experiences when receiving diagnoses and/or distressing information. Most findings are in agreement that families want honest information that is presented in a direct and caring manner (Gowen, Christy, & Sparling, 1993; Turnbull & Turnbull, 1990). Time should be allowed for families to digest and process the information, discuss the issues, come to terms with the issues and their feelings, and ask any questions. As has been stated previously, providing information to families in their preferred language and in the modality of their choice is essential. Often, families will need to have the information presented multiple times or in chunks. The families' language fluency and literacy level must be considered also so that information is not provided at a technical level that is not understandable to the family.

Whenever two or more people interact, the possibility exists for conflict, misunderstanding, or disagreement. It would be an unusual professional indeed who never experienced conflict when working with families.

Some methods of communication minimize misunderstandings and aid in achieving agreement when conflicts do occur, however.

Some Effective Techniques

Some of the techniques previously described may be particularly useful when communication breaks down. Listening actively (i.e., attentively, impartially, reflecting back, listening for feelings, summarizing; Edelman et al., 1992a) may prevent misunderstanding and help a service provider to move toward understanding when difficulties arise. Other techniques include monitoring nonverbal and verbal cues used by both parties engaging in the communication. These cues must be analyzed in light of each person's background and preferences. In some cultures, for instance, it is acceptable to cross one's legs or touch or pat another person on the arm or even kiss the stranger on the cheek or both cheeks, whereas in other cultures this would be deemed highly inappropriate, especially for a woman. These examples demonstrate how easy it is for misunderstandings to arise when we do not know one another well. Open and honest expressions are generally preferred. An individual can achieve clarity by offering illustrative examples or stories, speaking clearly, and choosing words carefully. At times it is useful to check the listener's perception of what was said to avoid misunderstandings in meaning or terminology. Even if each person speaks the same language, words and phrases may hold different meanings for the speaker and the listener.

Edelman, Greenland, and Mills (1992b) offered strategies for moving toward agreement when conflicts occur. Their work is an adaptation of information presented by Fisher and Ury (1981). The first strategy as described by Edelman and colleagues (1992b) is to *separate the person from the problem.* This involves agreeing that there is a disagreement and trying to put oneself in the other person's shoes. It is important to avoid blaming the other person and reacting too emotionally. The second strategy is to *establish interests, goals, and priorities.* At this point each person should articulate what they see as the problem and identify their goals and desired outcomes. Being flexible and creative helps to lead toward compromise and identification of mutual goals. The third strategy is to *generate options that can achieve a win-win position.* This is the brainstorming phase where all possible options are put on the table. If necessary other people can be brought into the discussion to help identify and expand the range of options. Finally, the fourth strategy is to *strive for agreement.* Everyone may need some time to weigh the information before making decisions. Ultimately it is the family who must make the decision that best fits their needs. This agreement also includes defining the next action steps for each party and what the follow-up will be. An example of one such conflict and its resolution is reflected in the following vignette.

THE DAVIDSONS

Mr. and Mrs. Davidson, the parents of Ross, a child with pervasive developmental disorder (PDD), came blazing mad to the semi-annual parent–

teacher conference with Ross's preschool classroom teacher. They had just spoken with another family, whose child was also diagnosed with PDD. This other couple had recently obtained a whole host of new services for their child from the school district, including a one-to-one paraprofessional who would help their child throughout the school day and increased speech therapy hours. The Davidsons believed that Ross deserved the same services and came to the school to demand that he receive them. The preschool teacher, Kathy, listened patiently to the Davidson's feelings and requests. She spent time endeavoring to understand their perspective. Then she paraphrased their concerns and requests to ensure that she understood their concerns. At that point she also suggested that she and the parents together re-examine Ross' educational goals and progress. When the teacher and parents looked at the observational data collected in the classroom and the outcome of recent assessments of his performance, they all agreed that Ross seemed to be making good progress and benefiting from the playgroup offered as part of the preschool program. His speech and language skills were advancing and he appeared to enjoy the classroom experience; he even had made a new friend. Kathy encouraged the parents to arrange play dates at home with this new friend.

Mr. and Mrs. Davidson were able to analyze this information Kathy had given them and look at the unique needs and goals for their son. They came to understand that what he needed may not have been identical to what another child might need. Kathy suggested that the classroom teachers and parents both make additional observations over the next month and revisit the goals and objectives at an appointed time the following month to consider if a shift in program or additional speech therapy was needed. The Davidson's went home reassured that their son was achieving his objectives and that his educational program would be reviewed for possible readjustment if necessary. Kathy was more aware of the parents' concerns and made a special effort to key into Ross's behavior and examine whether his current educational program was meeting his needs. Instead of an escalation in tensions that could have led to more meetings and even a fair hearing procedure, both parties were able to listen to one another, examine the options, and leave with a win-win understanding of one another's position and a plan for the future.

As this vignette demonstrates, both professionals and parents must learn to engage in problem-solving collaboration in order to achieve optimal goals for children in need of services. Open and honest communication is the underpinning for these skills.

RELATIONSHIP BUILDING AND COMMUNICATION IN ALL PHASES OF SERVICE DELIVERY

Effective communication and collaborative relationships are essential to all phases of the intervention process. From gathering information and assessment to the analysis and planning of service options and objectives to the actual delivery of service, the relationship and communication between families and professionals will largely dictate whether these intervention activities will meet the needs of children and their families.

Service providers are challenged to be flexible and culturally responsive in order to meet the needs of the diverse range of families and children with whom they work. Families will differ along many dimensions: culture, spoken language, race and ethnicity, literacy skills, spiritual practices, socioeconomic status, education level and background, family structure, lifestyle, living arrangements, geographical location (e.g., area of country, rural versus urban versus suburban), and the opportunities that they have. All these dimensions will influence methods of communication and relationship building.

Information Gathering and Assessment

Traditionally, professionals gathered information through interviews with families and by professional testing, often on a one-shot basis. A process of gathering information through extensive discussion with family members and using multiple observations and strategies has replaced the more traditional practices.

Appropriate practices now emphasize family involvement throughout the entire process (Greenspan & Meisels, 1996). Understanding children within the context of their most important environments, their families, is crucial to gleaning appropriate assessment information. Parents and other family members are the best and most knowledgeable informants regarding a child's needs, strengths, and developmental history. They also are best able to interact with the child and elicit the child's optimal performance. A collaborative alliance between professionals and families, thus, is essential to this process of information exchange.

This assessment and data gathering information phase requires professionals to individualize and make careful choices in the methods they employ in order to meet the needs of the vast range of children and families participating in services. Some common considerations are discussed in the areas of terminology, materials used, developmental values and expectations, type of needs assessment, and communication and interaction styles. Terminology must be carefully reviewed, particularly when interpretation or translation is involved. Some words do not readily translate or they may be misunderstood. Dale and Hoshino (1984) related one devastating and extreme example that demonstrates this point. They described a case in a neonatal intensive care unit involving a Hmong family in which the physicians recommended to the family that their child undergo a surgical procedure. When the word *surgery* was directly translated as *butchery* in the Hmong language, the family was understandably distraught and frightened. Most examples are not so emotionally laden. Given the number of acronyms and technical jargon used in most helping professions and the many languages and cultural backgrounds of families served, however, the potential often exists for grave misunderstandings. With respect to materials and symbols, professionals also are advised to choose carefully. Certainly it is crucial to choose materials that are nonbiased toward any race or gender. To ensure cultural sensitivity, one must also look to the ways that various cultures interpret symbols. Joe and Malach (1998) provided the example of an early interventionist who chose to meet an American Indian family at the Owl Café, not knowing that the owl was considered a bad omen in this family's culture.

Developmental values and behavioral expectations, too, will vary markedly from family to family. These values and expectations may differ from those of the professional as well, creating the potential for misunderstanding and miscommunication. For instance, families from various cultural and socioeconomic backgrounds may have quite different perspectives on the ages at which children are taught to use the toilet, sleep alone, and feed themselves. Families differ with respect to views about children's schedules and the degree of dependence or independence in child behavior that should be fostered.

The manner in which information is gathered is crucial to building effective working relationships and successful communication. In the "needs assessment" phase, different strategies may be employed from interviewing families to using written checklists or questionnaires. Some families will welcome a direct face-to-face exchange and the opportunity to tell their story, whereas other families will experience being selected for an interview as shaming and not allowing them to save face. When written materials are used, the language and reading skills of the family members must be considered, particularly since most adults who are unable to understand written materials are reluctant to admit this.

Families' preferences for communication and interaction style also vary. Some families prefer open, direct communication and are comfortable with discussing their particular situation. For others, more indirect communication techniques are preferred and experienced as appropriate. Some families expect formal data-gathering sessions and others prefer more informal situations and environments.

When working with families whose language is not spoken by the service provider, using interpreters or translators also requires planning and care. Guidelines for working with interpreters have been outlined in several publications (Chen, Chan, Brekken, & Valverde, 2000; Lynch, 2004; Ohtake, Fowler, & Santos, 2001). Major considerations when using interpreters include addressing remarks to the family members rather than the interpreter, avoiding culturally offensive language, learning some key words or phrases in the family's language if possible, speaking clearly and slowly as opposed to loudly, and allowing time for translation when presenting information (Lynch & Hanson, 2004).

Service providers must show sensitivity to families' socioeconomic and cultural backgrounds and to the meanings families ascribe to being interviewed or asked to divulge information. Guidelines for offering culturally competent services are provided in a number of publications (see Hanson, Lynch, & Wayman, 1990; Lynch & Hanson, 2004). The use of "cultural guides" or informants who are knowledgeable both about the family's cultural background and the service delivery system may be particularly beneficial to this process. Services can only be family centered if they are also culturally sensitive.

Collaborative Planning and Decision Making

The suggestions offered in the information-gathering discussion apply to the planning and decision-making process as well. Families will differ, often markedly, in their styles and preferences with respect to planning and decision making. Many families desire to be treated as equal partners in the process. Other families expect the professional to take the most active role and make the initial determination or recommendation for goals and service objectives. Again the family's background and experiences in their culture and social strata will affect their expectations and preferences.

Several concerns apply to all families, however. One is the need to focus on the child and family's strengths rather than the problems. It is difficult for any person to hear that they or their family members have problems. Information needs to be presented sensitively, clearly, honestly, and in a caring manner. Time must be allowed for family members to digest the information and express themselves. A collaborative and trusting relationship established at the outset between the service provider and family will bolster the communication when these difficult conversations must occur. Another concern centers on the need to look for solutions, not the causes of difficulties. When both the family and the professional are focused on the problem-solving aspects of the interaction, they are likely to more effectively design appropriate service objectives and prevent blaming and misunderstandings.

Implementation and Monitoring

As services are delivered, monitoring and communication with families must be ongoing. The style and manner in which the information is exchanged should vary in order to ensure that families' preferences are honored. In addition, service providers must consider the many demands and challenges that families face every day that go beyond the scope of services in which they are involved. Taking the family's perspective and imagining what it is like to live their lives can be an important professional goal. Families are challenged to meet the needs of all family members along many different dimensions. They may view the professional's involvement in their lives as taking up only a tiny fraction of their day or week, and the professional may not be high on their list of priorities. Conversely, the professional might be of tremendous import to the family, and thus professionals should not play down their roles too much, either. Families may view professionals as lifesavers and sometimes the professionals themselves give the families the impression that the child is not a high priority for them. Thus, flexibility and understanding of the entire range of demands families face and the tasks they must achieve is essential to monitoring and attaining respectful partnering and communication.

PROFESSIONAL ISSUES

Collaboration is hard work. Because professionals are engaged with a range of families and their work often involves meeting families in their homes or preferred environments, professionals will be faced with many challenges and decisions that must be made with each family. Several considerations are highlighted: the need to examine and implement professional standards and attention to professional sustenance.

Professional Standards

The collaborative relationships and family-centered services advocated in this text demand that professionals develop professional standards to work closely and respectfully with families. Several key concerns are discussed: confidentiality, ethical dilemmas and standards, and communication among professionals.

Confidentiality

Confidentiality is crucial. Professionals privileged to work closely with families will receive many intimate details regarding the family's life, especially when services are provided for young children and in families' homes. Professionals must adhere to strict standards of confidentiality in all phases of the intervention process to honor this partnership with families. This means that professionals should not discuss families' situations or divulge information to others about the family without the express permission of the family members.

Ethical Dilemmas

Professionals will at times be faced with ethical dilemmas. Such dilemmas often center on the need to divulge information such as in the case of potential abuse or neglect, or they may center on whether it is right to become more actively involved in the family's life to guide them to a more productive or optimal outcome. Sometimes the decision is clear-cut, as in the case of abuse, but at other times it is in a very gray area. The development of a guiding framework is useful to address these potential dilemmas (Beckman, Newcomb, Frank, & Brown, 1996; Wasik et al., 1990). It is recommended that intervention teams draw up a handbook of practices or operating principles that address issues of child and family risk and health, confidentiality, and visitation practices, for instance. Many professional organizations, such as the Council for Exceptional Children (CEC), also provide professional standards and/or a code of ethics. Such standards should be readily available to and practiced by the professional. These professional guidelines also can inform the guiding framework developed by the intervention team. Wrestling with professional dilemmas can be difficult. Practicing self-reflection, consulting with other professionals and team members, and discussing the situation with a supervisor are valuable strategies for addressing the concerns.

Communication

Communication issues among and between various types of professional service providers present special challenges as well. Most families end up working with a myriad of professionals. Many of these professionals even visit the family on different times and days. Although the child and family may benefit enormously from the expertise of a range of disciplines and professionals, the type of information and the way in which it is delivered may be burdensome to families. Beckman and Kohl (1993) documented some of these difficulties, including professionals' contradictions of one another when making judgments or recommendations and also turf disputes. Multiple service providers making multiple visits may disrupt family privacy and schedules, too. Thus, it is incumbent on professionals to communicate with one another and to reflect on the effects of their choices and priorities on the family's routine and lifestyle. The identification of a key contact person for the family among a team of professionals may help to alleviate some of these concerns articulated by families.

Professional Sustenance

Developing and sustaining human relationships is hard work. Professionals today are provided the opportunity to work with a panoply of children and families. The work can be highly rewarding because of the opportunities to meet people, learn new practices and skills, and form bonds with other individuals. The work can be stressful too. Relationship building does not always proceed as hoped or expected. Thus, professionals as well as families and children have needs. They must turn to strategies that help prevent or alleviate burnout and provide them with the opportunity to refuel.

Certain techniques nurture and sustain professionals' ability to work closely with families. The first strategy is *reflective practice*. Reflective practice includes a commitment of time and energy to consider one's work. Professionals may find it helpful to maintain a journal or a personal written log. They also may find it useful to engage in discussions with other professionals designed to reflect on the services provided. Strict confidentiality standards should be maintained in all such discussions and decisions should not be made about families without their participation; however, general discussions of strategies and concerns can be highly supportive to professionals and help them develop or hone their professional skills. Second, *team support* is crucial to the helping professions. Even when professionals are assigned as "home visitors" and spend the majority of their time working independently, support from other professionals is essential. Often the team will have to be constructed. Activities for group discussion, team building, team recreation, and information exchange among team members must be carefully planned and a commitment must be made to this process. Third, *supervision and mentoring* by senior staff members and/

or administrators are essential components to effective service delivery. In a busy world, these components are often the first to go. Effectively supervising and mentoring professionals, particularly those new to or entering the field, is essential to the maintenance of high standards of quality service delivery. Finally, professionals must take care of themselves. This need is reflected by an old expression, "If you don't take care of yourself, no one will." *Self-care* is a necessary and often overlooked component of effective service delivery, especially when services occur in high stress environments or situations. Different strategies of self-care will apply to different people but they may include employing relaxation techniques such as yoga or meditation, participating in recreational activities, spending special time with family or friends, or pursuing an avocation, to name a few. Regardless, these activities can assist the service provider to avoid burnout and gain needed refueling time in order to accomplish the demands of their employment.

SUMMARY

According to Vohs, "The absolute bedrock for true partnerships and collaboration is trust. It will only arise from talking and listening" (1998, ix). How simple and yet how complex this task is! Each professional and each family member brings so many personal characteristics and preferences to each interaction. Issues of culture, communication style, values, and beliefs all affect the interactions that occur.

Every single interaction that occurs is also a transaction. The interactions that take place will transform each participant and affect subsequent interactions. Developing collaborative partnerships and effective communication between families and professionals are the essential ingredients to positive outcomes for children and families served. These partnerships and collaborative relationships are forged over time and with commitment and effort on the part of both families and professionals. Given that all facets of intervention necessitate effective working relationships or partnerships between professionals and family members, the commitment to these collaborative and respectful practices is well worth the effort!

ACTIVITIES TO EXTEND THE DISCUSSION

1. **Map out or outline policies and practices in your agency or work site that form barriers to partnerships** (e.g., no transportation or child care, lack of interpreters or translators for presentations, home visits, meetings with families, discussions, materials [includes issues related to services for the hearing impaired]; staff members' attitudes; mismatch between services and family needs; modes of communication, such as written materials; and so forth). For each barrier, develop an action plan to overcome that barrier.

2. **Try a role-playing activity with several colleagues.** Ask one person to describe an emotionally charged incident he or she experienced in working with a family. The second person, as a listener, should attempt to use active listening skills. The third person can provide feedback on the listener's use of these skills.

3. **Think back on a challenging interaction that you have had with a friend or with a family with whom you have worked over the past 2 weeks.** Did you adequately employ clear and respectful communication skills in your interaction? As you work with colleagues and/or families over the next week, stop after the interaction and perform a self-reflection and self-rating of your skills. Which skills did you employ effectively? Which skills do you need to practice in order to enhance your communication with family members in the future?

REFERENCES

Beckman, P.J., & Kohl, F.L. (1993). Working with multiple professionals. In P.J. Beckman & G.B. Boyes (Eds.), *Deciphering the system: A guide for families of young children with disabilities* (pp. 21–38). Cambridge, MA: Brookline Books.

Beckman, P.J., Newcomb, S., Frank, N., & Brown, L. (1996). Evolution of working relationships with families. In P.J. Beckman (Ed.), *Strategies for working with families of young children with disabilities* (pp. 17–30). Baltimore: Paul H. Brookes Publishing Co.

Chen, D., Chan, S., Brekken, L., & Valverde, A. (Producers). (2000). *Conversations for three: Communicating through interpreters* [Videotape]. Baltimore: Paul H. Brookes Publishing Co.

Covey, S.R. (1989). *The seven habits of highly effective people.* New York: Simon & Schuster.

Dale, M.L., & Hoshino, L.B. (1984). Belief systems of Hispanic and pan-Asian populations in California: Implications for the delivery of care in the neonatal intensive care unit. *Journal of the California Perinatal Association, 4*(2), 21–25.

Dunst, C.J., & Paget, K.D. (1991). Parent–professional partnerships and family empowerment. In M. Fine (Ed.), *Collaborative involvement with parents of exceptional children* (pp. 25–44). Brandon, VT: Clinical Psychology Publishing Co.

Dunst, C.J., Trivette, C.M., & Deal, A.G. (1994). *Supporting and strengthening families Vol. 1. Methods, strategies and practices.* Cambridge, MA: Brookline Books.

Dunst, C.J., Trivette, C.M., & Johanson, C. (1994). Parent–professional collaboration and partnerships. In C.J. Dunst, C.M. Trivette, & A.G. Deal (Eds.), *Supporting and strengthening families: Vol. 1. Methods, strategies and practices* (pp. 197–211). Cambridge, MA: Brookline Books.

Edelman, L., Greenland, B., & Mills, B.L. (1992a). *Building parent/professional collaboration: Facilitator's guide* (2nd ed.). Baltimore: Kennedy Krieger Institute.

Edelman, L., Greenland, B., & Mills, B.L. (1992b). *Family centered communication skills: Facilitator's guide.* Baltimore: Kennedy Krieger Institute.

Fisher, R., & Ury, W. (1981). *Getting to yes: Negotiating agreement without giving in.* New York: Penguin Books.

Gowen, J.W., Christy, D.S., & Sparling, J. (1993). Informational needs of parents of young children with special needs. *Journal of Early Intervention, 17*(2), 194–210.

Greenspan, S.I., & Meisels, S.J. (1996). Toward a new vision for the developmental assessment of infants and young children. In S.J. Meisels & E. Fenichel (Eds.), *New visions for the developmental assessment of infants and young children* (pp. 11–26). Washington, DC: ZERO TO THREE: National Center for Infants, Toddlers, and Families.

Hanson, M.J. (2004). Ethic, cultural, and language diversity in intervention settings. In E.W. Lynch & M.J. Hanson (Eds.), *Developing cross-cultural competence: A guide for working with children and their families* (3rd ed.). Baltimore: Paul H. Brookes Publishing Co.

Hanson, M.J., Lynch, E.W., & Wayman, K.I. (1990). Honoring the cultural diversity of families when gathering data. *Topics in Early Childhood Special Education, 10,* 112–131.

Joe, J., & Malach, R. (1998). Families with Native American roots. In E.W. Lynch & M.J. Hanson (Eds.), *Developing cross-cultural competence: A guide for working with children and their families* (2nd ed., pp. 127–162). Baltimore: Paul H. Brookes Publishing Co.

Kalmanson, B., & Seligman, S. (1992). Family–provider relationships: The basis of all interventions. *Infants and Young Children, 4*(4), 46–52.

Lynch, E.W. (2004). Developing cross-cultural competence. In E.W. Lynch & M.J. Hanson (Eds.), *Developing cross-cultural competence: A guide for working with children and their families* (3rd ed.). Baltimore: Paul H. Brookes Publishing Co.

Lynch, E.W., & Hanson, M.J. (2004). *Developing cross-cultural competence: A guide for working with children and their families* (3rd ed.). Baltimore: Paul H. Brookes Publishing Co.

Lynch, E.W., & Hanson, M.J. (in press). Family diversity, assessment and cultural competence. In M. McLean, M. Wolery, & D. Bailey (Eds.), *Assessing infants and preschoolers with special needs.* Columbus, OH: Charles E. Merril.

McGonigel, M.J. (1991). Philosophy and conceptual framework. In M.J. McGonigel, R.K. Kaufmann, & B.H. Johnson (Eds.), *Guidelines and recommended practices for the*

Individualized Family Service Plan (2nd ed.) (pp. 7–14). Bethesda, MD: Association for the Care of Children's Health.

Ohtake, Y., Fowler, S.A., & Santos, R.M. (2001). *Working with interpreters to plan early childhood services with limited-English proficient families* (CLAS Technical Report #12). Urbana-Champaign: University of Illinois, Early Childhood Research Institute on Culturally and Linguistically Appropriate Services.

Rosin, P. (1996). Parent and service provider partnerships in early intervention. In P. Rosin, A. Whitehead, L. Tuchman, G. Jesien, A. Begun, & L. Irwin (Eds.), *Partnerships in family-centered care: A guide to collaborative early intervention* (pp. 65–79). Baltimore: Paul H. Brookes Publishing Co.

Salisbury, C. (1992). Parents as team members: Inclusive teams, collaborative outcomes. In B. Rainforth, J. York, & C. Macdonald (Eds.), *Collaborative teams for students with severe disabilities: Integrating therapy and educational services* (pp. 43–66). Baltimore: Paul H. Brookes Publishing Co.

Turnbull, A.P., & Turnbull, H.R. (1990). *Families, professionals, and exceptionality: A special partnership* (2nd ed.). New York: Merrill.

Walker, B., & Singer, G.H.S. (1993). Improving collaborative communication between professionals and parents. In G.H.S. Singer & L.E. Powers (Eds.), *Families, disability, and empowerment: Active coping skills and strategies for family interventions* (pp. 285–316). Baltimore: Paul H. Brookes Publishing Co.

Wasik, B.H., Bryant, D.M., & Lyons, C.M. (1990). *Home visiting: Procedures for helping families.* Beverly Hills: Sage Publications.

CONCLUSION

The Family as Possibility

I dwell in Possibility—
A fairer House than Prose—
More numerous of Windows—
Superior—for Doors—
—Emily Dickinson (from Poem #657)

Every individual begins life in a family, although the structures, inner-workings, and continuity of those families are as varied as the individuals themselves. Families are diverse in structure, size or composition, and membership. Families also vary in terms of how they define themselves and what roles they ascribe to individual family members. Families vary in cultural beliefs and practices, ethnicity, primary language(s) spoken, place of origin, and geographical location. Families diverge according to the risks they may encounter—including poverty, violent acts, ill health, unemployment, and homelessness. They also vary in terms of their resources—economic, social, spiritual, and formal and informal supports.

Families vary along every conceivable dimension. What is consistent is the family context as a *source of possibility*. For it is within the context of the family that individuals receive—at the most basic level—care and shelter as children, and it is within the family that individuals are socialized and supported as they grow. At times, that support must be bolstered or supplemented from outside or external structures when the family is unable to muster resources or fails to provide supports to its members. When professional services are needed or desired, practitioners are faced with decisions and challenges related to meeting family needs. The service delivery models advocated in this text are those that recognize and respect the diverse characteristics and needs of families and respectfully involve families as partners as family goals are identified and interventions are provided to facilitate family functioning.

THE INFLUENCE OF THE FAMILY CONTEXT: POSSIBILITIES FOR GROWTH AND DEVELOPMENT

Families typically function as a source of protection, nurturing, and support for all the members of the family. In some instances, however, families serve as a source of risk to one or all of the developing individuals within that family. Some aspect of family life or family relationships may constitute a risk at one point in development but a neutral or supportive force at another time.

This text has explored frameworks through which to view the development of the individual as well as through which to understand the family within the larger context of society. The transactional model has been advanced as one that fosters understanding of the effects of individuals' characteristics (e.g., personality, temperament, ability levels, health status, preferences, goals) as they interact with dimensions of the environment (e.g., quality of caregiving, educational opportunities, health and human service opportunities) in producing transactions or shifts in the individuals' development and behavior.

The ecological systems framework also was described in order to place individuals and families within the broader set of contexts in which they are nested and with which they continually interact. The framework depicts the interactions of individuals with their families and with other institutions such as education systems, health care facilities, child care, and community services. These interactions in turn are embedded within the larger web of structures and policies of the institutions and policies that affect these systems and services, as well as within the larger societal context. The influence on families of culture, geographical factors, and societal practices and philosophies, as well as the collective impact of families on those structures, is visible through this framework.

Dynamic Nature of Families: Possibilities for Change

Families are also dynamic and constantly changing. Throughout the life cycle of the family, significant changes occur in family composition and structure, in the relationships among family members, and in the function that the family may serve for a given member. For instance, in the final weeks in which this text was being completed, the authors of this book experienced the death of a parent, a child "leaving the nest" to attend college, a painful back injury, and a colleague's remarriage. These events all represent examples of family transitions or life changes. Such shifts in families underscore the dynamic nature of work with families. As professionals encounter families through their service environments, they must constantly be attentive to the changing needs and characteristics of the families with whom they work. Some events families encounter might disrupt their equilibrium or their abilities to perform their functions. In other instances, these events (even though traumatic) may enable positive shifts or adaptations. Professionals, hence, are presented with opportunities to support families in adjusting and adapting to changing circumstances.

FAMILY–PROFESSIONAL PARTNERSHIPS: POSSIBILITIES AND PATHWAYS FOR FAMILY SUPPORT

The service delivery approach advocated in this text emphasizes viewing the family as a system and recognizing that families must make decisions on their own behalf. Professionals are encouraged to bring their special knowledge and expertise to families through forming partnerships with families. The type of alliance will vary from family to family based on the families' preferences and belief systems, but effective alliances share a respect for family diversity and a commitment to assisting families to mobilize their resources and strengths. For some families who are faced with difficult circumstances, identifying and gaining access to resources may take longer or require more innovative and persistent measures. Regardless of the type or range of the family's need, the role of the professional is to support the family through a shared and collaborative service approach.

These collaborative partnerships can serve as a pathway through which families are helped to create new possibilities for resources and strategies to foster family competency and address the family's needs. They also fashion more positive working conditions for professionals and produce learning opportunities for them as well. Rather than dwelling on the difficulties and problems faced by families, this orientation opens windows of opportunities. Indeed, both families and professionals are invited to dwell in the possibilities.

INDEX

Page numbers followed by *f* indicate figures; those followed by *t* indicate tables.

241

Also by Eleanor W. Lynch & Marci J. Hanson!

ELEANOR W. LYNCH
MARCI J. HANSON

Developing
CROSS-CULTURAL COMPETENCE

A Guide
for Working
with Children and
Their Families

THIRD EDITION

"Hard to imagine that any professional working in the field today would not want this priceless resource."—Elizabeth J. Erwin, Ed.D., Queens College of the City University of New York

"Needs to be a desk reference [for] all professionals who work on behalf of children and families."—Jacqueline Thousand, Ph.D., California State University, San Marcos

The third edition of this bestselling text brings together detailed, accurate information on working with families and children with and without disabilities from specific cultural, ethnic, and language groups. Pre- and inservice early interventionists will

- Learn the basics of cultural competence. Readers will explore the ramifications of ethnic, cultural, and language diversity in intervention settings, and they'll get advice on communicating effectively and respectfully with families.

- Deepen their understanding of specific cultures. Nine chapters on different groups (see below) give readers up-to-date snapshots of traditions, family structure, values, and attitudes toward child rearing.

- Discover better ways to serve families. Readers will examine their own beliefs and values, and they'll get insightful guidelines on improving their practice.

Timely additions on South Asian roots, open-ended case studies on ethical dilemmas, and an expanded discussion of Middle Eastern roots make this a comprehensive, must-have reference for any early intervention professional working with families whose customs, beliefs, and values may differ from their own.

Practical insight on families with the following cultural roots:
Anglo-European • American Indian • African American • Latino • Asian
• Pilipino • Native Hawaiian and Samoan • Middle Eastern • South Asian

US$44.95 | Stock Number: 67441
2004 • 544 pages • 7 x 10 • paperback • ISBN 978-155766744-1